W9-AHN-978

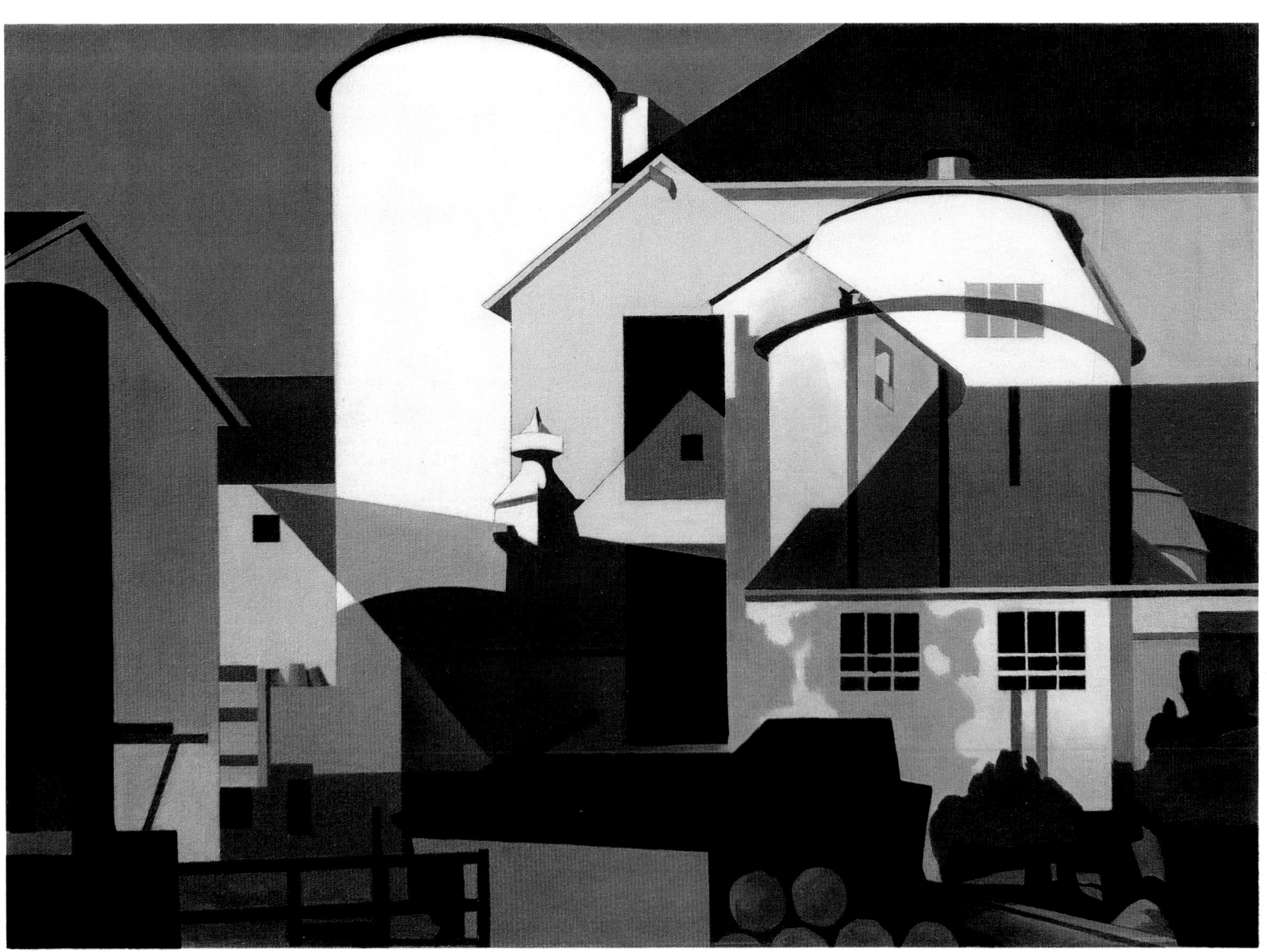

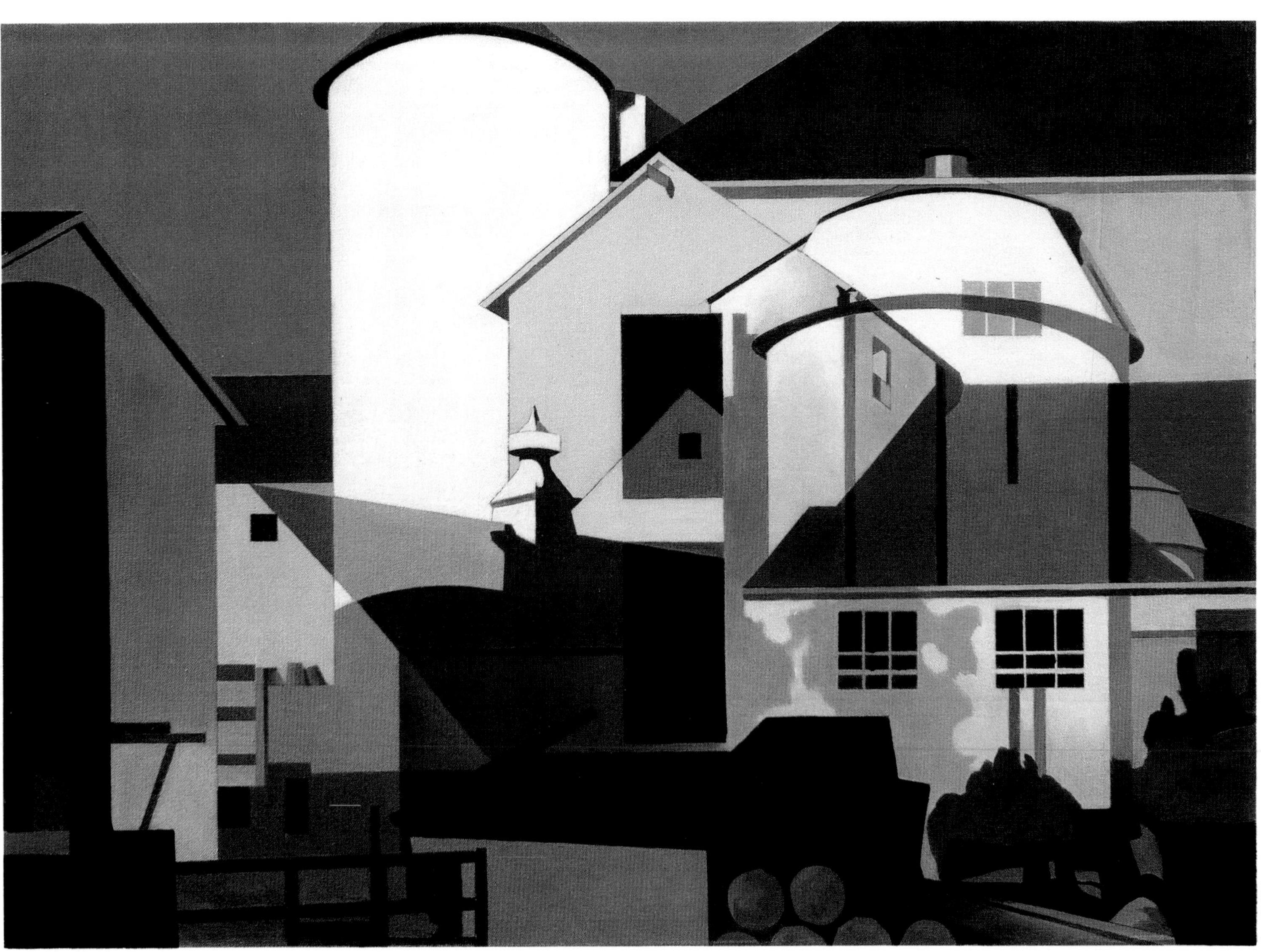

AMERICAN ORIGINALS

Selections from Reynolda House, Museum of American Art

Essay by Charles C. Eldredge

Catalog by Barbara B. Millhouse,
with the assistance of Robert Workman

ABBEVILLE PRESS PUBLISHERS NEW YORK
THE AMERICAN FEDERATION OF ARTS NEW YORK

Publication coordinator, AFA: Michaelyn Mitchell
Editor, Abbeville Press: Alan Axelrod
Manuscript editor: Amy Handy
Art director: Renée Khatami
Designer: Melissa Feldman
Production supervisor: Hope Koturo

This catalog has been published in conjunction with "American Originals: Selections from Reynolda House, Museum of American Art," an exhibition organized and circulated by The American Federation of Arts. The exhibition is a project of ART ACCESS, a program of The American Federation of Arts with major support from the Lila Wallace–Reader's Digest Fund. Additional support has been provided by the National Patrons of the AFA.

The national tour and catalog have been supported by a generous grant from Sotheby's.

Responsibility for the catalog entries is as follows: Barbara B. Millhouse, 1–3, 5–25, 27–32, 34, 35, 37, 38, 40–42, 44; Barbara B. Millhouse and Robert Workman, 4, 33, 43; Robert Workman, 26, 36, 39.

Exhibition Tour

Center for the Fine Arts
Miami, Florida
September 22–November 18, 1990

Palm Springs Desert Museum
Palm Springs, California
December 16, 1990–February 10, 1991

Whitney Museum of American Art
at Equitable Center
New York, New York
March 6–May 11, 1991

Memphis Brooks Museum of Art
Memphis, Tennessee
June 2–July 28, 1991

Amon Carter Museum of
Western Art
Fort Worth, Texas
August 17–October 20, 1991

Terra Museum of American Art
Chicago, Illinois
November 17, 1991–January 12, 1992

The Gilcrease Museum
Tulsa, Oklahoma
March 1–April 26, 1992

Founded in 1909, The American Federation of Arts is a nonprofit educational organization that serves the visual arts community. Its primary activity is the organization of exhibition and film programs that travel throughout the United States and abroad. Other services range from management training to reduced-rate programs in fine-arts insurance and transportation.

Printed and bound in Japan

First edition

Copublished in the United States of America by The American Federation of Arts and Abbeville Press, Inc.

Library of Congress Cataloging-in-Publication Data
American originals.
Catalog of an exhibition organized by the American Federation of Arts, to be held Sept. 22–Nov. 18, 1990 at the Center for the Fine Arts, Miami, and at other museums.
Includes bibliographical references and index.
1. Painting, American—Exhibitions. 2. Reynolda House—Exhibitions. I. Eldredge, Charles C. II. Millhouse, Barbara Babcock. III. Workman, Robert G. IV. Reynolda House. V. American Federation of Arts. VI. Center for the Fine Arts (Miami, Fla.)
ND205.A657 1990 759.13′074′73
90-634
ISBN 1-55859-067-6 (cloth)
1-55859-122-2 (paper)

Contents

Foreword

There is no shortage in this country of museums with respectable collections of American art. Only a handful, however, have collections as thoroughly first rate as that of Reynolda House. The Reynolda House collection has the distinction of including only important works by artists of major significance in the history of American art—a particularly impressive and unique accomplishment for such a young museum. For the AFA it is truly a pleasure to be able to bring to museum audiences and readers everywhere a collection that provides such an illuminating chronicle of the key developments in American art.

We are, first and foremost, indebted to Reynolda House's president, Barbara B. Millhouse, and executive director, Nicholas B. Bragg, for allowing the AFA to organize a national tour during a time when their lovely museum—in which paintings are exhibited as part of a home rather than in a gallery setting—will be undergoing renovation. At Reynolda House, we also wish to thank Joanne Viren, who has assisted throughout the project.

To Barbara Millhouse, we also want to express our appreciation for her important and thoughtful contribution to this catalog. Charles C. Eldredge's essay has also made an insightful contribution, for which we are most grateful.

We want to acknowledge the museums presenting the exhibition: the Center for the Fine Arts, Miami; the Palm Springs Desert Museum, Palm Springs, California; the National Academy of Design, New York; the Memphis Brooks Museum of Art, Memphis, Tennessee; the Amon Carter Museum of Western Art, Fort Worth; and the Terra Museum of American Art, Chicago.

Those on the AFA staff who have worked diligently to make the exhibition and publication a reality include J. David Farmer, director of exhibitions; Robert Workman, administrator for exhibitions, who has contributed a number of fine entries to this catalog; Michaelyn Mitchell, head of publications; and Andrea Farnick, associate registrar. I also want to acknowledge the efforts of our director of development and public affairs, Susan J. Brady, and our public information director, Jillian Slonim. Finally, we wish to express our appreciation to the Lila Wallace-Reader's Digest Fund for their support through the AFA's ART ACCESS program, and to Sotheby's for a generous grant supporting the national tour and this publication. We also wish to thank the national patrons of the AFA, who have designated this project as the national patron exhibition of 1990.

Myrna Smoot
Director, The American Federation of Arts

Preface and Acknowledgments

The formation of this collection, which is exhibited in the former home of Katharine Smith and Richard Joshua Reynolds (founder of the R. J. Reynolds Tobacco Company in Winston-Salem, North Carolina), is the means by which the founding board of directors chose to fulfill its charter as a nonprofit corporation dedicated to "the encouragement and advancement of the arts and education." The house was established as such in 1963 by the Reynolds' son-in-law, Charles H. Babcock, Sr., who until his death in 1967 devoted his efforts to ensuring its continued vitality.

Plans to establish a permanent collection of American art were initiated in 1966 by the board of directors of Reynolda House and the initial selection of works began that year. The original acquisition committee was composed of Nancy Susan Reynolds, the daughter of Katharine Smith and R. J. Reynolds; their son-in-law, Charles H. Babcock, Sr.; and two granddaughters, Anne Cannon Forsyth and Barbara Babcock Millhouse. They invited Stuart P. Feld, then associate curator of American art at the Metropolitan Museum of Art, New York, to serve as their advisor, and with funds pooled from three family foundations—the Mary Reynolds Babcock Foundation, the Z. Smith Reynolds Foundation, and the Reynolds, Bagley, Verney Foundation (now called Arca)—they selected nine works of art that set high standards for the future growth of the collection.

On September 8, 1967, the small but well-selected collection, comprised of nine paintings by Joseph Blackburn, Gilbert Stuart, Frederic E. Church, Martin J. Heade, Eastman Johnson, Albert Bierstadt, William Harnett, William Merritt Chase, and Childe Hassam, was opened to the public. In his presentation speech Thomas Hoving, then the director of the Metropolitan Museum, said: "People touring the house are going to be struck repeatedly by certain paintings. The names of artists, in some cases, are not going to mean much to them. The quality of the work is." This remark reveals the neglected state of American art at this time and demonstrates the foresight the committee exercised in its initial selection.

The collection grew rapidly in the 1960s and '70s when many gifts were acquired. As each member of the original acquisition committee began to make personal donations they were joined by another Reynolds' granddaughter, Betsy Babcock, who contributed *Tree, Cactus, Moon* by Joseph Stella, which she purchased at the Edith Halpert estate sale. A broad range of donors soon looked to Reynolda House as the setting where a major work of art could find an appreciative audience. Those generous individuals whose paintings are traveling in this exhibition are R. Philip Hanes, Emily and Milton Rose, Lawrence A. Fleischman, Lee A. Ault, and Dorothy and Maynard Weber. The continued participation of Barbara Babcock Millhouse has been especially significant in the growth of the collection, and her insistence on quality has been an important factor in maintaining the excellence established by the founding committee.

One of the delights of this collection is that it can be seen in a home that, though grand, is warm and comfortable. Completed in 1917 as the center of a large estate, Reynolda House was occupied for nearly fifty years by descendents of the Reynolds family. Since 1970 it has been my pleasure to develop an education program at Reynolda House that today attracts almost half of our annual visitors. My staff and I make every effort to bring in a diverse public and encourage them to understand art within the cultural context of American literature, music, and history. That this collection now goes forth and finds a wider public is gratifying to me and a treat awaiting a new audience.

After the board of directors approved a capital campaign to support the installation of an environmental control system, the American Federation of Arts was sought out as the best organization to mount a traveling exhibition of selected works from the collection during the renovation. This joint endeavor has enlisted the considerable talents of Robert Workman and Michaelyn Mitchell from the American Federation of Arts and Joanne Viren from Reynolda House.

Major contributors to the preliminary work of this catalog were the National Endowment for the Arts, Richard H. Jenrette, the James G. Hanes Memorial Fund/Foundation, and the John W. and Anna H. Hanes Foundation.

In preparation for the exhibition a generous grant from the Institute of Museum Services enabled several paintings to be treated by David Goist, chief conservator, North Carolina Museum of Art, and his assistant, Janet Hessling. Throughout the project a dedicated effort to secure funds was made by Elizabeth Morgan, assistant director for finance and development.

We are grateful to the president of our board, Barbara B. Millhouse, for the major contribution she has made to the research and writing of a large portion of this catalog. Her volunteer efforts both in a presidential and curatorial role have been essential to the success of this project.

Nicholas B. Bragg
Executive Director, Reynolda House

I am most grateful to those who have contributed over the years to the information and insights included in the text of this catalog: Gerald Carr, Bruce Chambers, Elaine Dee, Stuart P. Feld, Robert Graham, Judith W. Harvey, Robert Hobbs, John Kasson, Constance Kay, Sarah Hunter Kelly, Claudia Brush Kidwell, James Kraft, Joseph L. Lee, Townsend Ludington, Chad Mandeles, Nancy Mowll Mathews, Jody A. Mellenthin, Nicholas Millhouse, Emily Mills, Mollie Neal, Andrew Oliver, Ronald Pisano, Nona Porter, Jules Prown, George Rickey, Richard Rust, Margaret Supplee Smith, Kendall Taylor, Elizabeth L. Tebow, Carol Troyen, Mrs. H. Rembrandt Woolridge, and Jeffrey J. York. I am also grateful to my assistants, Nancy Fichman, Carson Joyner, and Linda A. Long.

Lastly, I want to acknowledge the professors and participants in American Foundations, the Reynolda House/Wake Forest University summer graduate program, for so generously sharing their knowledge from a broad range of disciplines: James Barefield, Cyclone Covey, James Dervin, Gloria Fitzgibbon, Doyle Fosso, Louis Goldstein, Annette Le Seige, Robert Mielke, Terry Radomski, and our many students who have brought their insights to bear on these works of art.

Barbara B. Millhouse

American Art At Reynolda House

In 1865 Emanuel Leutze painted a portrait of his longtime friend, the artist Worthington Whittredge, working at the easel. The painting is today in the collection of the Reynolda House Museum of American Art. There, amidst other fine works of more familiar authorship and larger scale or brighter hue, Leutze's small, dark composition might at first be easily overlooked by the visitor. Yet, like so many of the Reynolda treasures, *Worthington Whittredge in His Tenth Street Studio* (cat. no. 17) rewards our attention, and ultimately reveals much about American art and aspirations in the middle of the nineteenth century.

Leutze's portrait came from the last in a series of sittings that the handsome Whittredge—a favorite subject for many of his colleagues—had given since the two men first met in Germany in 1849. On that occasion, Whittredge, an aspiring landscapist from Cincinnati, had been enlisted by Leutze, the American master of the Düsseldorf school, to pose for his historical masterwork, *Washington Crossing the Delaware*. Wearing a replica of the general's costume, Whittredge assumed the hero's role, and also modeled for the figure of the steersman. In an 1856 portrayal by Leutze, Whittredge appeared as himself, albeit still garbed in period costume. The "contemporary" gentleman did not appear until 1861, in the imposing portrait by which Whittredge is now represented in our pantheon of artistic achievement, the National Academy of Design.

By that date, the two friends had relocated to New York where they were both elected to the prestigious Academy. They were also fellow occupants of the Tenth Street Studio Building, the fashionable artists' enclave in which Leutze painted the likeness of Whittredge at his easel. Within the privileged precinct of the artist's studio, Leutze captured an informal moment, without many of the conventions of artifice that marked portraiture of an earlier era. The Tenth Street Studio Building was something of a landmark in mid-century Manhattan, a unique congregation of artists within the burgeoning American art capital. Many of the leading painters of the day worked at the address, and newcomers like Whittredge were invariably drawn to the artistic mecca. For its occupants, the building was an important social center as well as a work space. By the 1880s, William Merritt Chase's elaborately decorated Tenth Street studio (cat. no. 24) was the centerpiece for artistic life in New York; but, even in earlier decades, the rooms of the gregarious Whittredge were often the site of dinner parties "graced by the city's loveliest ladies, whose billowing skirts filled the small space to overflowing."[1] Yet as Leutze portrayed it, the Whittredge studio was not crowded with crinolines, but was instead a place for creativity in solitude; in comparison to Chase's, its decor was almost Spartan. One frequent visitor to the artists' haven described it as "a cluster of somewhat dim apartments resembling cells in a convent," a cloistered effect that Leutze captured in his depiction of artistic industry and inspiration.[2]

The painting is part of a long tradition of American portrayals of artists and craftsmen, extending from John Singleton Copley's famous portrait of Paul Revere to the present day, which suggests the natural and ongoing attraction of artists to other creative forces. Yet unlike Revere, who gazes directly at the viewer, Leutze's subject directs his attention toward the unseen canvas on his easel, lost in the creative reverie of the moment. The light that falls evocatively into the tenebrous space accents the painter's pate and hand, suggesting an equation of mental and manual products. Leutze's objective seems ultimately larger than simply recording a likeness; within the modest dimensions of his composition and simple motif, he celebrates the very act of artistic creation.

The Whittredge portrait of 1865 is imbued with an ineffable mood, to which small details contribute tellingly. Through the high studio window we glimpse a sliver of sky and pink blossoms, evoking the landscapist's traditional inspiration in nature, the probable subject—to judge from the oil studies strewn at his feet—of Whittredge's unseen canvas. The foliage suggests that the portrait was completed sometime during the spring, probably late April or early May, before New York's painters made their annual exodus to their favored summer haunts. But the spring of 1865 was different from most, a season of sorrows, when lilacs last in the dooryard bloom'd. Whittredge, like most of his compatriots, had been powerfully moved by the murder of the president on April 14, just five days after Lee's surrender, which concluded the divisive turmoil of civil war. The artist had been a strong advocate of the Union's cause; he had tried unsuccessfully to enlist in Lincoln's army in 1861, and subsequently used his artistic talents to support the war effort by assisting with fairs, exhibitions, and other benefits. In the cataclysmic wake of Appomatox and assassination, it seems significant that the artist chose to be portrayed in the solace of the studio, working with the beneficent themes of nature. In that creative sanctuary, the portrait implies, one might find redemption through art.

Such a notion would have been alien to an earlier generation of American painters. A century before Whittredge and Leutze, John Singleton Copley had complained of his fellow Bostonians: "A taste of painting is too much Wanting to afford any kind of helps; and was it not for preserving the resembla[n]ce of particular persons, painting would not be known in the plac[e]. The people generally regard it no more than any other useful trade, as they sometimes term it, like that of a Carpenter tailor or shoemaker, not as one of the most noble Arts in the World. Which is not a little Mortifying to me."[3] Prior to Copley, immigrant artists such as Jeremiah Thëus (cat. no. 1) and Joseph Blackburn (cat. no. 2) had brought from Europe to the Colonies their firsthand knowledge (however imperfect) of current portrait fashions; native-born talents also borrowed from European precedent, conveyed to these shores through engraved or painted copies. In both cases, artists lavished attention on stagey poses and the material facts of sitters and their environs. In that prephotographic era, a premium was placed on illusionism (or the best approximation possible); this was especially evident in attention given to rendering the sumptuousness of silk, the delicacy of lace, the round sheen of a pearl—particulars that might distract from problems with anatomy or the "resemblance of particular persons."

In his youthful productions, Copley similarly composed with an eye toward foreign models and standards. Yet his paintings were quickly recognized as superlative in his native Boston, and by the 1760s his rank as the Colonies' leading portraitist was secure. Copley's ascendancy among Boston patrons may have hastened the departure of the once-influential Blackburn from that arena.

What ultimately distinguished a talent like Copley's was his ability to combine a fidelity to facts with an evocation of unique personality, as in *John Spooner* (cat. no. 3). Using a simple oval format with figure posed against neutral ground, devices borrowed from mezzotint copies of British examples then in vogue, Copley surpassed his contemporaries in the ability to quicken the likeness with a sense of distinctive character. This ability, evinced early in the Spooner portrait, lent force to later, more complicated productions, such as the portrait of Paul Revere, which dispense with formula to discover the power of portrayal through direct, intense observation.

While Copley's aspirations to the grand manner of the Royal Academy—and his Tory sympathies—led eventually to his departure for London and a preoccupation with history painting, many others remained in the newly united States to satisfy the continuing demand for likenesses. Among the most prominent was Charles Willson Peale of Philadelphia, whose encyclopedic interests define a native product of the Enlightenment. A patriot, inventor, scientist, and founder of the first American museum, Peale was also a painter who established a distinguished line of artists that remained active well into the 1800s. For more than a quarter century, Peale enjoyed the patronage of distinguished sitters, many of them among the founders of the Republic, before other pursuits (chiefly his museum) led to the 1794 announcement of his retirement from the field of portrait painting. Though this, like prior notices of similar intent, proved somewhat premature, after the mid-1790s Peale did generally confine his painting to subjects from his large family, such as the imposing double portrait of his daughter, Angelica Kauffmann Peale, and her husband, Alexander Robinson (cat. no. 4). His daughter's handsome face and finery were faithfully recorded in precise detail, painted with a sureness and grace typical of Peale's style; painting his vain and pretentious son-in-law, however, Peale found a "disagreeable business. . . . [He] seemed to have so little disposition to give me a chance to do justice to my reputation as a painter."[4] Whatever the cost to family concord—apparently considerable, for the artist did not see Angelica for nearly a decade thereafter—Peale's artistic reputation did not suffer from the experience.

Peale's precise style, like Copley's, relates more to his empirical approach to the world than to the dictates of classical draftsmanship. In Barbara Novak's memorable phrase, it was a uniquely American "conceptual realism—idea . . . amplified to become form." In Copley's late colonial paintings, she found "the roots of an enduring American vision" in which "abstract knowledge is fortified by the *stuff* of empiricism, distinctive and tactile properties of objects, qualities of weight and texture." It was, she concluded, "one of the great art historical mysteries, an alchemistic transmutation of paint into texture."[5] This tradition of remarkable literalism extended into the late nineteenth century in the trompe l'oeil still lifes of William M. Harnett (cat. no. 23) and, subject to changing conditions and tastes, into our own time with the Precisionists and magic realists of the decades between the world wars, and even to the more recent Photorealists.

The tradition found its complement in the loose and coloristic approach of Gilbert Stuart, who, following Copley's departure, was Peale's main challenger for the mantle of premier portraitist. Stuart early eschewed the copyism of others, determined "to find out what nature is for myself, and see her with *my own eyes*." He disparaged the instruction of Benjamin West and other leaders whom he encountered during his long residence in Britain: "When Benny teaches the boys, he says, 'yellow and white there,' and he makes a streak, 'red and white there,' another streak. . . . But nature does not color in streaks. Look at my hand; see how the colors are mottled and mingled, yet all is clear as silver."[6] It was the challenges of flesh that motivated Stuart in his distinctive portraits, which emphasized not the material attributes of his sitters but the luminosity of skin tones and the expressiveness of a face. In the portraits of his mature years (cat. no. 5), fluent brushwork and glowing tones capture the sitter's evanescent personality. Stuart's was the sensibility of a proto-Impressionist, so different from the linear precision of the "conceptual realists," and represents the essential other pole of American painting practice.

While none could surpass Stuart's dextrous ability, many were inspired by it. The Philadelphia portraitist Thomas Sully, for instance, admired the vitality of Stuart's images, remarking of one that "it was a living man looking directly at you."[7] In his own portrait *Jared Sparks* (cat. no. 7), Sully's dashing technique owes much to Stuart (with whom Sully studied in 1810) and indicates the importance of his legacy for artists of the nineteenth century. Incipient in Stuart's work was the romantic spirit, which in the *Sparks* portrait is given full flower. The intellectual sitter was posed looking "off camera," as if momentarily contemplating some idea from his reading; the subject's attention averted from the viewer toward intellectual activity anticipates the creative contemplation in which Leutze caught Whittredge several decades later. This exaltation of intellectual prowess and achievement links the portraits of the 1830s and 1860s with the later interests of Thomas Eakins; albeit dramatically different in style, Eakins's paintings (cat. no. 29) were stamped with a strong sense of individual character, informed by proto-psychological insights that extended the motif of creativity and cerebration into the modern era.

If the eighteenth century was the great age of portraiture in America, the nineteenth was that of the landscape. Obviously, the need for portraits continued, but in the first quarter of the century the artist's attention was increasingly captured by the abundant wilderness of North America. From the time of the initial settlement, the indigenous flora and fauna of the New World had excited the European imagination, and aspects of America's scenic splendors had found their way into many decorative motifs. It was, however, only with the time and security that settlement offered that the American landscape came to the fore as a major artistic preoccupation. The rise of a landscape school also coincided with the breakdown of the rigid hierarchy of artistic themes imposed by the Royal Academy, guardian of traditional values that had long favored idealized compositions and historical motifs over lowlier pursuits, which included landscape, still life, and genre subjects.

Joshua Shaw was among the numerous immigrants to the new nation who were captivated by its scenic wildness. Steeped in the late eighteenth-century conventions of view painting in his native England, Shaw transferred those traditions to New World subjects. His *Witch Duck Creek* (cat. no. 8) is typical of his mature Romantic style, with its careful delineation of foliage tracery and the poetic spell of moonlight. Shaw's portfolio of prints featuring *Picturesque Views of American Scenery* (1819–21), while heavily reliant upon British precedent in format and media, was innovative in its focus upon the "unsung and undescribed" splendors of American wilderness. Shaw's views were enormously influential in directing attention to "the majesty and loveliness of nature [which were nowhere] more strikingly conspicuous than in America . . . present[ing] to the eye every variety of the beautiful and sublime."[8]

In the same year that Shaw began the serialized publication of his *Views*, Thomas Doughty listed himself in the Philadelphia directory as "landscape painter," the first native-born artist to declare such a specialty. Rather than Shaw's specific views, Doughty's carefully ordered compositions emphasized more generalized pastoral delights of nature. *In the Cats-*

kills (cat. no. 9), like many of his works, depends upon Claudian formula in its arrangement of water and distant peak enframed by dark foliage, a favorite arrangement for his contemplations of the wilderness's grandeur. Doughty's lyric celebrations of nature earned immediate success when exhibited in the early 1820s, and helped to establish the new vogue among his compatriots.

The important contributions of Shaw, Doughty, and their contemporaries notwithstanding, the title "father of American landscape painting" was early and often accorded to Thomas Cole. The honorific was bestowed in recognition of his transformation of the scenic view tradition to a nobler allegorical plane where subjects from nature came to enjoy the authority and dignity once conferred upon painted histories and personifications. The transition was not, however, uncomplicated. As did Copley, the young Cole complained of the narrowmindedness of patrons who wished mere "portraits" of their real estate holdings, rather than grander allegorical compositions based on wild subjects. As recounted by Cole's biographer, one particularly vexing patron, a land speculator who employed the artist in the winter of 1825–26, "had neither the mind to appreciate, nor the honesty to reward the ability he had entrapped into his service. . . . For the kind of picture which Cole then delighted to paint he affected a contempt, and advised him to turn his pencil to the bullocks of his farm-yard."[9]

Happily for Cole, others proved more receptive to his imaginative compositions, and he was spared a career based on bullocks. His paintings were distinguished from earlier descriptions of specific places by the moral imperative that lay behind their creation. In nature, Cole discovered not simply the scenic, but something more profound. Like Emerson, whose transcendentalist philosophy developed simultaneously and in parallel with his aesthetic, Cole regarded nature as a divine textbook in which the discerning viewer could discover meaning and metaphor. In his famous essay *American Scenery*, the painter advised that "He who looks on nature with a 'loving eye' . . . feels a calm religious tone steal through his mind, and when he has turned to mingle with his fellow men, the chords which have been struck in that sweet communion cease not to vibrate." American nature was distinguished from that of cultivated Europe by its undefiled wildness, which "cast [the mind] into the contemplation of eternal things."[10] Such subjects provided important evidence of God's immanence in the world—and of His favoritism for the American garden. It was in this benevolent, native Eden that Cole situated his major tributes to the landscape, such as the nostalgic *Home in the Woods* (cat. no. 11).

Cole's painted paeans to American scenery were initially inspired by—even if they did not specifically depict—the wilderness of the Hudson valley and the Catskills, thereby earning him and his followers the sobriquet "Hudson River School." The "school" was never geographically confined, however, nor was it limited to familiar vistas. Well-known marvels—Niagara, for example, or Virginia's Natural Bridge (cat. no. 14)—bolstered the association with the New World. The morally uplifting lessons inherent in nature were made more emphatic by these grand incidents in the native landscape, which likely accounts for the appearance of the Natural Bridge in the background of Edward Hicks's *Peaceable Kingdom of the Branch* (cat. no. 6). But the beneficence of the American wilderness was not localized; it existed more as a state of mind than a place on a map, and its reflection in paintings was not solely reliant upon famous tourist sites. The view from Jasper Cropsey's country home toward Mounts Adam and Eve (cat. no. 21) would not likely have been a familiar stop on mid-century treks through the Catskills, but the unique autumnal tints make it an unmistakably *American* scene whose theistic tinge is reinforced by the biblical reference of its motif.

The landscape vogue that Cole helped to launch led not only to broad panoramas of American scenery, but also to detailed examinations of nature's forms and forces. Asher B. Durand, who was among the first to discover and acclaim Cole's paintings in 1825, followed the example of the younger artist and in the 1830s turned his attention from portraiture, historical subjects, and engraving to depictions of nature. After Cole's premature death in 1848, Durand inherited the mantle of leadership in the flourishing landscape school. While some of his pastoral views share Cole's idealization of nature, Durand's carefully studied compositions generally eschewed the rhetorical overtones of Cole at his most allegorical, instead emphasizing fidelity to natural fact garnered through precise drawings and oil studies. In his series "Letters on Landscape Painting," published in 1855, Durand advised that "all Art is unworthy and vicious which is at variance with Truth."[11] To attain such truthfulness, he emphasized the need for continual practice at drawing, and recommended the close study of nature's details in oil studies completed outdoors. In a study such as *Rocky Cliff* (cat. no. 13), we can almost share the forest sensations that surrounded the artist—feel the dampness of the mosses, smell the humus, sense the rough fracture of granite. In the intimate study of nature's specifics, Durand's intensely literal vision released sensory responses, even—paradoxically—poetry. A similar merger of science and sentiment was accomplished by a number of painters of that period, most notably Frederic Edwin Church, whose exotic Andean views of the 1850s (cat. no. 12) at once address concerns peculiar to nineteenth-century scientific theory and to Christian symbolism, and Martin Johnson Heade, who, likely inspired by Church, also turned his attention to tropical subjects (cat. no. 18) rendered with scientific precision yet loaded with cryptic sensuality.

The pictorial rewards of Durand's close scrutiny of nature were shared by others of his generation and later. Worthington Whittredge, for instance, upon his return from a decade abroad, sought to reimmerse himself in his native environs, believing that "a landscape painter is only at home when he is out of doors."[12] He had been impressed by Cole's precedent, but found Durand's less allegorical, more native subjects to his greater liking. Inspired by the older artist, he also took to the woods, certain "that if I turned to nature I should find a friend." In contrast to orderly European forests picked clean by generations of fagot gatherers, the American prospect was marked by "nothing but the primitive woods with their solemn silence reigning everywhere."[13] His brooding forest interiors of the 1860s, such as *The Old Hunting Grounds* (cat. no. 16), hauntingly evoke the primeval wilderness and reveal that Whittredge was a faithful student of American nature.

The habit of metaphorical statement is deeply engrained in American arts, providing a persistent foil to the tradition of literal vision and presentation. The later nineteenth century, an era that Lewis Mumford aptly labeled the "Brown Decades," was particularly infected by the subjective temper, which found outlet in diverse expressions of mood and personal symbolism. Many painters tended toward traditional forms of allegory and personification in responding to the tumultuous epoch, such as Elliott Daingerfield in his *The Spirit of the Storm* (cat. no. 30). Others escaped into realms of reverie (Elihu Vedder's dreamy *Dancing Girl*, cat. no. 19) and fantasy (William Rimmer's *Lion in the Arena*, cat. no. 22), putting, in Mumford's words, "the ugliness of contemporary life at a distance." Their imaginative motifs seemingly illustrate his discovery of that "something wistful in the American character that shrinks from the harsh forms of reality."[14] Even such a confirmed realist as Thomas Eakins was touched by the spirit of the time, his insightful portraits capturing his sitter's psyche as well as the physique.

Among the works most overtly endowed with mood are the late landscapes of George Inness. Equally scornful of the Impressionists' "pancake of color," of the morally uplifting intent of earlier landscapists, and of the overly literal styles of Pre-Raphaelite and other mid-century painters, Inness instead sought a subjective response to his subjects, and to provoke the same response in the viewer. To a query regarding the aim of an artist, he replied that it is "simply to reproduce in other minds the impression which a scene has made upon him. A work of art does not appeal to the intellect. It does not appeal to the moral sense. Its aim is not to instruct, not to edify, but to awaken an emotion. . . . The true beauty of the work consists in the beauty of the sentiment or emotion which it inspires."[15] Although a near contemporary of many of the great landscapists of the mid-nineteenth century, Inness was, in an age of Nature, a champion of Art.

The mid-nineteenth century's reverence for nature merged with the subjective spirit of its final decades, constituting a vital legacy for painters maturing in the early 1900s. Georgia O'Keeffe, for example, at Lake George in the 1920s was inspired by the same vistas and seasonal cycles that had captivated the artists of the Hudson River School. Like them, she found inspiration in the close study of nature's forms and forces, but the discoveries she found therein were expressed in a modern idiom, less imitative and more personal than her ancestors'. Her well-known floral enlargements examine the intricacies of growth and pattern, concerns that appear in her landscapes as well, both those at Lake George and later of the Southwest. In *Pool in the Woods, Lake George* (cat. no. 34), for instance, the sensual curve of green mountains, echoed on the water's still surface, suggests the organic vitality of verdant nature. The composition of lake and mountains is centered around a dark oval, just as Whittredge's forest scene is organized around a central recess; O'Keeffe's rounded form simultaneously suggests the specific pool of the title as well as a more general energy source intuited through her close attention to natural rhythms.

Nature's inspiration elicited a number of subjective and formally innovative responses from early modernists, particularly those of O'Keeffe's circle such as Arthur Dove who distilled, as did she, the essence of nature in designs both representational and abstract. The propensity to nature's motifs was found among other contemporaries as well. Joseph Stella, for example, moved in his later years from designs based on urban, man-made structures to elaborate botanical compositions energized by throbbing celestial orbs and pulsing vegetal forms (cat. no. 37). For Charles Burchfield, the sounds and rhythms of nature were a lifelong preoccupation, dating from his early watercolors of 1915 to such late, grand compositions as *The Woodpecker* (cat. no. 41). In their celebration of nature and the organic principle, O'Keeffe and her like-minded contemporaries were the beneficiaries of earlier traditions of metaphysics and subjectivity. In a modern, secular age, a specific analogy between such motifs and any conventional religious credo is unexpected and undiscovered. Nevertheless, as Mumford noted, "Even when the connection between the Brown Decades and our time is not direct, one is conscious of kindred impulses."[16] Or, in the apt words of one recent critic, O'Keeffe was "a transcendentalist without God."[17]

The antipodal strains of objective vision and subjective response that characterized much American art in earlier generations continued into the twentieth century. Not every modernist sought inspiration in nature, and even those who did responded in various ways. Some were drawn to landscape and figure studies by the possibilities they presented for formal invention rather than metaphoric statement. Inspired by their French counterparts, American Impressionists such as Mary Cassatt (cat. no. 27) and Maurice Prendergast (cat. no. 32) experimented with color and technique. Their efforts were succeeded by similar trials in other stylistic veins. When Alfred Maurer painted the sunstruck Provencal landscape (cat. no. 31), for instance, he was more interested in the formal qualities of Matisse's bold palette and stroke than in the natural energies that animated Stella's tree. Even more influential on American modernists was the revolutionary style of the Cubists, which represented a new way of seeing. Their fractured forms and simultaneous perspectives were echoed in diverse manners by American painters, from the faceted designs of Lyonel Feininger's town- and landscapes (cat. nos. 33, 36) to the precisely drawn geometries of Charles Sheeler's architectural and mechanical subjects (cat. no. 40).

The Cubist inventions continue to inspire new adaptations even in our own day, albeit in subjects often remote from Picasso's Paris of eight decades ago. The flattened shapes and stylized patterns of Jacob Lawrence's urban scenes, such as *Builders No. 2* (cat. no. 44), provide a distant but strong echo of those earlier innovations. In his paintings of the quotidian pursuits of his time and place, Lawrence continues a long tradition of American genre imagery dating back to the early nineteenth century. William Sidney Mount's *The Card Players* (cat. no. 10) and Eastman Johnson's rural types in a New England maple sugar camp (cat. no. 15) heralded a new cast of characters in the American artistic repertoire. In the traditional canon of the eighteenth-century Academy, such concerns had not ranked highly; but the democratic fever of the 1820s and '30s brought with it a new permissiveness in pictorial pursuits and with it these new subjects. Once established, the interest in genre motifs was enduring, persisting into our own era in the work of Lawrence, Thomas Hart Benton (cat. no. 35), and a host of others.

Lawrence's *Builders* extends and enriches this tradition. The image recalls the sights of Harlem in the 1930s, where Lawrence spent his formative years and where his interest first turned to art. The *Builders'* basis in childhood memories links its inspiration to Horace Pippin's painted recollections of his mother's tales of slavery (cat. no. 38). Unlike the brutality of Pippin's incident, however, Lawrence selected a more pacific and productive moment.

The artist admitted that this theme, which he has treated numerous times over several decades, had for him more than anecdotal interest: "The *Builders* came from my own observations of the human condition." In emphasizing the dignity of the builders' work and the significance of their craft, Lawrence's subject echoes concerns that have persisted in our visual history. Like Copley's *Revere* or Leutze's *Whittredge*, the carpenters are involved in constructive pursuits, with their hands and minds building for the future. However, unlike the silversmith or landscapist working alone, the builders act as a group; theirs is the product of harmonious community, not of the solitary genius.

In the tumult of the late 1960s, Lawrence could "not forget . . . that encouragement which came from the black community" decades earlier. From his youth he recalled the Harlem carpenters and their communal craft, and turned the subject to a larger purpose. "I like the symbolism," he later explained. "I think of it as man's aspiration, as a constructive tool—man building."[18] A century after Leutze's celebration of art in the midst of calamity, Lawrence also turned to the theme of constructive endeavor, but discovered there a different pictorial prescript, one perhaps more appropriate to his time.

Charles C. Eldredge

NOTES

1. Mary Sayre Haverstock, "The Tenth Street Studio," *Art in America* 54 (September–October 1966): 51.
2. S.G.W. Benjamin, "William H. Beard," in *Our American Artists* (Boston: D. Lothrop, 1879), n.p.
3. Copley to Benjamin West (or Capt. R. G. Bruce?), 1767(?), in *American Art, 1700–1960: Sources and Documents*, ed. John McCoubrey (Englewood Cliffs, N.J.: Prentice-Hall, 1965), 18.
4. Quoted in Edgar P. Richardson et al., *Charles Willson Peale and His World* (New York: Harry N. Abrams, 1982), 217.
5. Barbara Novak, *American Painting of the Nineteenth Century* (New York: Praeger, 1969), 15, 20.
6. Quoted in William Dunlap, *History of the Rise and Progress of the Arts of Design in the United States* (1834), ed. Alexander Wyckoff, vol. 1 (New York: Benjamin Blom, 1965), 216, 220.
7. Quoted in Dunlap, *History of the Rise and Progress of the Arts*, vol. 1, 253.
8. Edward J. Nygren, *Views and Visions: American Landscape Before 1830* (Washington, D.C.: Corcoran Gallery of Art, 1986), 46.
9. Louis Legrand Noble, *The Course of Empire, Voyage of Life and Other Pictures of Thomas Cole, N.A.*, 1853; reissued as *The Life and Works of Thomas Cole*, ed. Elliot S. Vesell (Cambridge, Mass.: Harvard University Press, 1964), 37.
10. Thomas Cole, *Essay on American Scenery* (1835), in McCoubrey, *American Art*, 100, 102.
11. Quoted in John K. Howat et al., *American Paradise: The World of the Hudson River School* (New York: Metropolitan Museum of Art, 1987), 112.
12. Quoted in Edward H. Dwight, *Worthington Whittredge* (Utica, N.Y.: Munson-Williams-Proctor Institute, 1969), 16.
13. Worthington Whittredge, "Autobiography," in McCoubrey, *American Art*, 119.
14. Lewis Mumford, *The Brown Decades: A Study of the Arts in America, 1865–1895* (New York: Dover, 1955; first published 1931), 197, 198.
15. George Inness, "A Painter on Painting," *Harper's New Monthly Magazine* 56 (February 1878): 458.
16. Mumford, *The Brown Decades*, 236.
17. Kenneth Baker, "What Went Wrong? A Reappraisal of Georgia O'Keeffe," *Connoisseur* 217 (November 1987): 173.
18. Quoted in Ellen Harkins Wheat, *Jacob Lawrence, American Painter* (Seattle: University of Washington Press, 1986), 143.

MRS. THOMAS LYNCH, 1755

JEREMIAH THËUS

1716–1774

Elizabeth Allston Lynch (b. 1728) was the daughter of William and Esther Allston of South Carolina. Her father was the son of John Allston, who came to South Carolina in 1682. Her mother, Esther Bruce de Marboeuf of St. Thomas and St. Denis's Parish, was the daughter of a physician, Dr. Joseph La Bruce. In 1745 Elizabeth Allston married Thomas Lynch, who was to become a delegate to the First and Second Continental congresses.[1] Their son, Thomas Lynch, Jr., became a signer of the Declaration of Independence.

Born in Chur, Switzerland,[2] Jeremiah Thëus became the leading portrait painter in Colonial Charleston. The resemblance of his style to eighteenth-century Swiss portraits suggests that he received early training in his homeland before 1735, when he emigrated to Charleston with his family and a large group of other Protestants. For thirty years he painted portraits of South Carolina's leading citizens using the soft, pastel colors that suggest that he had some knowledge of the French rococo style.

Elizabeth Allston's rigid pose and static smile indicate that Thëus had not engaged her in animated conversation as was the practice of later portrait painters, but transferred her onto the canvas with the self-conscious expression of a sitter concerned with the importance of the occasion. Family history records that her mother refused flatly to sit for Thëus.[3] Whether this was motivated by modesty, superstition, or the belief that he could not do her justice cannot be determined, but the fact remains that posing was not a casual experience.

There are reasons to suspect that Elizabeth may not have completed her sitting for Thëus. The date of her husband's remarriage, recorded as December 18, 1755, occurs the same year as the date on the portrait. The timing of his remarriage suggests that Elizabeth, whose death date is unknown, died during or soon after the completion of the portrait. Since she bore no children after 1749, the possibility that the portrait is posthumous must also be considered.[4]

The elaborate gown in which Elizabeth Allston is portrayed was taken from a popular mezzotint (c. 1752) of the duchess of Hamilton that was engraved by Richard Houston from a portrait by Francis Cotes, a leading English artist (fig. 1). It was used frequently in portraits by Thëus and other artists of the period.[5] The gown in the mezzotint and, likewise, in the portrait, is distinguished by fur-trimmed scalloped sleeves and fine lace that encircles the neckline, which is further embellished with an artificial nosegay.[6] The taffeta shawl, a rococo device that seems to float behind the sitter, appears in both the mezzotint and the portrait. Thëus copied this same dress with slight variations in two other known portraits: Mrs. Charles Lowndes (Sarah Parker), c. 1759–63, in the Carolina Art Association/Gibbs Art Gallery, Charleston; and Susannah Holmes (signed and dated 1758), in the collection of the Charleston Museum.[7]

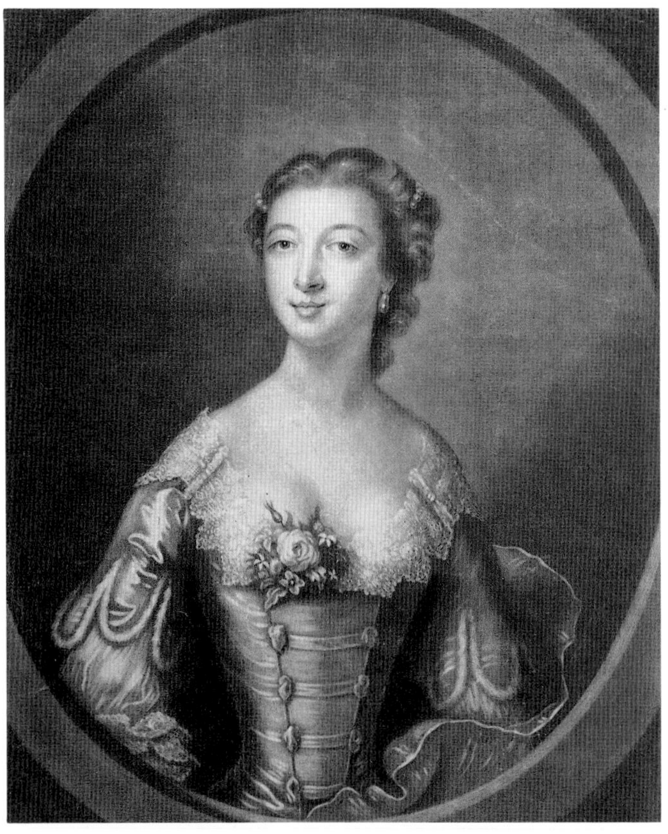

Figure 1 RICHARD HOUSTON, AFTER FRANCIS COTES
Portrait of the Duchess of Hamilton Brandon, c. 1752
The Henry Francis du Pont Winterthur Museum, 65.2595A

Although the use of mezzotints as prototypes for poses and fashion was common among both Colonial and provincial English artists, the popularity of this particular mezzotint may be connected as much with the reputation of the sitter as with the fine attire in which she is portrayed. The original wearer of this gown

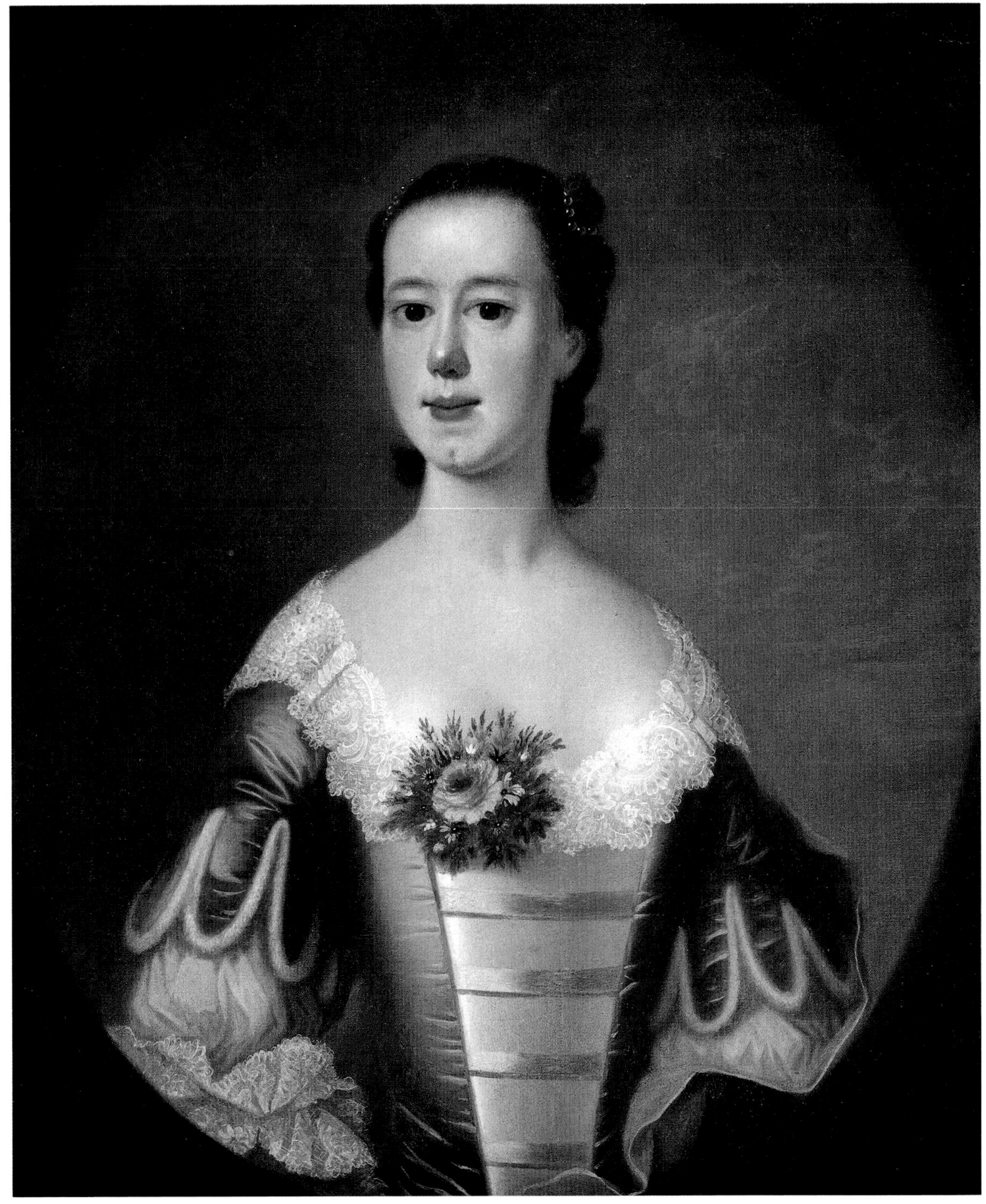

1 Oil on canvas, 29⅞ x 24⅞ in. (75.9 x 63.2 cm)
Signed and dated at lower right: THËUS, 1755
Gift of Barbara B. Millhouse

was Elizabeth Gunning, a young lady from impoverished Irish gentry, who, with her sister, Maria, captured the attention of the court of George II. They became so celebrated for their beauty and amiable dispositions that they were mobbed by crowds wherever they went.[8] Sir Horace Walpole records with humor the courtship of Elizabeth by the duke of Hamilton, which culminated in marriage in the 1750s. The publicity brought to the duchess at this time through the proliferation of London newspapers must have caught the attention of Charlestonians, who were known for their close ties to England. It is possible, then, that the appropriation of her costume may reflect the sitter's admiration for this charming duchess as much as for the costliness of her attire.[9]

Notes

1. Margaret Simons Middleton, *Jeremiah Thëus: Colonial Artist of Charles Town* (Columbia, S.C.: University of South Carolina Press, 1953), 145.
2. Louise Dresser, "Jeremiah Thëus: Notes on the Date and Place of His Birth and Two Problem Portraits Signed by Him," *Worcester Art Museum Annual* 6 (1958): 43.
3. Middleton, *Jeremiah Thëus*, 110.
4. Lois Davidson Hines, compiler, *Lynch Families of the Southern States, Lineages and Court Records* (Naugatuck, Conn.: Dorothy Ford Wulfeck, 1966), 163.
5. Waldron Phoenix Belknap, Jr., *American Colonial Painting: Materials for a History*, (Cambridge, Mass.: Harvard University Press, 1959), 317.
6. Elisabeth McClellan, *Historic Dress in America 1607–1870*, vol. 1 (New York and London: Benjamin Blom, n.d.), 213.
7. Martha A. Severins, "Jeremiah Thëus of Charleston: Plagerist or Pundit?" *Southern Quarterly: A Journal of the Arts in the South* 24 (Fall–Winter 1985).
8. Ruth M. Bleackley, "The Beautiful Misses Gunnings" Part II, *Connoisseur* 12 (August 1905): 232.
9. The Gunning name became a household word connoting good fortune. The kindest wish of good fortune one could receive in Dublin was, "May the luck of the Gunnings attend you."

Detail of *Mrs. Thomas Lynch*

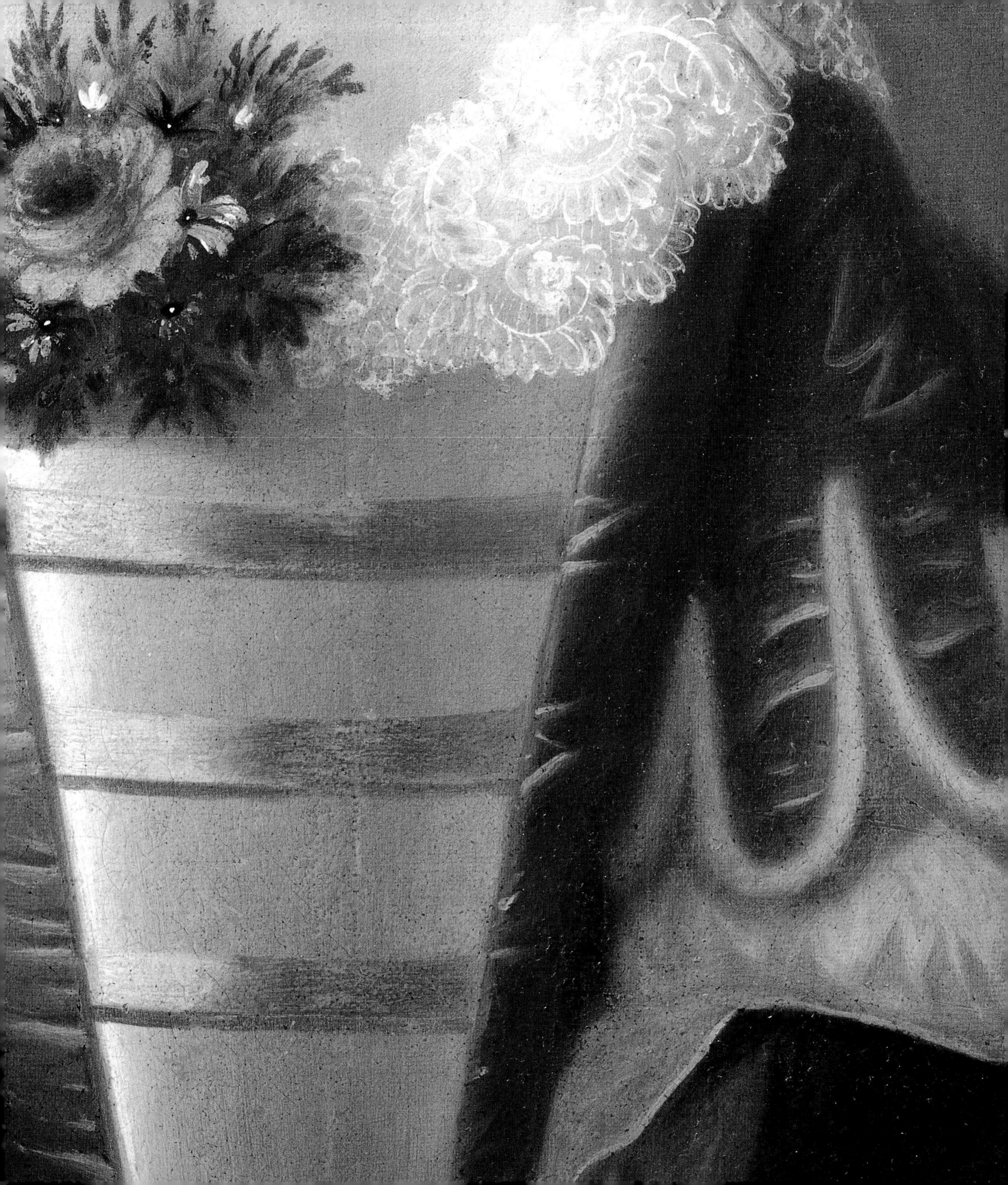

ELIZABETH BROWNE ROGERS, 1761

JOSEPH BLACKBURN

(active in America 1754–63)

Joseph Blackburn's style of portraiture places him in the school of Thomas Hudson (1701–1779), the teacher of Sir Joshua Reynolds, and Allan Ramsay (1713–1784), a Scottish artist who became a leading London portraitist. Although Blackburn could not model a face as adeptly as his British contemporaries, he brought to America enough knowledge of the fashionable rococo style to draw a prominent clientele soon after his arrival in New England. His ability to imbue his portraits with this new taste for elegance and fluidity made a significant impact on a young Boston artist, John Singleton Copley, whose style was transformed during the nine years that Blackburn worked in the Colonies. Copley surpassed Blackburn, whose reliance on drawing rather than modeling the features suggests that he did not have the advantage of academic training in painting the face. He may have worked either as a provincial English or Scottish painter who relied on engravings for pose or as a drapery painter specially trained in painting costumes, accessories, and backgrounds.

Elizabeth Browne Rogers (1741–1812) was twenty years old when Blackburn painted this portrait. She was the daughter of the Anglican rector Arthur Browne, of Queen's Chapel, Portsmouth, New Hampshire, and his wife, Mary Coxe, daughter of the vicar of St. Peter's in Drogheda, Ireland.[1] Like many other New Englanders, she must have spent her teenage years following the courageous feats of Robert Rogers (fig. 2) and his recruits, whose successful encounters with the Indians near Lake George during the Seven Years War were widely reported in the local newspapers. Between military encounters, the six-foot-tall hero visited Portsmouth, where he was a member of the Masonic lodge of which Elizabeth's father was the chaplain. On July 3, 1761, the *New Hampshire Gazette* reported: "Last Tuesday Evening was Married here Major Robert Rogers (who has so eminently distinguished himself in the Services of his King and Country) to Miss Betsey Browne, youngest Daughter of the Rev. Mr. Arthur Browne, of this Place." This portrait, dated the same year, is thought to be her wedding portrait.

Shortly after their marriage Robert wrote to Betsey: "O could I but be where I now wish with you Betsey, once more to feast my Eyes on her who so suddenly made me prisoner to Love." Only six days after what appears to have been an impetuous marriage, Robert, who had served in the militia since age fifteen, was off to South Carolina to seek another military expedition. For the next five years Betsey lived with her parents, her husband returning home only for short periods. During this time rumors of the major's "prodigality" and "gratification of unlawful pleasure and passion" abounded, but Betsey appears to have remained loyal.[2]

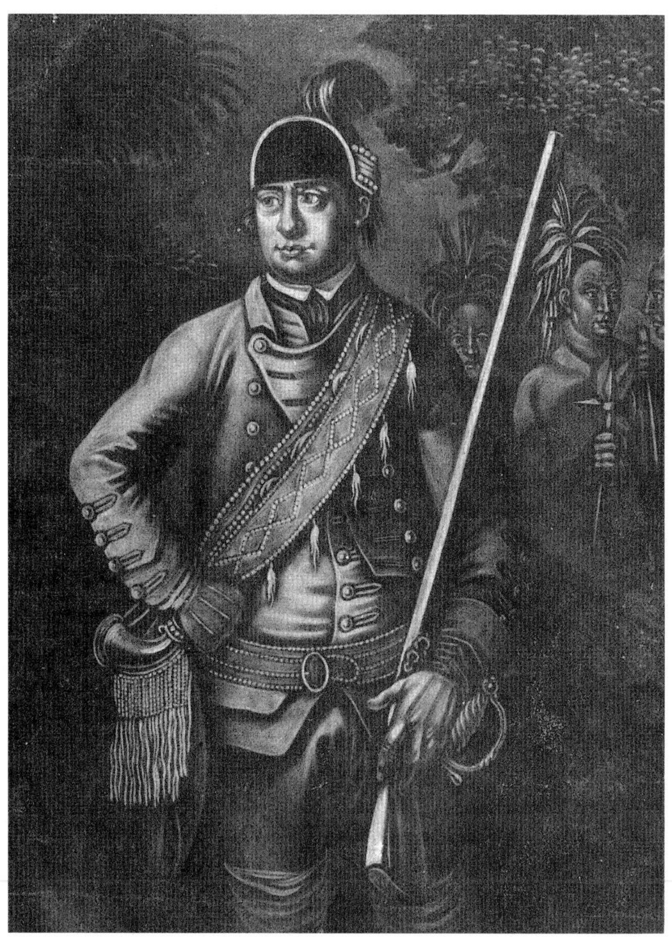

Figure 2 Major Robert Rogers, 1776
Reynolda House, Museum of American Art

When Rogers was appointed commandant in 1766 at Fort Michilimackinac, a strategic military and trading post that England maintained on the western frontier, Betsey accompanied him there. Because Rogers had offended his superior officers by seeking his appointment as commandant directly from King George III, a conspiracy against him was soon brewing. After only sixteen months in command, Rogers was falsely accused of

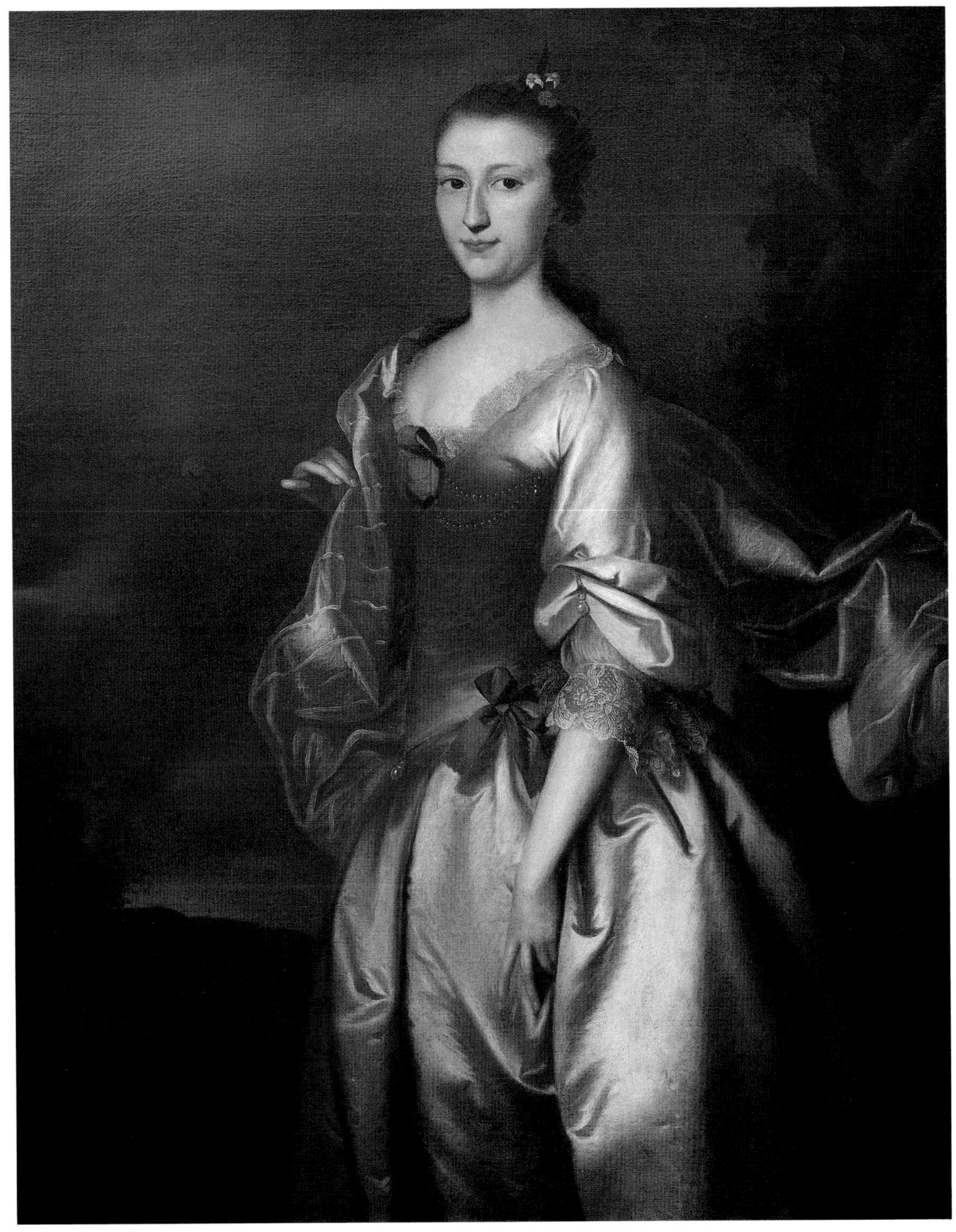

2 Oil on canvas, 50 x 40 in. (127 x 101.6 cm)
Signed and dated at lower left: I BLACKBURN PINXIT 1761
Original purchase fund from the Mary Reynolds Babcock Foundation, Z. Smith Reynolds Foundation, Area Foundation, and Anne Cannon Forsyth

treason and confined to the guardhouse until the spring thaw, when the rivers and lakes opened up and he could be taken to Montreal for trial. With her husband in prison Betsey was left dishonored and defenseless in this remote outpost. The proceedings of Roger's court martial in October 1768 document that Mrs. Rogers was insulted for attempting to speak with her husband through the prison window and that a sergeant "kicked her arse away."[3] Daniel Morison, the surgeon's mate, kept a diary in which he listed one of Ensign Robert Johnstone's violent exploits: "[He] quarreled with Major Rogers, and used uncommon freedom with his wife, common fame says to the extent of carnal conversation with her."[4]

Although Rogers was acquitted at the Montreal trial, his reputation had been seriously tarnished. By 1778, after seventeen years of marriage—during which Betsey enjoyed little of the happy domestic life that she must have expected when this portrait was painted—she petitioned successfully for a divorce. No sooner had she divorced one heavy drinker and philanderer, however, than she married another. Her second husband, Captain John Roche (1737–1811), native of Cork and commander of the *Ranger* before John Paul Jones, also had an unsavory reputation. The well-known author Kenneth Roberts, a former owner of this portrait, wrote the historical novel *Northwest Passage* about the ordeals of Betsey and Robert Rogers.

Neither the artist Joseph Blackburn nor this proud bride could have foreseen the hard life in store for her when this portrait was painted in 1761. Blackburn portrays Betsey Browne posed elegantly against a landscape with the last glow of sunset on the horizon. With her dark eyes set on the viewer, she appears to be a determined and spirited woman whose strong character is forcefully conveyed despite the artist's limited artistic training. She is dressed in the fashion of the day, and the blue of the decorative bow is echoed in one of the tiny wild flowers in her hair. It is possible that Betsey Browne may not have actually worn all this finery. The artificiality of the hands and the floating shawl betray the possible source of the pose and dress as an engraving after leading English portrait painters.[5] The two outstretched fingers on the left hand direct the viewer's attention to the sensuous surface of the satin, while her gentle fingering of the edge of the gossamer shawl suggests a mannerism associated with sizing up costly fabrics. These commonly used mannerisms underscore the importance of eighteenth-century portraiture as a means of suggesting the sitter's wealth and social position.

Notes

1. Lawrence Park, *Joseph Blackburn: A Colonial Portrait Painter with a Descriptive List of His Works* (Worcester, Mass.: American Antiquarian Society, 1923; reprinted from *Proceedings of the American Antiquarian Society*, October 1922).
2. John Cuneo, *Robert Rogers of the Rangers* (New York: Oxford University Press, 1959), 150–57.
3. "Mackinac History, an Informal Series of Vignettes," leaflet 10 (Mackinac Island, Mich.: Mackinac Island State Park Commission, 1967).
4. Daniel Morison, "The Doctor's Secret Journal, a True Account of Violence at Fort Michilimackinac written in 1764–1772," edited by George S. May (Mackinac Island, Mich.: Mackinac Island State Park Commission, 1960). Morison was the surgeon's mate.
5. Elizabeth Browne Rogers's left hand is identical to the left hand in Allan Ramsay's 1746 portrait *Mrs. Madan*, located in Thorton Manor, Thorton Hough, Cheshire, England (no. 222–27b, Frick Library). A similar striped gossamer shawl can be found in the portrait *Mrs. Baumont* by Thomas Hudson (222–26b, Frick Library).

Detail of *Elizabeth Browne Rogers*

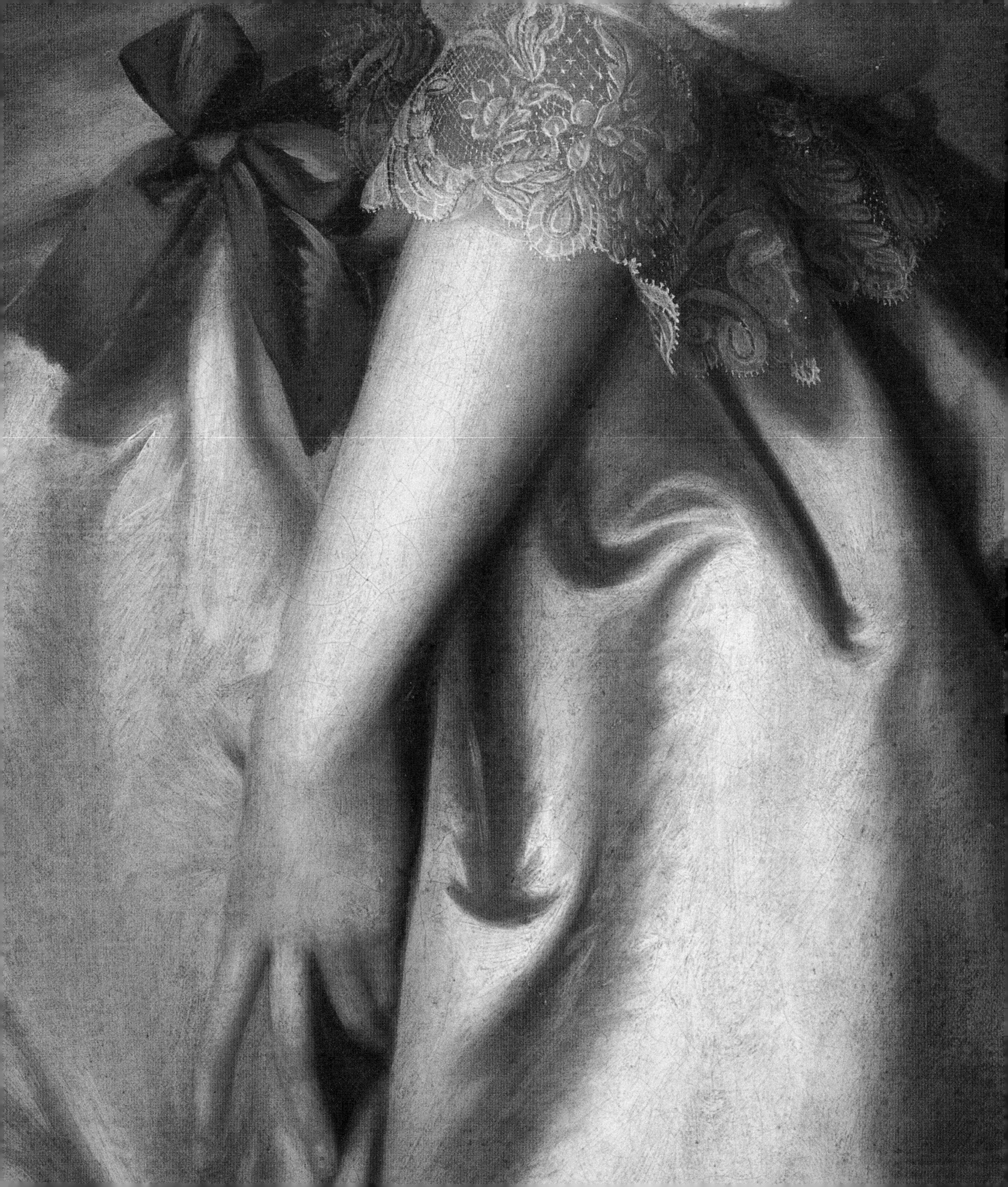

JOHN SPOONER, 1763
JOHN SINGLETON COPLEY
1738–1815

The merchant John Spooner sat for this portrait one year after his second marriage, to Margaret Oliver, whose family was one of the wealthiest and most influential in Boston. Her father, Andrew Oliver (1706–1774), served as Secretary of Massachusetts from 1756 to 1771, and then as Lieutenant Governor under his brother-in-law Thomas Hutchenson (1711–1780), the last royal governor of the colony. Born in 1728, John Spooner was the son of John and Elizabeth Wells Spooner. His first wife was Hannah, the eldest daughter of John Jones of Boston, whom he married in 1756.[1] This portrait was probably precipitated by John Spooner's marriage to Margaret Oliver in 1762 or by the birth of their son the following year.

Like the majority of Copley's sitters, John Spooner was a Congregationalist and had a median income of one hundred to five hundred pounds per year.[2] He was also a High Tory and therefore shared political sympathies with the Oliver family, who, by the mid-1760s, had begun to receive threats from the radicals. Andrew Oliver was appointed stamp officer after the passage of the Stamp Act of 1765, and was consequently hanged in effigy between the figure of Lord Bute and George Granville on the large elm tree called the Liberty Tree. On the same day, August 14, 1765, mobs demolished the stamp office and ransacked the Oliver home. John Spooner and Margaret must also have suffered from hostilities directed toward British sympathizers. To escape the turmoil that gripped pre-Revolutionary Boston, John, Margaret, their son Andrew, and possibly other children set sail for England on July 24, 1768.[3] Only seven months later, on March 18, 1769, *John Boyle's Journal of Occurrences* reported from Boston the sitter's death: "On the 18th of December last died in London of a mortification of his Bowels, Mr. John Spooner, late of this town, Merchant, who with his Lady went from hence 24th July last."[4]

In this portrait, painted early in his career, Copley has placed the sitter's head against an olive-green background within a brown oval, a framing device common in British portraiture of the period. Although the size of the portrait precludes the use of props, Copley has taken measures to indicate Spooner's social position through his carefully coiffed powdered wig and his fashionable attire. His right hand, though not visible, seems to be placed akimbo on his hip in a dignified pose used frequently in full-length eighteenth-century portraiture. His gold-braided waistcoat remains partly unbuttoned so that his hand can be inserted in a gesture that indicated the proper deportment of a gentleman of high social position.[5] As evidenced by the *pentimenti* on Spooner's left side, Copley made an adjustment to his shoulders to slope them in a somewhat exaggerated but fashionable manner.

By 1763 Copley had learned how to create a convincing physical likeness that far surpassed anything known in the Colonies at that time. Spooner's features are animated with a mobility that departs radically from the linear eyes and static smiles of Copley's influential English predecessor Joseph Blackburn. By maintaining transparency in the shadows and building up thick layers of impasto in the highlights Copley reveals his knowledge of sophisticated painting techniques.

Copley was the first American artist with skills developed solely in the Colonies whose artistic achievement matched the quality of the work of professionally trained London artists. Though his overworked application of paint and pasty fleshtones confess to his lack of direct access to European art centers, he was able—through careful study of the few oil paintings and engravings available in Boston and through trial and error—to raise his art to a level far beyond his Boston colleagues. Moreover, because his style developed independently of artistic circles, it reveals a forceful realism characterized by hard outline and hidden brushstroke that has been identified as a distinguishing American feature.

NOTES

1. Barbara Neville Parker and Anne Bolling Wheeler, *John Singleton Copley, American Portraits* (Boston, Mass.: Museum of Fine Arts, 1938), 187–88.
2. Jules David Prown, *John Singleton Copley In America, 1738–1774*, vol. 1 (Cambridge, Mass.: Harvard University Press, 1966; published for the National Gallery of Art, Washington, D.C.), 114.
3. "Andrew Spooner was educated in England, returned to America, and married Ann Howard in Newport, Rhode Island, June 16, 1787. They had a daughter . . . and a son. . . . Andrew Spooner's wife Ann died in 1791, and in 1798 he married Elizabeth Sparhawk, who died in 1800. . . ." Letter from Andrew Oliver, Jr., Director, Museum Program, National Endowment for the Arts, Washington, D.C., to Barbara Millhouse, October 27, 1987.
4. Parker and Wheeler, *John Singleton Copley*, 187–88.
5. Aileen Ribeiro, *Dress in Eighteenth-Century Europe, 1715–1789* (New York: Holmes & Meier Publishers), 120.

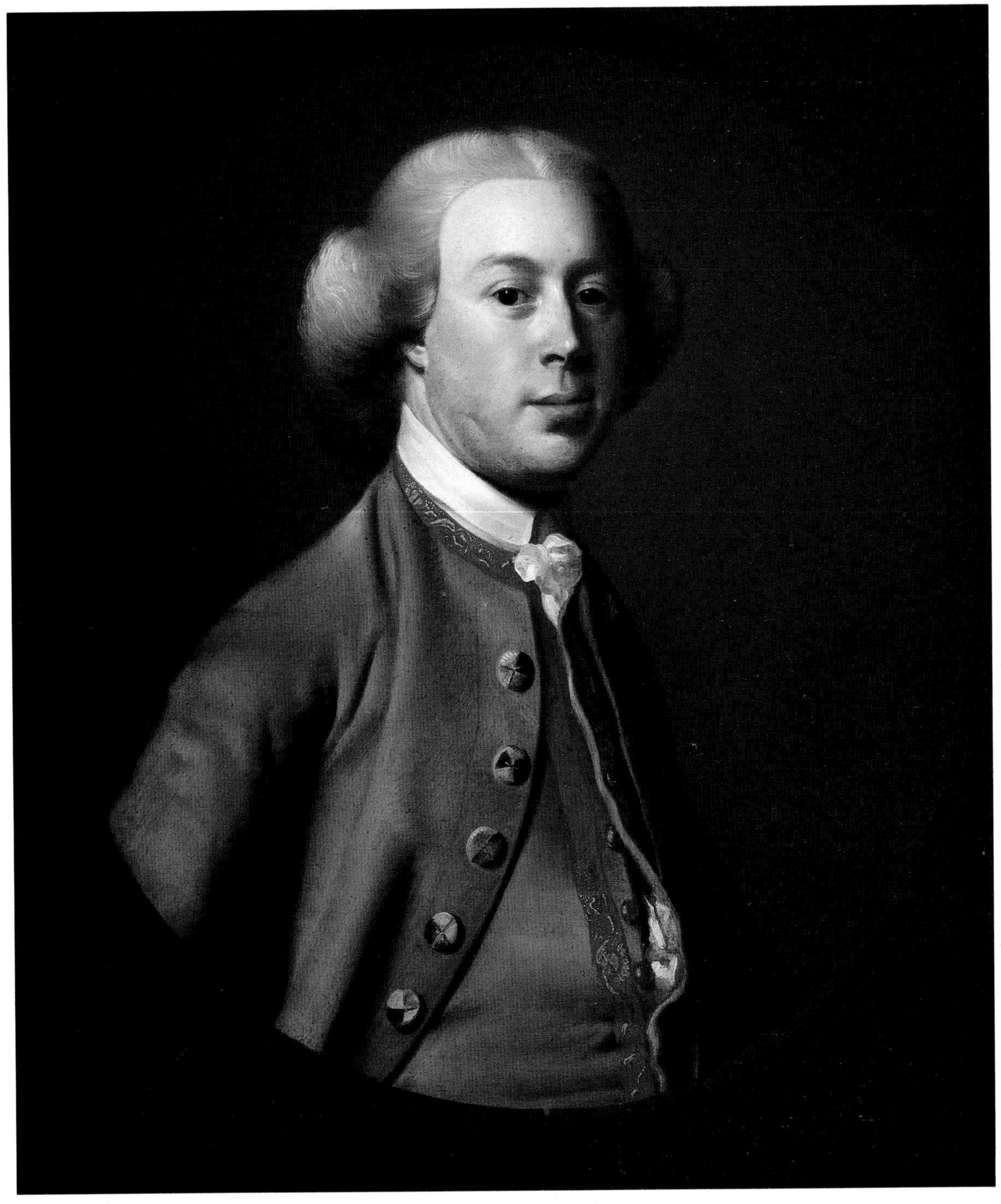

3 Oil on canvas, 30 x 25¾ in. (76.2 x 65.4 cm)
Signed and dated at lower right: J. S. COPLEY/PINX 1763
Bequest of Nancy Susan Reynolds

Mr. and Mrs. Alexander Robinson, 1795
Charles Willson Peale
1741–1827

Charles Willson Peale was the leading portraitist in this country between the careers of John Singleton Copley and Gilbert Stuart. Noted for his contributions in the natural sciences, for his inventions, and for his establishment of the first museum in America, Peale supported his diverse interests through his art. After apprenticeship to a saddler he took painting instruction from a local portraitist. In 1767 a group of local businessmen paid for Peale's passage to London, where he spent two years in Benjamin West's studio. Importantly, Peale concentrated his energies on portrait painting—particularly miniatures—instead of the more grandiose history painting that West's career was built upon. Through West, Peale was introduced to many important colonists, most notably Benjamin Franklin. Upon his return to Maryland he quickly established his position as a talented and fashionable artist.

Angelica Kauffmann Robinson and Alexander Robinson, the sitters for this portrait, were the daughter and son-in-law of the artist. Alexander Robinson was a wealthy Englishman who had come to America in 1781 in search of a younger brother reported killed during the Revolutionary War. Mr. Robinson owned a plantation in Virginia and a house in Baltimore where the couple lived in a particularly grand style. In spite of Charles Willson Peale's prominence as an artist, Robinson considered his father-in-law's profession degrading and seriously curtailed his wife's contact with her family.

The occasion for this painting was the anticipated birth of the couple's first child; as custom dictated, it was important that a likeness of husband and wife be produced before the potentially life-threatening event. According to Peale's diary the sittings for this painting were particularly unpleasant for both artist and subject: "I may say that I never found a more disagreeable business, altho' the object was certainly as much to oblige him as myself, yet he sat with a bad grace, and with very much labor I at last completed the original and made a copy unfinished and the face of Mr. Robinson not quite equal to the first, and was contented to have it so rather than plague a man who seemed to have so little disposition to give me a chance of doing justice to my reputation as a painter."[1]

The Reynolda House portrait, the second version mentioned by Peale, hung for many years in the dining room of the artist's home near Germantown, Pennsylvania. Again from the artist's diary we know that the painting was somewhat reworked. From a comparison of the two versions, it is clear that Peale altered the composition slightly, for the garden balustrade placed between the couple in Angelica's version was removed in the other painting. Perhaps even more telling than the removal of the barrier solidly placed between husband and wife is the tender clasping of hands that replaced it. This alteration suggests that the artist's irritation with his son-in-law may have subsided somewhat by the end of his life.

Unlike the more baroque paintings produced by Copley after he left the Colonies for England in 1774, Peale focused on the naturalism of both the sitter and the environment. His subjects are presented in sympathetic surroundings that reinforce the attitude of the person depicted. In this double portrait Mr. and Mrs. Alexander Robinson are shown in tender association, inspired as much by the artist's love for his daughter as by the nature of the relationship between husband and wife. A glimpse into their complex characters is provided by Peale's clear and precise handling of their astute faces and clasped hands. Their position in life is defined by the fine and delicate clothing, as well as the lush garden backdrop that echos their prosperity.

Note

1. C. C. Sellers, *Portraits and Miniatures by Charles Willson Peale* (New York: Scribner's, 1952), 183.

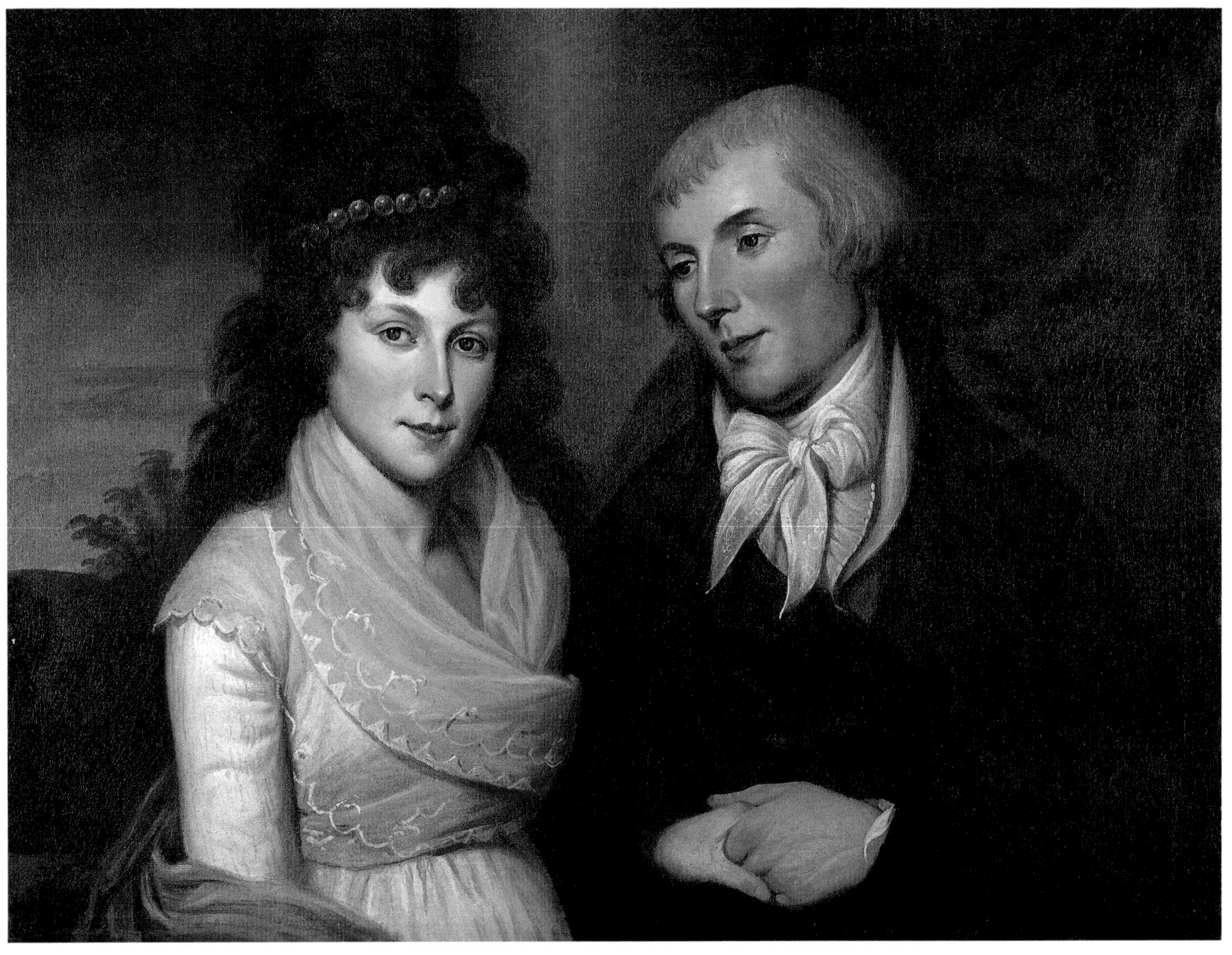

4

Oil on canvas, 27¼ x 36⅛ in. (69.2 x 91.8 cm)
Gift of Barbara B. Millhouse

Mrs. Harrison Gray Otis, 1809

Gilbert Stuart

1755–1828

Sally Foster Otis (1770–1836), shown here in her thirty-eighth year, was the daughter of William Foster, a prominent Boston merchant, and his wife, Grace Spear. On May 31, 1790, she married a Harvard graduate, Harrison Gray Otis, who served as a congressman during the John Adams administration and as a senator under James Monroe. By 1809, when this portrait was painted, Sally had given birth to ten children and her last was to be born the following year. After dining with her in 1816, former president John Adams wrote: "I never before knew Mrs. Otis. She has good Understanding. I have seldom if ever passed a more sociable day."[1]

At the time of this portrait the Otis family lived in the last of the three houses they built; all were designed by the finest Federalist architect, Charles Bulfinch. This house, at 45 Beacon Street, Boston, is preserved today as the headquarters of the American Meteorological Society, where a companion portrait of Harrison Gray Otis is exhibited (fig. 3). Otis was instrumental in developing Beacon Hill into a fashionable location and made a fortune through these and other real estate speculations. He and Sally enjoyed an extraordinary devotion to each other, as documented in letters written during Otis's political career.

In 1797 when the American artist John Vanderlyn encountered in Paris the classical style of dress depicted in this portrait, he found it "very licentious . . . the Coiffure à la Grec (for men and women) is all the mode here."[2] Sally Otis's low-cut sheer white dress, chased gold amulet, and coiffure became fashionable during the Napoleonic era. Sally, like many wealthy American ladies, kept her couture dresses in a trunk for a few years until the latest modes caught on at home.[3]

Although Sally Otis is posed according to a formula that Stuart used frequently in his female portraits, the alert expression, glowing flesh tones, and loose brushwork mark this portrait as one of the finest of his Boston period. Stuart's best paintings reveal a remarkable ability to interpret character through features brushed on with a few rapid strokes—a skill he acquired during his years of training in England. For twenty years after his return to the United States in 1792, his talents were sought after by nearly every person of importance in Federalist America.

In this portrait, however, there is visual and documentary evidence that Stuart began with the intention of including Sally's two-year-old son, Alleyne, whose overly large head is visible through the partly transparent paint on the left. Mrs. Charles

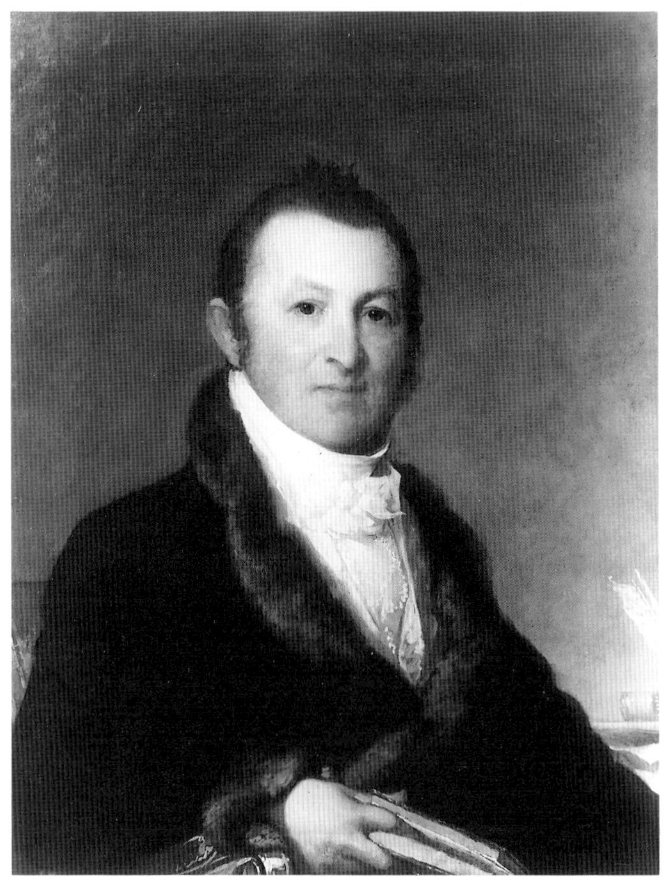

Figure 3 Gilbert Stuart
Portrait of Harrison Gray Otis, 1809
The Society for the Preservation of New England Antiquities

Davis, whose portrait was also being painted by Stuart at this time, wrote to her mother of a visit she made to Stuart's studio a few days earlier: "Mrs. Otis's picture is as perfect as it can be. She is taken with her younger son in her arms and a most beautiful one it is. I asked Mr. Stuart how it was possible to get a correct likeness of children, who are always in motion, 'I shoot flying,' was the answer."[4] An infrared photograph provides further evidence that her arm was placed originally around her son's shoulders with her fingers visibly gripping his arm in a pose resembling one of Stuart's rare double portraits, *Mrs. George Calvert and Her*

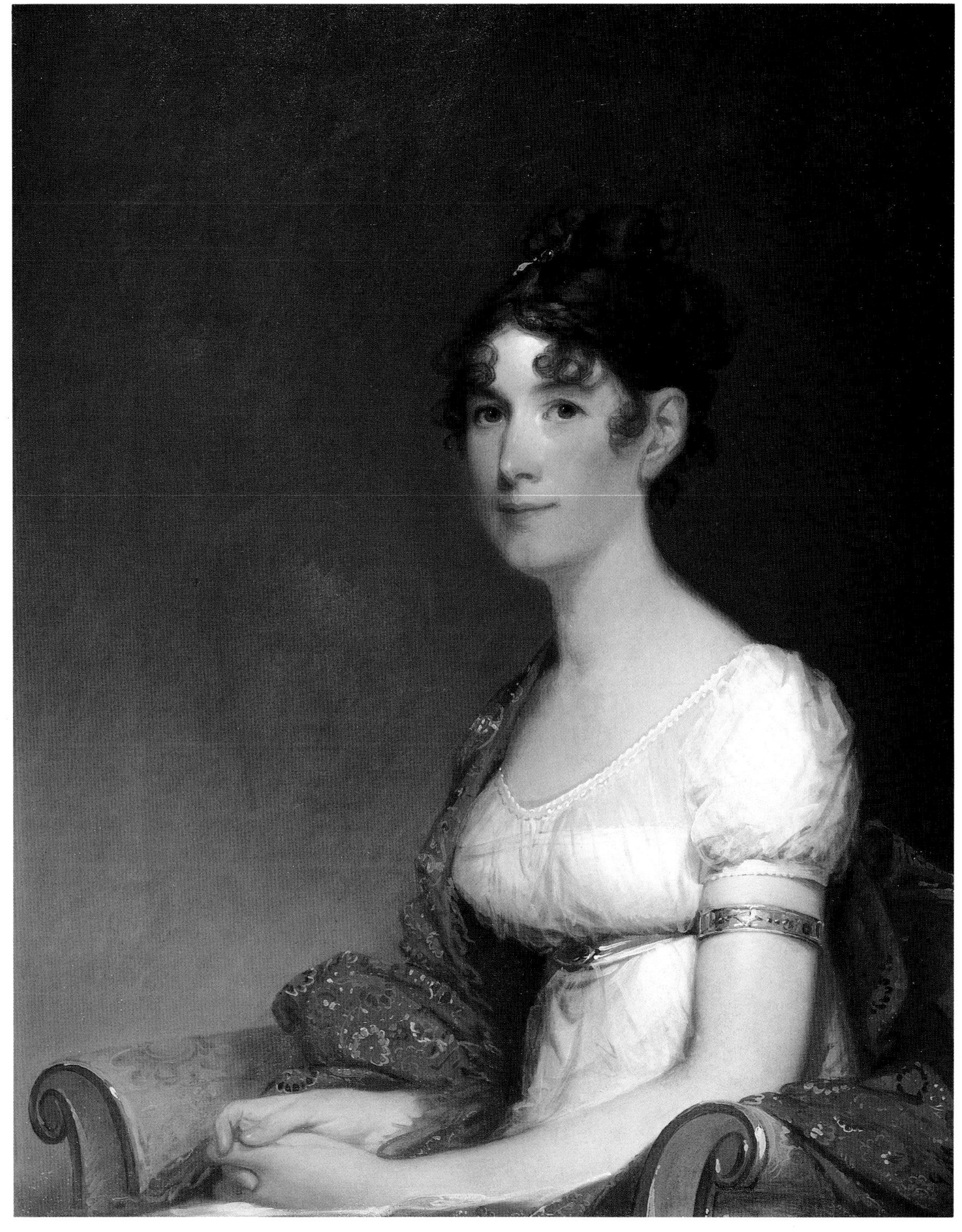

5

Oil on mahogany panel, 32 x 26 in. (81.3 x 66 cm)
Original purchase fund from the Mary Reynolds Babcock Foundation, Z. Smith Reynolds Foundation, Area Foundation, and Anne Cannon Forsyth

Daughter Caroline.[5] The reason Alleyne's head was painted out is not known, but Stuart did not make preparatory drawings for his portraits, and, if the correct proportions and likeness had not been caught at first try, he probably would have left the canvas unfinished. In this portrait, however, he preferred to paint out the image rather than lose the spontaneous brushwork and transparent tones that are the hallmark of his style.

NOTES

1. Samuel Eliot Morison, *Harrison Gray Otis, 1765–1848: The Urbane Federalist* (Boston: Houghton Mifflin, 1969), 192.
2. Letter from John Vanderlyn to Peter Vanderlyn, Paris, Aug. 14, 1797, in the New-York Historical Society, quoted in *The Classical Spirit in American Portraiture* (Providence, R.I.: Brown University, 1976), 41.
3. Morison, *Harrison Gray Otis*, 187, note.
4. Lawrence G. S. Park, *Gilbert Stuart: An Illustrated Descriptive List of his Works*, 4 vols. (New York, 1826), 565.
5. Park, *Gilbert Stuart*, no. 159.

Detail of underpainting

Peaceable Kingdom of the Branch, c. 1826–30

Edward Hicks

1780–1849

In the 1820s, soon after becoming deeply embroiled in the Quaker Separatist movement led by his cousin Elias, Edward Hicks, a Quaker preacher from Newton, Pennsylvania, began to make oil paintings of the peaceable kingdom based upon the description found in Isaiah 11:6. This painting is one of four extant versions of *Peaceable Kingdom of the Branch* that includes the Natural Bridge (Virginia's famous landmark) and belongs to Hicks's earliest period.[1] The conviction with which Hicks portrayed his longing for peace in his paintings of this period stands in ironic contrast to the fact that he and Elias led the dispute that so severely disrupted Quaker harmony. Although the Hicksites put an end to the controversy in 1827 when they withdrew from the Philadelphia Yearly Meeting, Hicks continued to paint variations of the biblical vision of peace for the following thirty years.

In this engaging example Hicks depicts the domestic animals named in the scriptural verse—a lamb, a goat, and a calf—reposing contentedly with their natural predators. The child leads them with an arm resting casually on the lion's mane. This scene of everlasting peace is set against a backdrop composed of hollow stumps and ravaged trees—Romantic imagery that was just beginning to enter mainstream American painting in the 1820s. Its use at this time is ironic in that it seems to rank a back-country painter as a forerunner of the American Romantic movement, but the appropriation of nature symbolism in this painting seems only to reflect the immediate anguish caused by the Quaker schism. In the background the Natural Bridge and beneath it the tiny figures engaged in the signing of William Penn's treaty offer models for unification used by both nature and man.

Earning his living as a decorative painter, Hicks was accustomed to the practice of copying ready-made motifs onto the wagons, chairs, milk buckets, floor cloths, and signboards he decorated. He followed the same procedure in his oil paintings, choosing images he found in the Bible, maps, and penny booklets that he combined into compositions that expressed his peaceful aspirations. Although Hick's pictorial vocabulary was limited by this practice, he nonetheless achieved an authoritative and innovative synthesis of biblical, natural, and historical emblems whose originality and complexity surpass the usual ambitions of folk artists.

Hicks's curious selection of the Natural Bridge as a counterpart to the biblical vision of the peaceable kingdom is best explained by descriptions in current travel accounts. In 1798 Isaac Weld attempted to account for this geological curiosity: "Two sides of the chasm were once united, but by what great agent they were separated, whether fire or water, remains hidden."[2] The Natural Bridge thus served as the appropriate symbol for the once united, now separated Quakers. Hicks's inclusion of the signing of William Penn's treaty functions similarly as a testament to man's fulfillment of the peaceful kingdom on earth.

The word *branch* in the title refers to the biblical passage in Isaiah 11:1, which announces the Messiah's descent as a "Branch" from the royal line of David, son of Jesse. The grapevine and branch held by the child represent the sacrificial blood of Christ—a curious choice for a leading spokesman for the inner light rather than outward sacrament as the true means of salvation. The single branch loaded with autumn leaves and growing out of the hollow stump also seems to provide a visual counterpart to the title, as though the new growth on old wood represented the prevalence of the Hicksites over the Orthodox Quakers.[3]

Hicks produced over sixty versions of the peaceable kingdom between 1820 and 1849.[4] Today he is celebrated as this country's foremost representative of nineteenth-century folk painting.

Notes

1. Eleanore Price Mather, *Edward Hicks, His Peaceable Kingdoms and Other Paintings* (Newark, N.J.: University of Delaware Press, 1983). Mather illustrates three other versions containing the Natural Bridge: no. 2, p. 95 (Yale University Art Gallery), no. 3, p. 96 (Abby Aldrich Rockefeller Folk Art Collection), and no. 4, p. 97 (Mead Art Museum, Amherst College). These date between 1822 and 1826. No. 6, p. 99, is titled *Peaceable Kingdom of the Branch*, but does not contain a Natural Bridge. A later painting (1846–47), titled *Peaceable Kingdom of the Pensive Lion*, no. 57, p. 150 (Denver Art Museum), contains a natural bridge.
2. Isaac Weld, *Travels through the States of North America* (London, 1798), 221.
3. Letter from Judith W. Harvey, Director, Friends Center, Guilford College, Greensboro, N.C., to Barbara B. Millhouse.
4. Mather, *Edward Hicks*, p. 21.

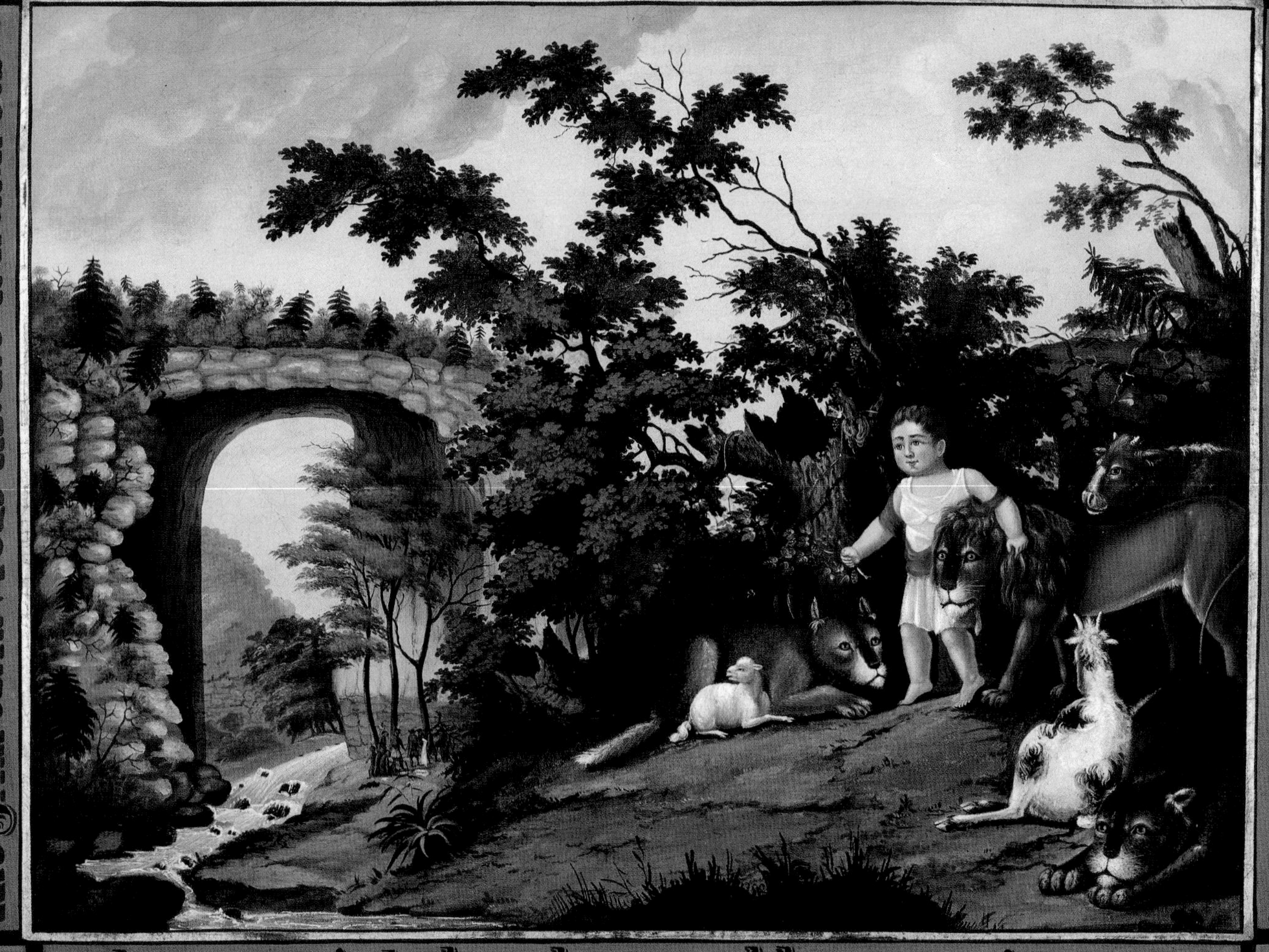

6

Oil on canvas, 23½ x 30¾ in. (59.7 x 78.1 cm)
Gift of Barbara B. Millhouse

Jared Sparks, 1831
Thomas Sully
1783–1872

On February 7, 1831, the prominent Bostonian William H. Eliot wrote to his Harvard classmate Jared Sparks: "You could not do Margaret (who continues well) and me a greater favor than sitting for your portrait to Sully, now decidedly the first portrait painter in the country. As a production of his pencil it will have great value to me, but as a souvenir of its subject I will not attempt to say how dear it will be to us both."[1] In his *Account of Pictures* Sully entered March 15, 1831, as the day of the portrait's completion and the receipt of one hundred dollars as payment.[2] During his lifetime Sully painted over two thousand portraits—a prolific output that resulted in uneven quality, but the balance established between idealization and individuality, as well as its apparent ease of execution, makes this portrait one of Sully's finest.

Born in Horncastle, Lincolnshire, England, Thomas Sully emigrated at age nine to Charleston, South Carolina. He was able to acquire enough training in Charleston and Richmond, Virginia, so that in 1809 when he was offered a trip to London, he was already an experienced artist. In London he studied with Benjamin West, an American neoclassical artist serving as history painter to George III, but it was the Romantic exuberance of the

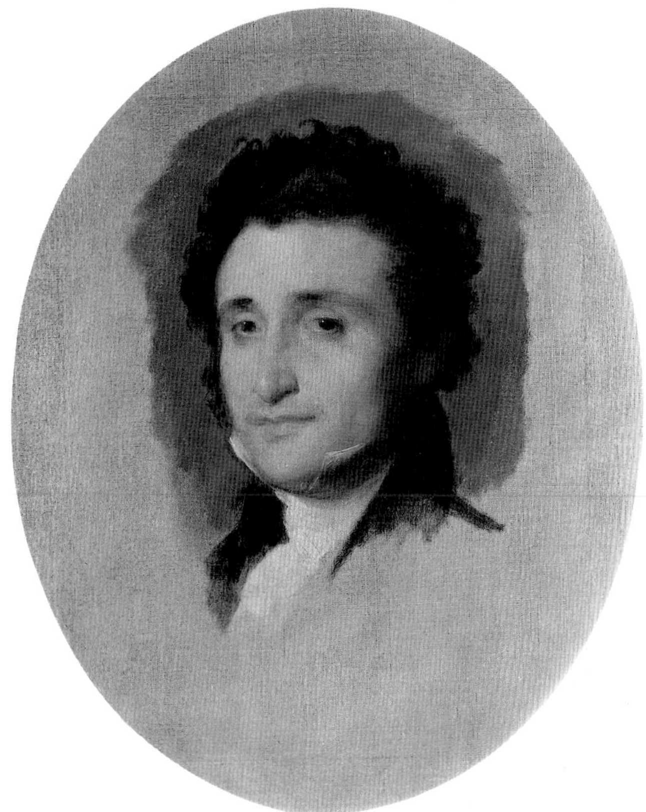

Figure 4 Gilbert Stuart
Jared Sparks, n.d.
New Britain Museum of American Art, Connecticut,
Stephen Lawrence Fund and Charles F. Smith Fund, 1955.6

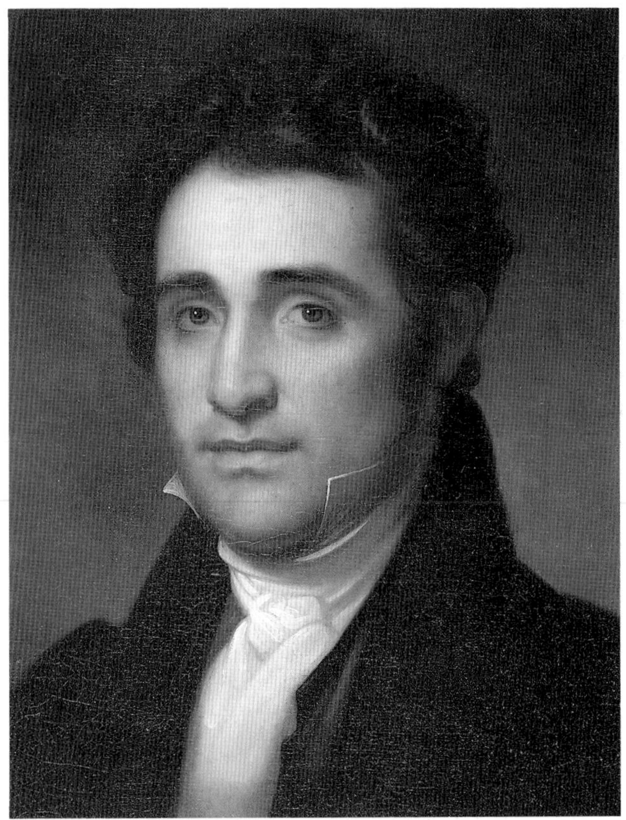

Figure 5 Rembrandt Peale
Portrait of Jared Sparks, n.d.
The Harvard University Portrait Collection, Harvard University,
Cambridge, Massachusetts,
Bequest of Lizzie Sparks Pickering, H244

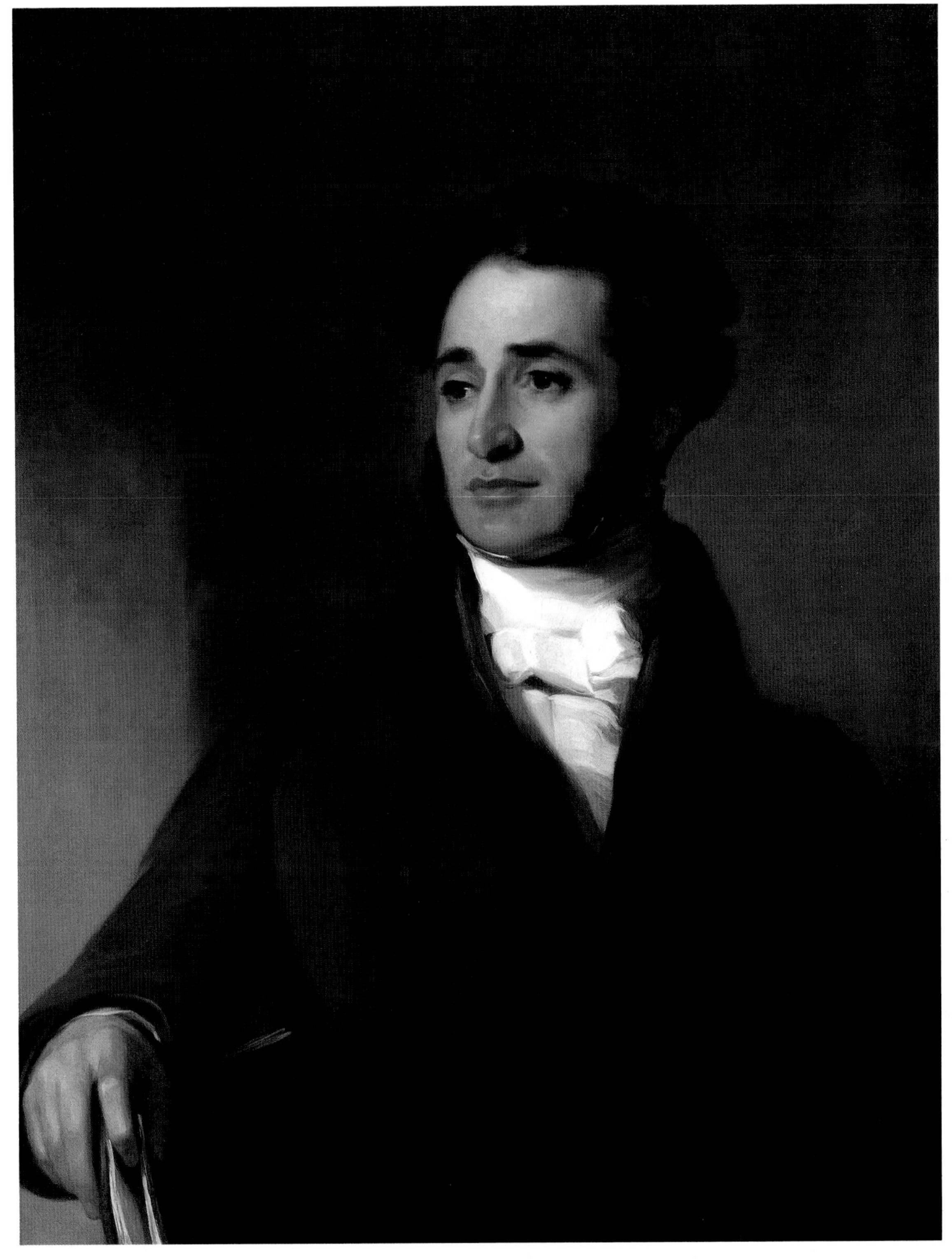

7 Oil on canvas mounted on panel, 36⅜ x 28¼ in. (92.4 x 71.8 cm)
Signed and dated at lower left: TS. 1831
Gift of Barbara B. Millhouse

leading British portrait painter Sir Thomas Lawrence (1769–1830) that left its mark permanently on Sully's style.[3] After only nine months abroad, Sully returned to the United States and settled in Philadelphia, where his inclination to improve upon his sitter's features and his effortless brush attracted a large clientele, making him the leading portrait painter in this country after the death of Gilbert Stuart.

The subject of this portrait, Jared Sparks (1789–1866), grew up in a poor family on a farm in Willington, Connecticut, where in his youth he worked as a carpenter in the summer and a school teacher in the winter. Recognizing his scholarly aptitude, the clergy raised funds to send him to Phillips Academy in Exeter, New Hampshire. In 1815 he graduated from Harvard with honors and in 1819 he was ordained as the pastor of the new Unitarian Church in Baltimore. After four years in the ministry, he resigned, moved to Boston, and purchased on credit the *North American Review*, which under his editorship grew into a distinguished periodical. Simultaneously, he had begun to compile and edit letters and documents for a twelve-volume publication entitled *The Diplomatic Correspondence of the American Revolution.* Perhaps the completion of this monumental task in 1830 or the anticipation of his forthcoming three-volume biography, *The Life of Gouverneur Morris*, occasioned his civic-minded classmate, William H. Eliot, to commission this portrait.

To establish Spark's scholarly profession Sully has used one of Stuart's favorite devices of placing his sitter with his finger marking a place in a book. This also gives the sitter the appearance of being caught at a momentary interruption from his reading. Sparks is portrayed as a vigorous, dashing young man belying his forty-two years and his cerebral life-style. Derived from his studies with Sir Thomas Lawrence, the sweeping movement of the figure is achieved through the forward thrust of his right arm—the forceful diagonal that reaches from his hand to his head—and the subtle twist of his body. The low viewpoint, narrow shoulders, elongated neck, curly black hair, and sparkling dark eyes combine to transform this Harvard scholar into an ideal of masculine elegance.

Few men in Spark's time had such a penchant for exhaustive scholarship, yet Sully portrays him with the remote gaze of a visionary and a dreamer. In the eulogy presented on March 14, 1866, William Reed Deane contradicted such a portrayal: "Imagination and fancy were not characteristic of [Sparks's] mind. He was methodical and indefatigable in every work he had immediately in hand."[4] The combination of a brilliant scholar and an artist who aimed for romantic idealization resulted in a portrait that speaks as much of the sentiment fashionable in their time as of the power of personality.[5]

Notes

1. Herbert Baxter Adams, *The Life and Writing of Jared Sparks* (Cambridge, Mass.: Riverside Press, 1893), 548.
2. Sully's *Account of Pictures* dates this painting as begun Jan. 25, 1831, finished March 15, 1831. Its price was $100. Apparently the portrait was already in progress when Eliot wrote the letter.
3. Thomas Sully, "Recollections of an Old Painter," *Hours at Home* 10 (November 1869): 69–74.
4. William Reed Deane, *In Memoriam Jared Sparks, LL.D.* Obit, March 14, 1866.
5. For comparison there are two other known portraits of Jared Sparks: one unfinished portrait by Gilbert Stuart (fig. 4) and another by Rembrandt Peale (fig. 5).

Detail of *Jared Sparks*

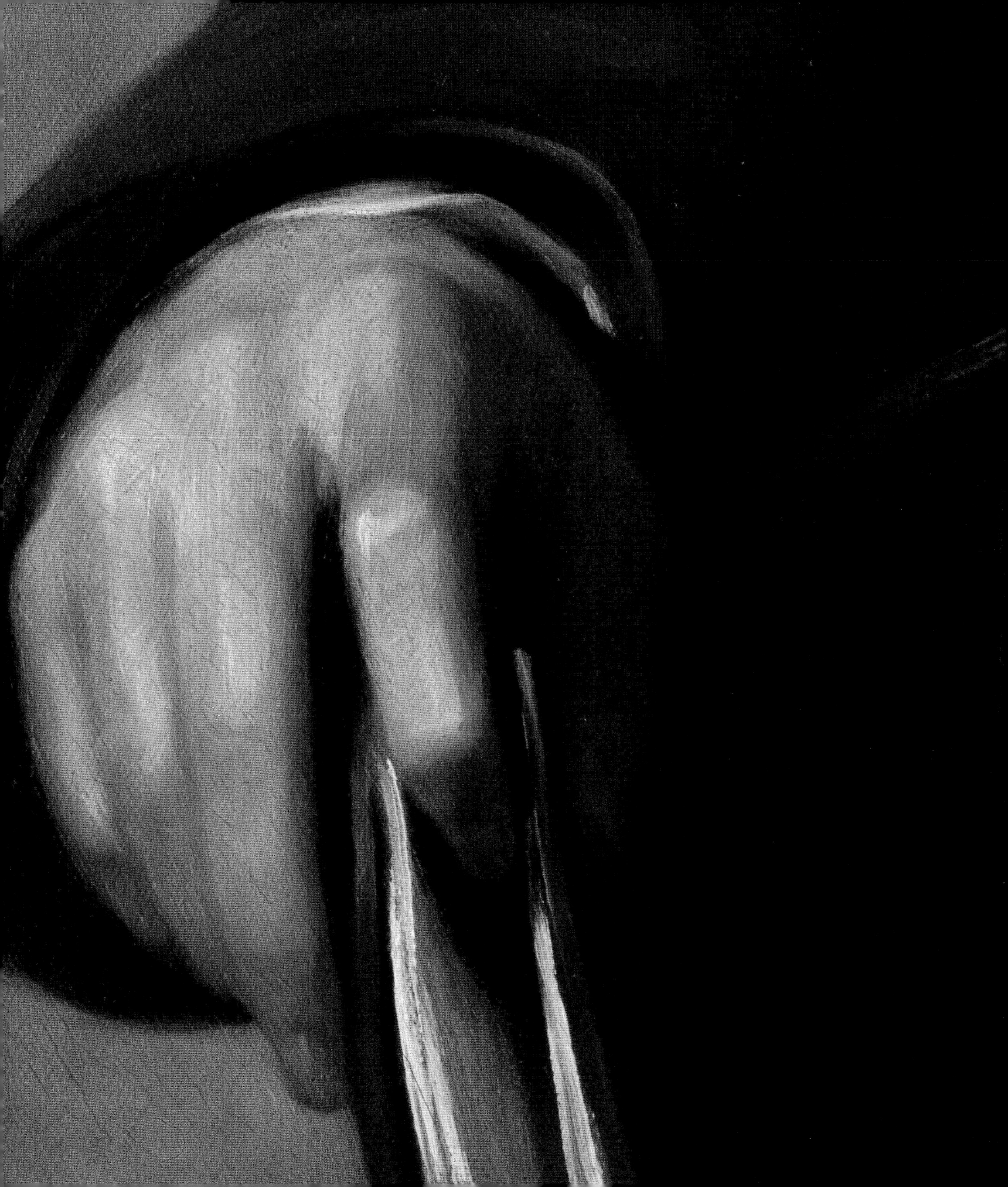

WITCH DUCK CREEK, c. 1835

JOSHUA SHAW

c. 1777–1860

English-born Joshua Shaw achieved fame in his homeland as a landscape painter with *The Deluge* (undated; Metropolitan Museum of Art, New York), a painting more highly received than Turner's work of the same theme. In 1817 Shaw settled in Philadelphia, and shortly thereafter began traveling from Massachusetts to Georgia, painting what had "rarely been made the subject of pictorial delineation."[1] He painted views of such obscure locales as Spirit Creek, Georgia; Fayetteville, North Carolina; Passaic River, New Jersey; and Witch Duck Creek, Norfolk, Virginia. Assembled in a portfolio entitled *Picturesque Views of American Scenery*, the aquatints were published in 1819–21 in collaboration with the engraver John Hill. The prints were bought by the hundreds, and the portfolio became both a milestone in American printmaking and a pioneer effort in the depiction of the American landscape in a Romantic mood.

Witch Duck Creek was discovered in London as one of a pair of paintings. Both have cream-colored borders, an indication that

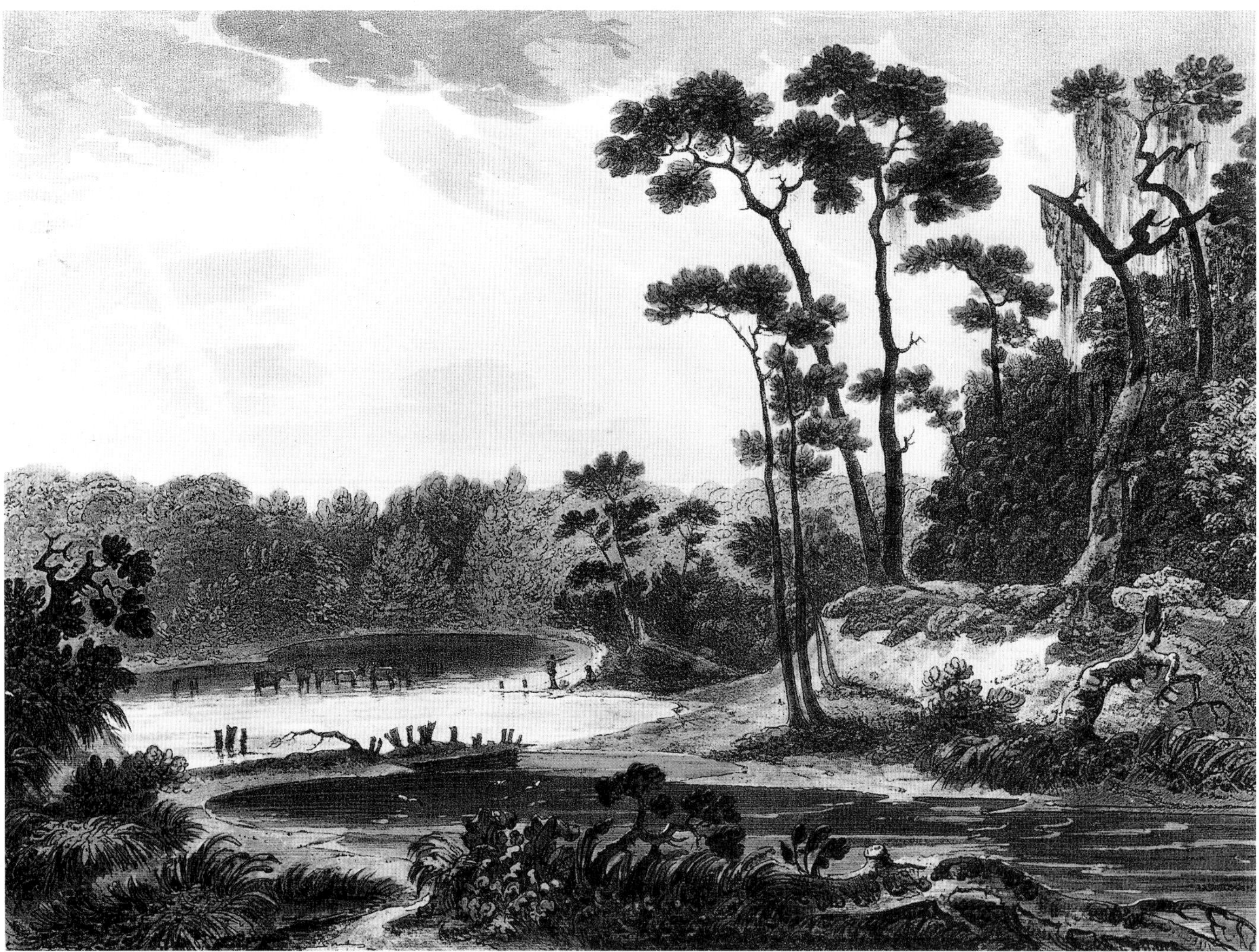

Figure 6 JOHN HILL, after Joshua Shaw, *Oyster Cove, Lynhaven River*, n.d. The New-York Historical Society, New York City

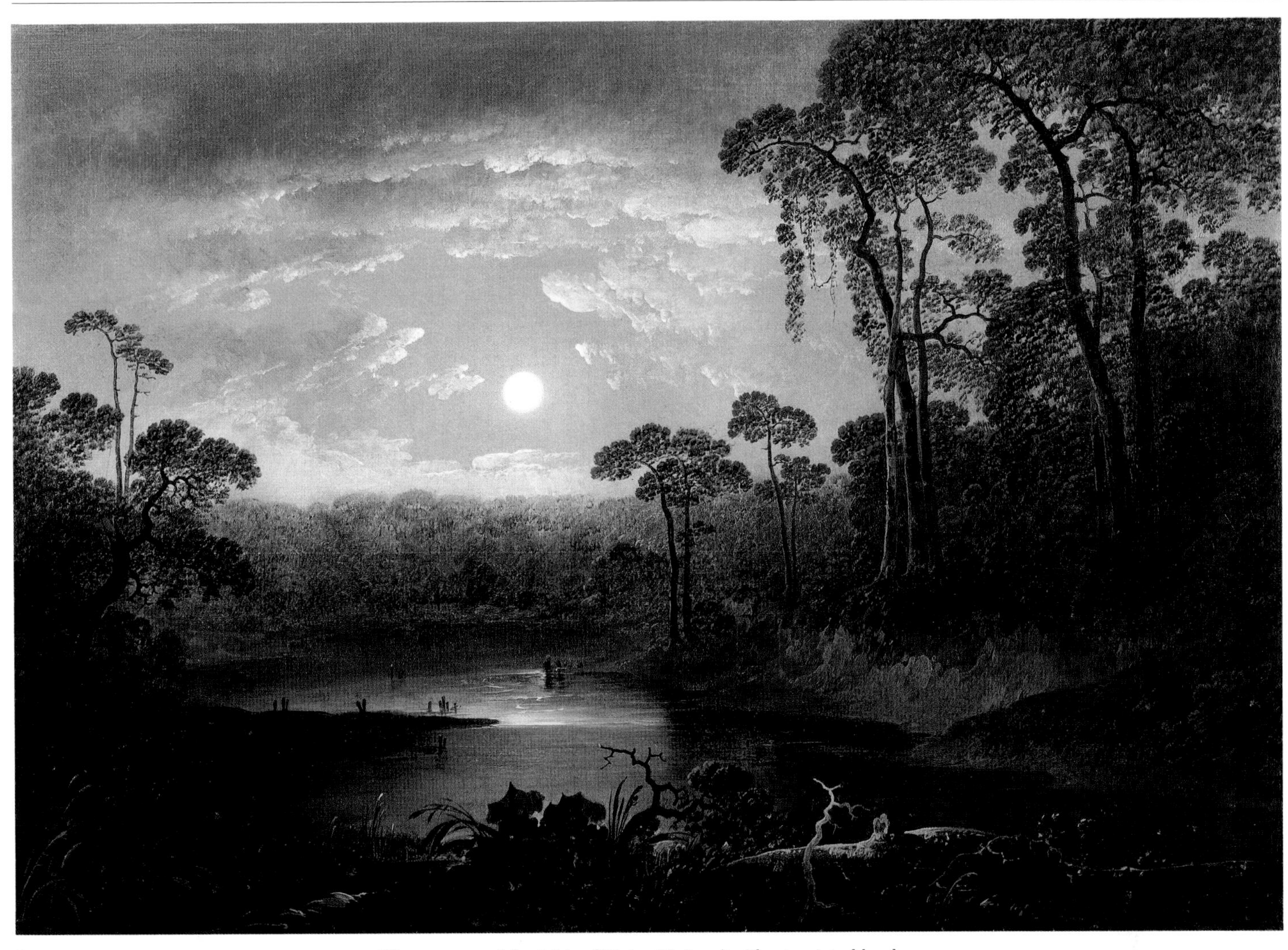

8 Oil on canvas, 10 x 14 in. (25.4 x 35.6 cm) without painted border;
13½ x 18 in. (34.3 x 45.7 cm) with painted border
Inscribed by the artist on the original stretcher:
NO. 12, WITCH DUCK CREEK
Gift of Charles H. Babcock, Sr.

they were intended to be reproduced as engravings. One was inscribed on the stretcher in Shaw's handwriting: "No. 11, Scene, North Carolina." The other was inscribed: "No. 12, Witch Duck Creek." The former was exhibited in 1835 at the Artists' Fund Society in Philadelphia as "No. 230, A Scene in North Carolina, approaching the Allegheny Mountains, one of a series about to be published in London by Fisher, Son, and Co., in the finest line manner, with letter press descriptive of the subjects, historical and domestic." *Witch Duck Creek* was undoubtedly a part of the same series, which seems never to have been published.

The date of *Witch Duck Creek* is unknown but the appearance of painting no. 11 in the 1835 exhibition suggests that *Witch Duck Creek* was painted about that time. Another painting of the same size that seems to belong to this series is inscribed in Shaw's handwriting: "Wood and Prairie on fire by night as it appeared to the artist in the State of Georgia 1821. Joshua Shaw, painted 1835." The inscription indicates that Shaw was using sketches from his earlier trips throughout the South as a basis for the later series. The similarity between Hill's aquatint *Oyster Cove, Lynhaven River* (a site near Norfolk; fig. 6)—published in *Picturesque Views of American Scenery*)—and *Witch Duck Creek* is unmistakable; both were probably based on sketches made during his trip to this area in connection with the publication of *Picturesque Views of American Scenery*. With its coves and inlets, seaside grasses, and scrawny trees, the area is today relatively unchanged from when Shaw painted it over 130 years ago.

The eerie moonlight in *Witch Duck Creek* gives the painting an ambiance appropriate to its name. History tells us that a woman named Grace Sherwood, accused by local authorities of witchcraft, was thrown into Lynhaven Bay and informed that if she could swim, she was a witch; if she drowned she was innocent. The outcome of her grim watery judgment can only be surmised, but since this episode the area has been called Witch Duck. As depicted by Joshua Shaw, the emanating mood was one consistent with the Romantic spirit that was beginning to emerge in the early decades of the nineteenth century.

NOTE

1. Joshua Shaw, *Picturesque Views of American Scenery* (Philadelphia: M. Carey and Sons, 1819-21), 1.

Detail of *Witch Duck Creek*

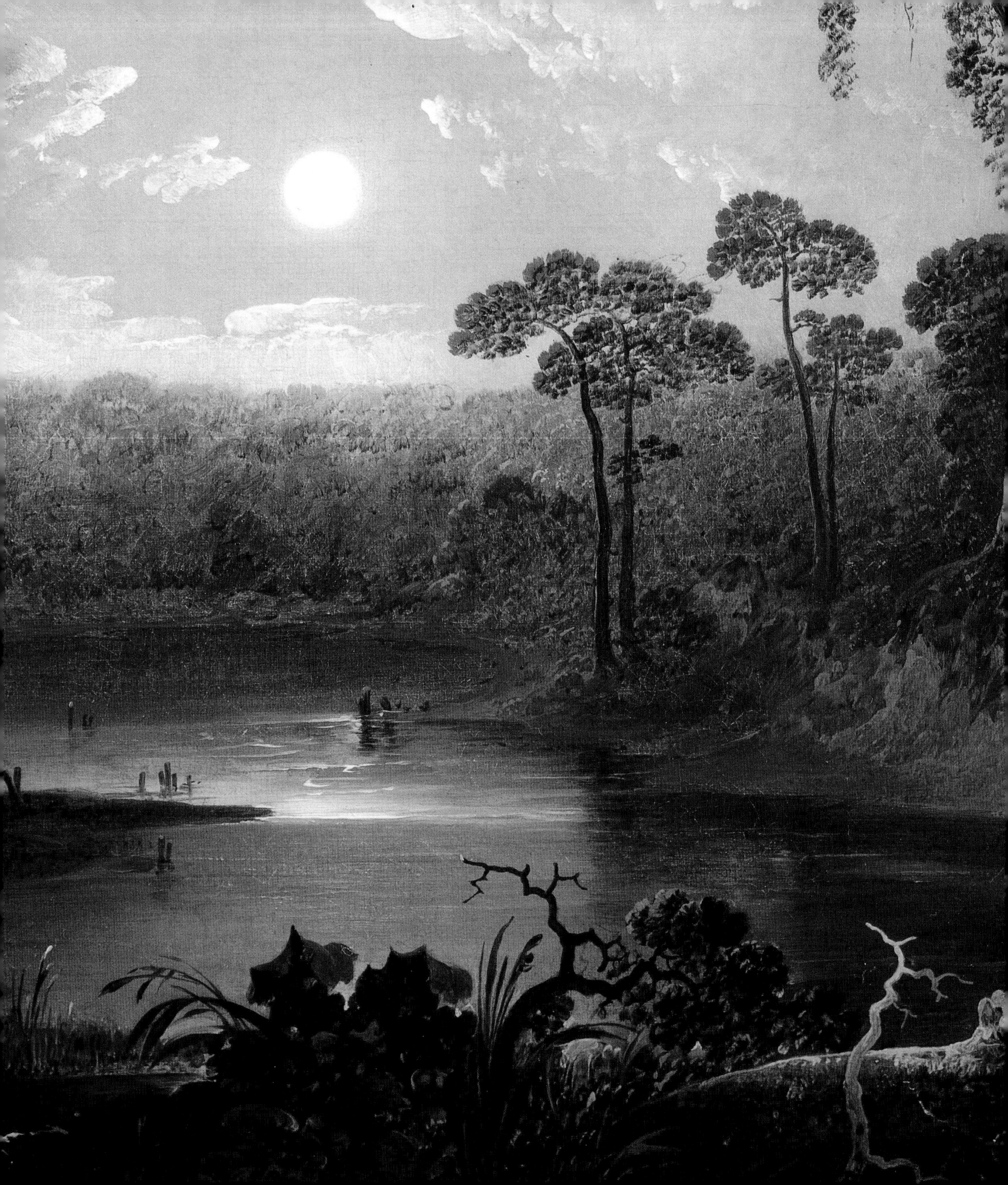

In the Catskills, 1836
Thomas Doughty
1793–1856

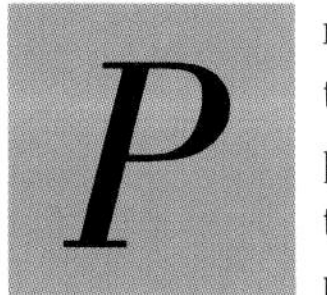

Preceded by generations of English writers arguing the qualities of the sublime, the beautiful, and the picturesque, Thomas Doughty set out to address these issues using the contours of the Catskill mountains. By so doing, he became one of the first to portray the natural features of American landscape according to the dictates of the sublime and the beautiful. Although he never achieved the mastery of color, light, and atmospheric conditions that were to appear in later landscape paintings, the silvery tonalities of Doughty's work create an appealing harmonious effect. During a visit to the Pennsylvania Academy of the Fine Arts in 1826, Thomas Cole, the artist who was to become the leader of the first American school of landscape, was inspired by the Doughty landscapes on exhibit there.[1]

In an effort to make a better living in 1832, Doughty moved with his wife and five children from Philadelphia to Boston. Although he was known to have made frequent trips from Boston to the Catskills in 1836 and 1837, it is doubtful whether he found intact this prescription of mountain, reflecting lake, and cascade. So replete with philosophical and religious meaning was this formula that for forty years artists searched far and wide for these natural elements, sketched them individually on the spot, and reworked the drawings into a variety of studio compositions. As late as the 1870s Albert Bierstadt, for example, was attracting celebrity for shaping these very same natural features to the contours of the Rocky Mountains and the Sierra Nevadas.[2] Unfortunately, like many early self-taught artists in this country, Doughty could not acquire the professional training to convey the full impact of a Romantic landscape. Doughty's early attempts in this branch of art, however, laid the foundation for this country's first native school of landscape painting.

Like most subsequent Hudson River School artists, Doughty derived a compositional formula from the seventeenth-century landscapes of Claude Lorrain. In this painting, for example, Doughty arranges trees and boulders like stage scenery on either side of the view and places the foreground, middle, and background in distinct planes that lead the eye into the distance. The monochromatic tonality suggests that Doughty, who was never to achieve convincing color, had greater access to engravings than original oil paintings. The diminutive figure gazing into the sunset became a frequent motif in subsequent landscape painting and affirms man's feeling of insignificance in the face of the overwhelming forces of nature. Although the single figure can also be found in European Romantic landscape painting, its westward gaze and ubiquity in American landscape seem to reflect a growing national consciousness of the immense size of this continent. Through this intermediary the contemporary viewer can share the awe and wonder that Americans experienced as they began to interpret natural beauty as signs of God's blessing upon this nation. The works of Washington Irving, James Fenimore Cooper, and William Cullen Bryant contain numerous verbal descriptions of the feeling Doughty translated into pictorial form.

Notes

1. William Dunlap, *History of the Rise and Progress of the Arts of Design in the United States*, vol. 3 (New York: Benjamin Blom, 1965; first published 1834), 148.
2. Albert Bierstadt's *Sierra Nevada* in the Reynolda House collection shares the same natural features with Doughty's *In the Catskills:* Both have a central mountain peak, a waterfall, and a reflecting lake.

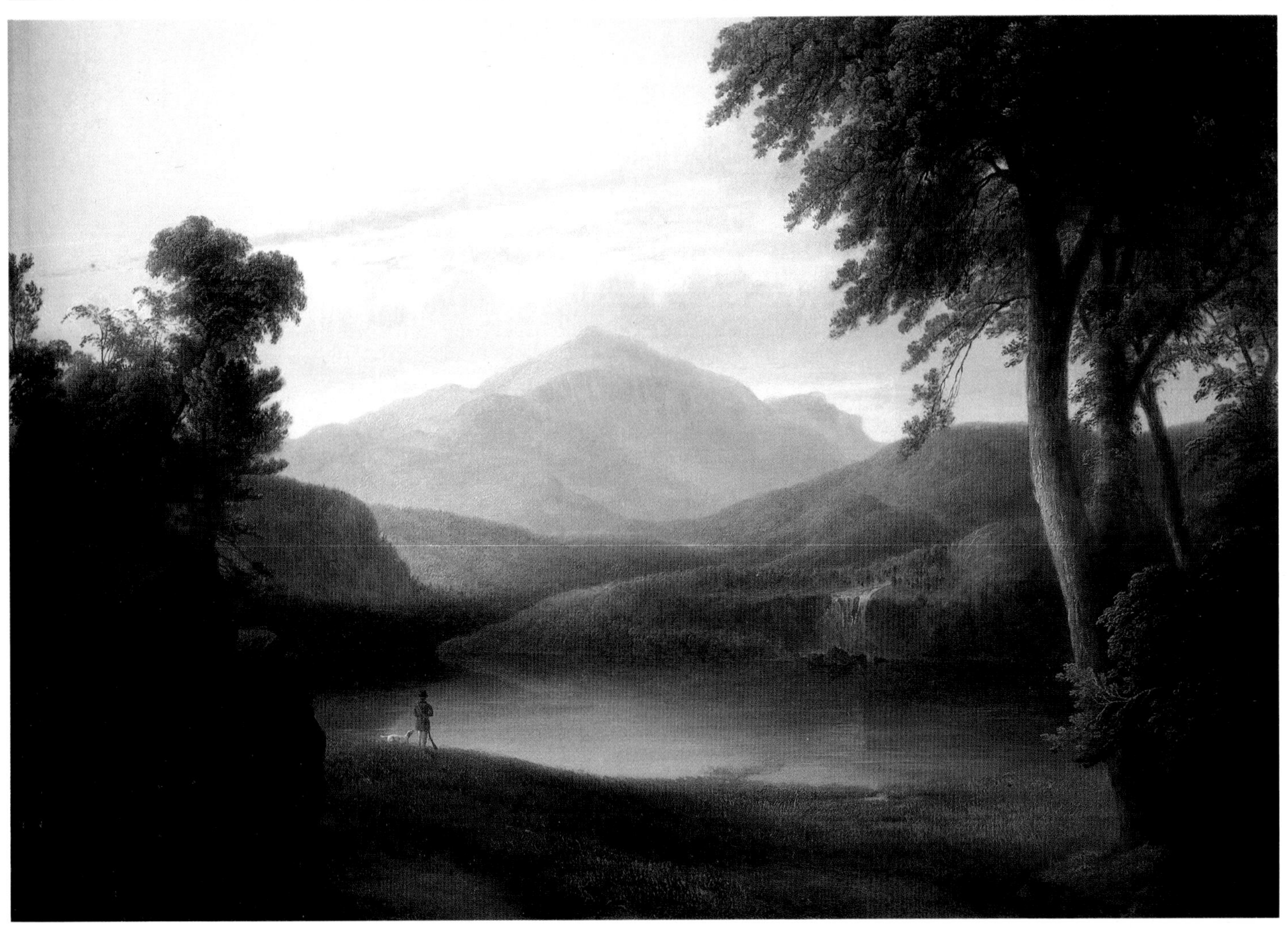

9

Oil on canvas, 25 x 35 in. (63.5 x 88.9 cm)
Signed and dated at center left: T DOUGHTY/1835
Gift of Barbara B. Millhouse

The Card Players, c. 1847–50

William Sidney Mount

1807–1868

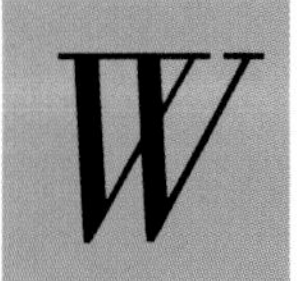

William Sidney Mount was the first American-born artist to achieve widespread fame for the depiction of everyday life. He accommodated American concerns into a genre tradition that reaches back to seventeenth-century Dutch painting. This tradition was transmitted to Mount primarily through the engravings by the eighteenth-century English satirist William Hogarth and the nineteenth-century Scottish genre painter Sir David Wilke. Although Mount took his scenes from his native village of Stoney Brook, Long Island, his art transcends the boundaries of his village and raises issues that probe the moral concerns of Americans during his time.

At first glance the confident attitude of the coatless player facing the viewer seems to suggest he holds the winning hand. On closer observation, his bleary eyes, unbuttoned trousers, and the jug between his feet undermine his apparent assuredness by casting doubt upon his sobriety. His opponent, dressed more formally, is hesitantly pulling a card from his hand. Through masterly control of the facial expressions and gestures, Mount has expertly conveyed the intensity of this decisive moment, but he seems to have left the outcome of the game open to conjecture.

Rather than present his scene in a public place, Mount has removed his players to a broken-down shack behind a house, which implies they are partaking in an activity that does not meet accepted ethical standards of the community. The narrative unfolds in subtle details: A single gold coin on the three-legged bench substituting as a card table indicates that they are gambling, and the earthenware on the chimney, doorjamb, and floor also seem to enhance the story. In the manner of the English satirist William Hogarth, the pitcher, chamberpot, and mortar and pestle have emblematic implications that suggest gluttony, disgust, and ill health.

The seriousness of the misconduct of these two men is underscored by another detail. A crumpled scrap of paper, lying under debris in the overturned barrel, contains the title "SERMONS by Rev. L. D———." Once again Mount heightens the drama by avoiding settled conclusions. His intent in including the sermon might be a warning against the sin of card playing on the Sabbath, but it might also indicate that a clergyman is equally susceptible to human failure, and having scrapped his sermon, he passes the afternoon gambling with the local farmer.

Throughout his life the pitfalls of idleness troubled Mount. Hogarth's popular series of engravings *The Rake's Progress* and *Idleness and Industry* graphically illustrate the ruin that besets those who reject a life of hard work and virtue. The subject was treated articulately in a widely read book of sermons entitled *Seven Lectures to Young Men* published in 1844 by the Indianapolis preacher Henry Ward Beecher, who later became a famous pastor in Brooklyn.[1] In this painting the state of decay into which the outbuilding has fallen signifies the inevitable state of ruin into which these reprobates will fall—a metaphor also used in Beecher's sermons. Therefore, even though Mount hoped this painting would elicit a chuckle, its moral admonition is nonetheless clear.

Note

1. I am endebted to John F. Kasson, professor, Department of History, University of North Carolina at Chapel Hill, for this observation.

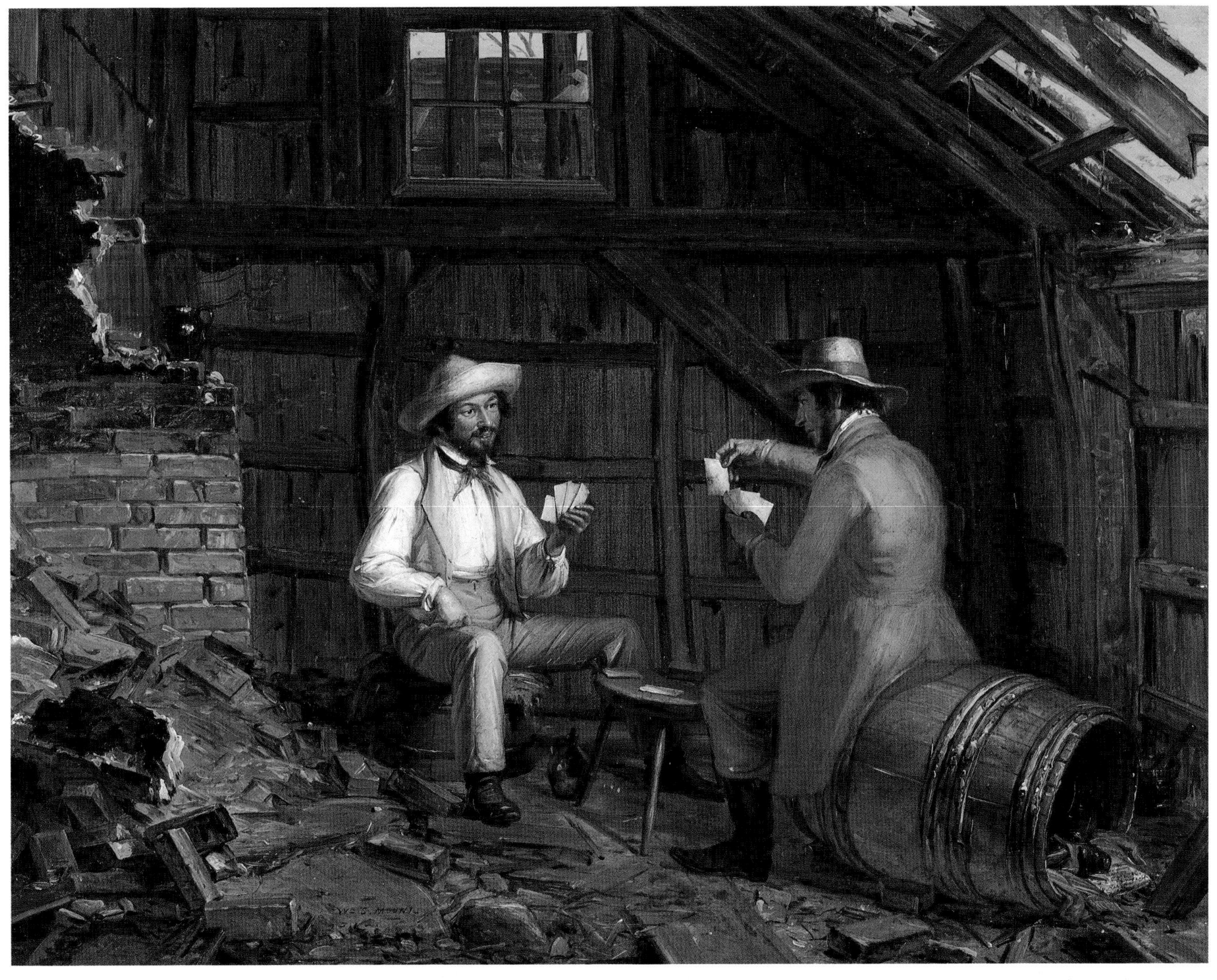

10

Oil on panel, 19 x 24¾ in. (48.3 x 62.9 cm)
Signed at lower left: WM. S. MOUNT-
Gift of Barbara B. Millhouse

Home in the Woods, 1847
Thomas Cole
1801–1848

On February 26, 1847, Thomas Cole received a letter from the American Art Union in New York City offering him five hundred dollars to paint a landscape, the subject and size to be of his own choice. By November of the same year, the completed painting *Home in the Woods* was listed in the Art Union catalog. In this painting Cole has located a pioneer family on the shore of a lake in view of Mt. Chocorua, the most spectacular peak in the Sandwich range of the White Mountains in New Hampshire. Cole first visited the area in 1828, and used the famous peak in a number of subsequent paintings.[1] Because it had a lake at its base, and could be seen in view of Lake Winnipesaukee and Squam Lake as well, it supplied a readily available combination of the beautiful and the sublime.[2]

The foreground of *Home in the Woods* confronts the spectator with a tangle of forest debris whose sawed trunks and mangled limbs take on a turbulent anthropomorphic quality, as if the pristine wilderness had been witness to a catastrophic military defeat. The broken limb in the foreground has been appropriated from Jacob Ruisdael's *The Jewish Cemetery* (1668), which was well known in Cole's time. Cole has flanked these fallen trees and branches with emblems of the vanishing wilderness. The ax-hewn stump records destruction by man and the lightning-struck tree destruction by nature. The hellebore, strategically placed

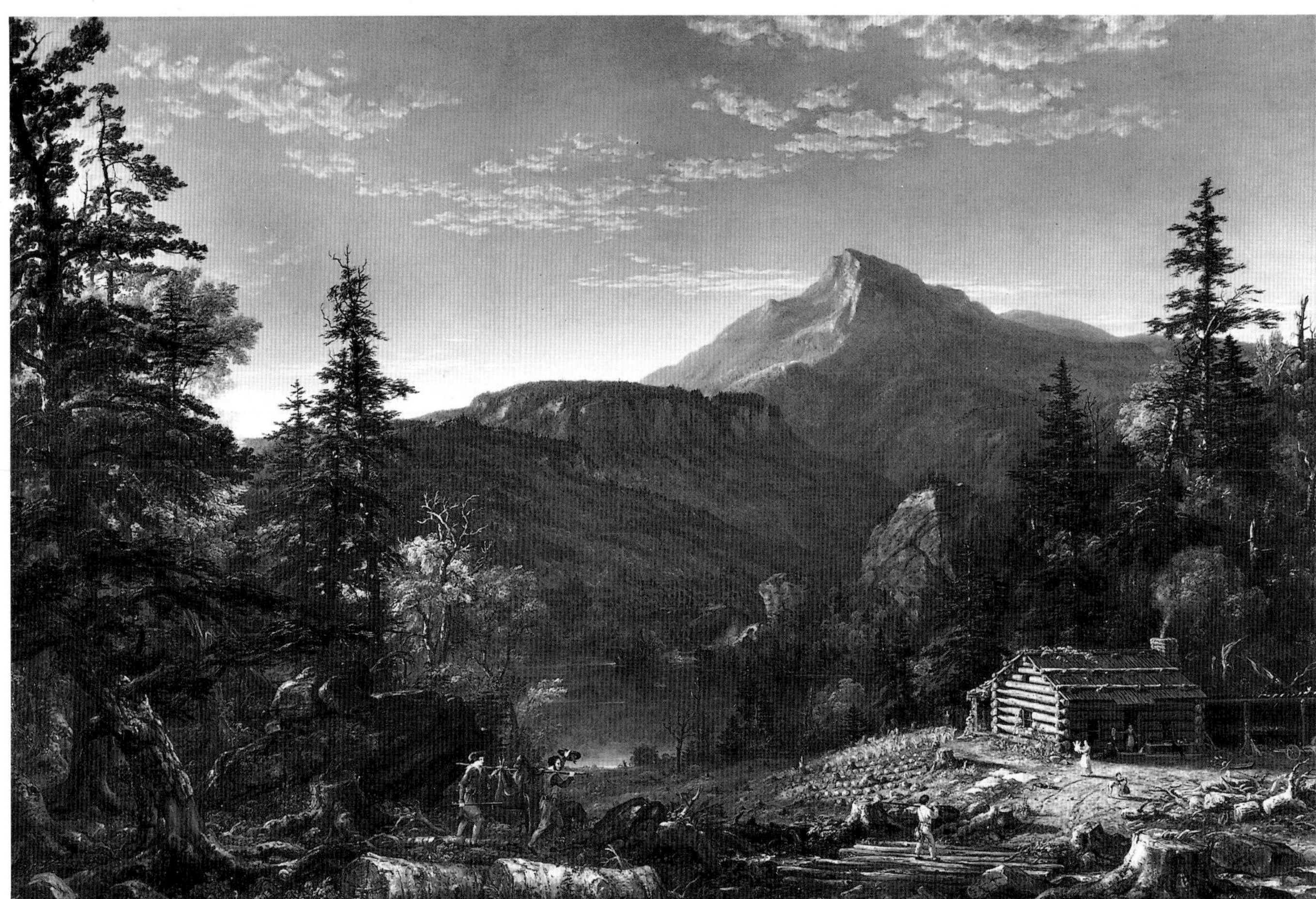

Figure 7 Thomas Cole, *The Hunter's Return*, 1845. Amon Carter Museum, Fort Worth, Texas, 156.83

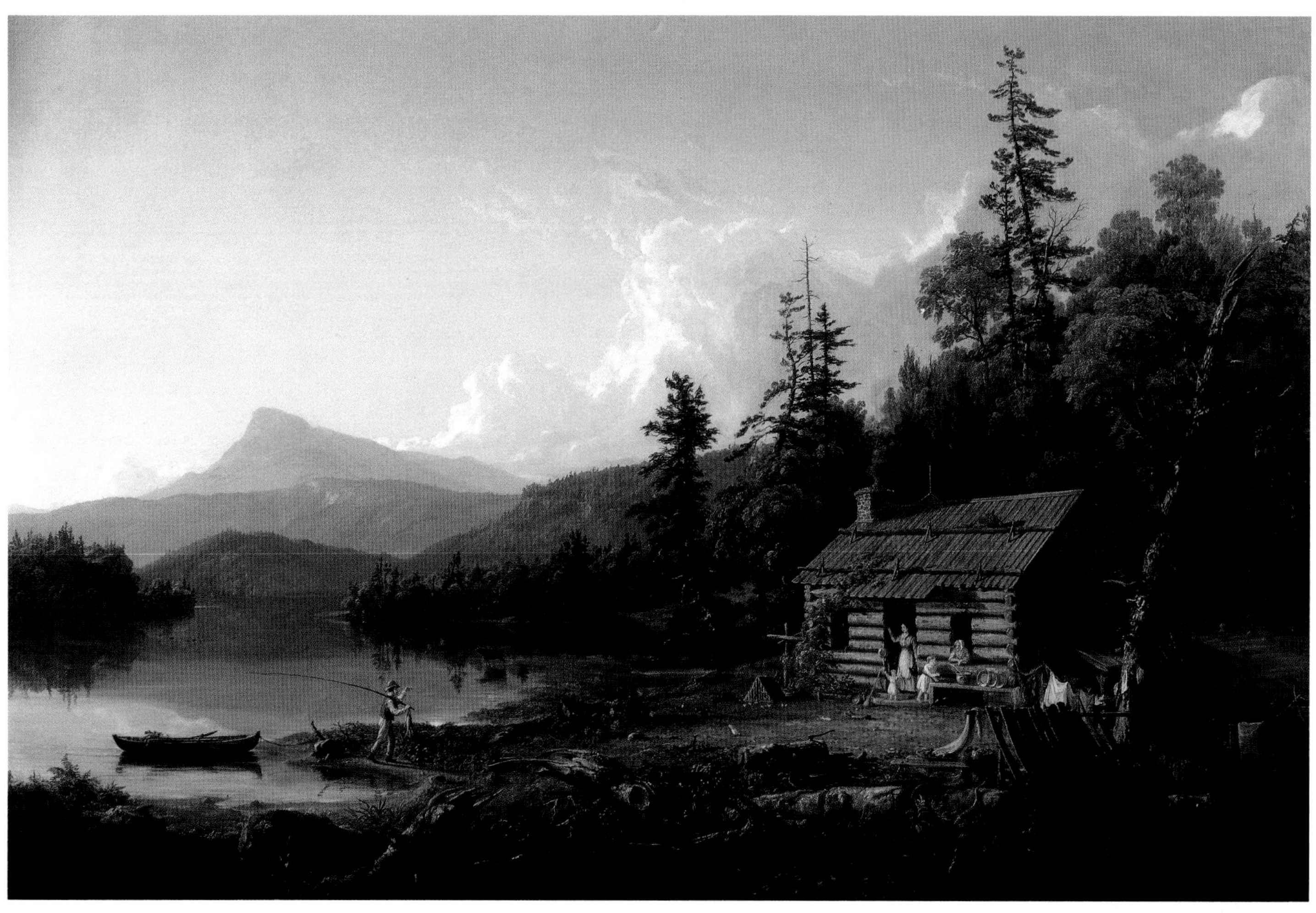

11

Oil on canvas, 44 x 66 in. (111.8 x 167.6 cm)
Signed on the barrelhead at lower right: T Cole
Gift of Barbara B. Millhouse

between the sawed ends of a felled tree in the foreground, provides a further clue to Cole's attitude. Appearing frequently in Hudson River School paintings, this plant was in Cole's time a well-known antidote for melancholy—a sign that reinforces Cole's despair over his disappearing wilderness.[3]

Cole's genius for injecting his imagery with many layers of meaning can be seen clearly in the iconography associated with the passage of time. Evening light appears not so much for its rosy hue as for its suspension between day and night—a transitional time that calls for quiet contemplation of change and loss. Cut out of the wilderness, the sprouting garden behind the cabin alludes to the seasonal transition from spring to summer. The brilliantly colored and centrally located butter churn, no longer facing the drying effects of the morning sun, is not a mere detail of pioneer life, but another device through which the passage of time can be perceived. These transitory aspects of nature are measured against the larger symbol of permanence and hope for eternal life found in the unchanging contours of the majestic mountain peak that presides over the entire scene.

Under the influence of his friend and biographer, the Reverend Louis LeGrand Noble, Cole joined the Episcopal Church in 1842, and became preoccupied with the cross as a principal subject for his paintings. It may therefore be possible to read the triangles and the items that appear in this painting in threes as intentional symbols of the Trinity. Scholars have interpreted the wooden support at the left of the cabin as a Christian cross,[4] though it is composed of not two but three sticks and is evidently intended to support a vine.

Although he was only forty-seven years old when he painted *Home in the Woods*, Cole's health had been failing for a year. In February 1848 he died of pneumonia. *Home in the Woods*, one of his last major paintings, seems invested with a sense that human life is transcended by a life hereafter.

NOTES

1. Mt. Chocorua also appeared in *The Last of the Mohicans* (1827), *The Hunter's Return* (1845; fig. 7), and *The Pic-nic* (1846), as well as a number of lesser-known paintings.
2. Donald D. Keyes, *The White Mountains: Place and Perceptions* (Hanover, N.H.: University Press of New England, 1980), 88. The cows in *Home in the Woods* may refer to the legend of Chief Chocorua, for whom the peak is named. He is purported to have uttered a curse as he died that made the countryside uninhabitable to cattle.
3. Robert Burton, *The Anatomy of Melancholy, what it is, with all the kinds, causes, symptoms, prognostics, and several cures of it. In three Particians*, by Democritus Junior (Philadelphia: J. W. Moore, 1855), 400–401, 406.
4. Matthew Baigell, *Thomas Cole* (New York: Watson-Guptill Publications, 1981), 78.

Detail of *Home in the Woods*

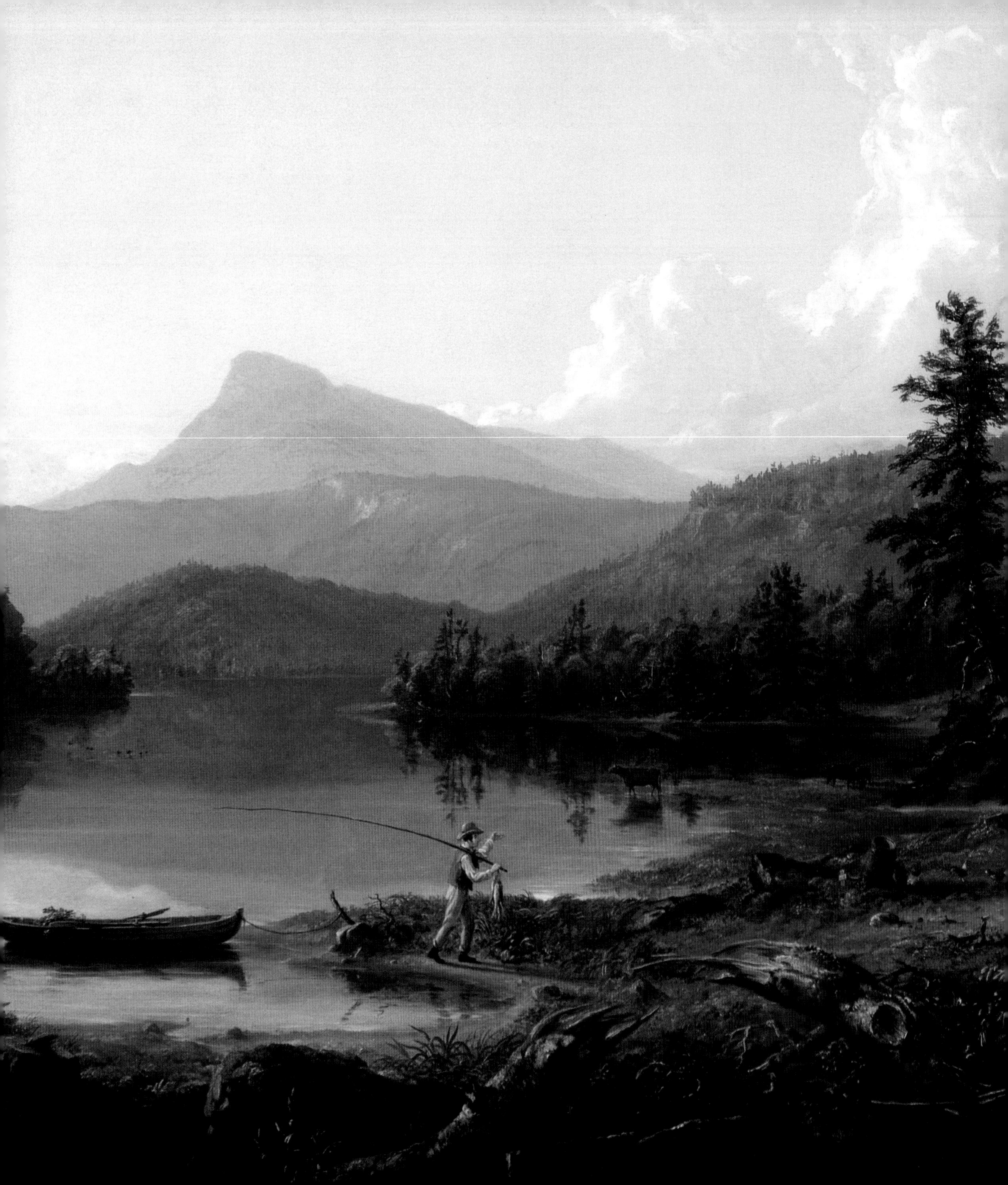

THE ANDES OF ECUADOR, 1855
FREDERIC EDWIN CHURCH
1826–1900

Painted after Frederic Church's first trip to Ecuador, *The Andes of Ecuador* combines the scientific and religious concerns of Church's time into one grand panorama. The infinite botanical detail, the terrifying depths of the abyss, and the overwhelming sense of unlimited space combine to communicate a powerful sense of the sublime. As landscape became the primary vehicle for communicating this intense feeling of awe, artists became proficient in creating the illusion of infinitely receding vistas, and Church mastered the imagery more skillfully than any other American artist in mid-nineteenth-century America.

In the 1850s Church had been following in the footsteps of his teacher, Thomas Cole, painting New England scenery in the Hudson River School manner, when he became absorbed in a recently published four-volume book, *Cosmos,* written by the great German scientist Baron Alexander von Humboldt. In this brilliant effort to describe the geographical features of the world as an organic whole, Humboldt declared Ecuador without equal in its rich display of "the phenomena of physical effects in their general connection," a place where nature could be seen as "one great whole, moved and animated by internal forces." He challenged the artist to go "in the humid mountain valleys of the tropical world to seize . . . on the true image of the varied forms of nature."[1] In April 1853 Frederic Church, then only twenty-seven years old, accepted the challenge and set out with his friend Cyrus W. Field for Colombia and Ecuador.

After several months Church returned to his New York studio where he used his pencil sketches as the basis for a number of small South American landscapes. The critics, however, followed the progress of a larger panorama, which was described in the *Crayon* as "his most important work yet."[2] *The Andes of Ecuador* was exhibited at the Boston Atheneaum in 1855 and at the National Academy of Design in New York in 1857, drawing glowing descriptions from the press.

According to his pupil William James Stillman, Church spent a long time arranging the details into a single composition, but once decided, he painted "with a rapidity and precision which were simply inconceivable by one who had not seen him at work."[3] In this masterpiece of his first trip to South America, Church has described the topographical section of the entire country by flanking a wide plateau with the double chain of the Andes. On the right he has placed the smoking cone of Cotopaxi, and on the left the quiescent peak of Tungurahua, which contemporary critics thought to be the famed Chimborazo, although its jagged contours differ from Chimborazo's rounded dome.[4]

Like Humboldt before him Church was fascinated by the novelty of a country where the "different climates ranged the one above the other."[5] In this painting he illustrates Humboldt's description by condensing into a single view the moist rain forest, the dry savannah, the wind-swept paramo, and the snow capped peaks. To an age that interpreted seasonal change as an emblem of life's cycle, this new equatorial configuration—where perpetual summer prevails in the river valleys and perpetual winter prevails on the mountain peaks—required a new symbolic reading. The eternal summers of the tropical regions seemed to provide evidence of the long-lost Garden of Eden. The variety and richness of tropical vegetation, painted with loving precision, was believed to be unmistakable evidence of a bountiful God.

Tracing the flow of water in *The Andes of Ecuador* provides a lesson in the diversity and unity inherent in the divine plan. On the left, countless threads of cascades spill down the distant slopes and converge into a barely perceptible lake. These placid waters flow into a rushing river that glides across a verdant valley and finally disappear into a deep gorge. On the right, another stream follows a similar alternation of repose and motion as it swirls around the rocks and plunges down the cliff into a natural basin, joining the other river in a gorge that passes out of the picture far beneath the viewer. With his all-inclusive sensibility Church has mastered the portrayal of water through its many manifestations (liquid, foam, vapor, cloud, snow, and ice) in a demonstration of a primary condition of nature—perpetual change.

In Thomas Cole's allegories the river represented man's voyage through life, but in the great Ecuadorian panorama of his student Church, the river's countless sources, lengthy journey, and elusive transmutations discourage an analogy with human life and mortal time and seem instead to embody the great eons associated with geology. The water's flow, moving from numerous streams in the background into a single torrent in the foreground, symbolically pursues a course from the remote past into the immediate present. Suspended over the precipice, the viewer stands at a point of transition—at the moment of a civilization's genesis.

The work of the great English landscape painter J.M.W. Turner, whose engravings Church knew and whose original oil paintings he could have seen at the National Academy of Design,[6]

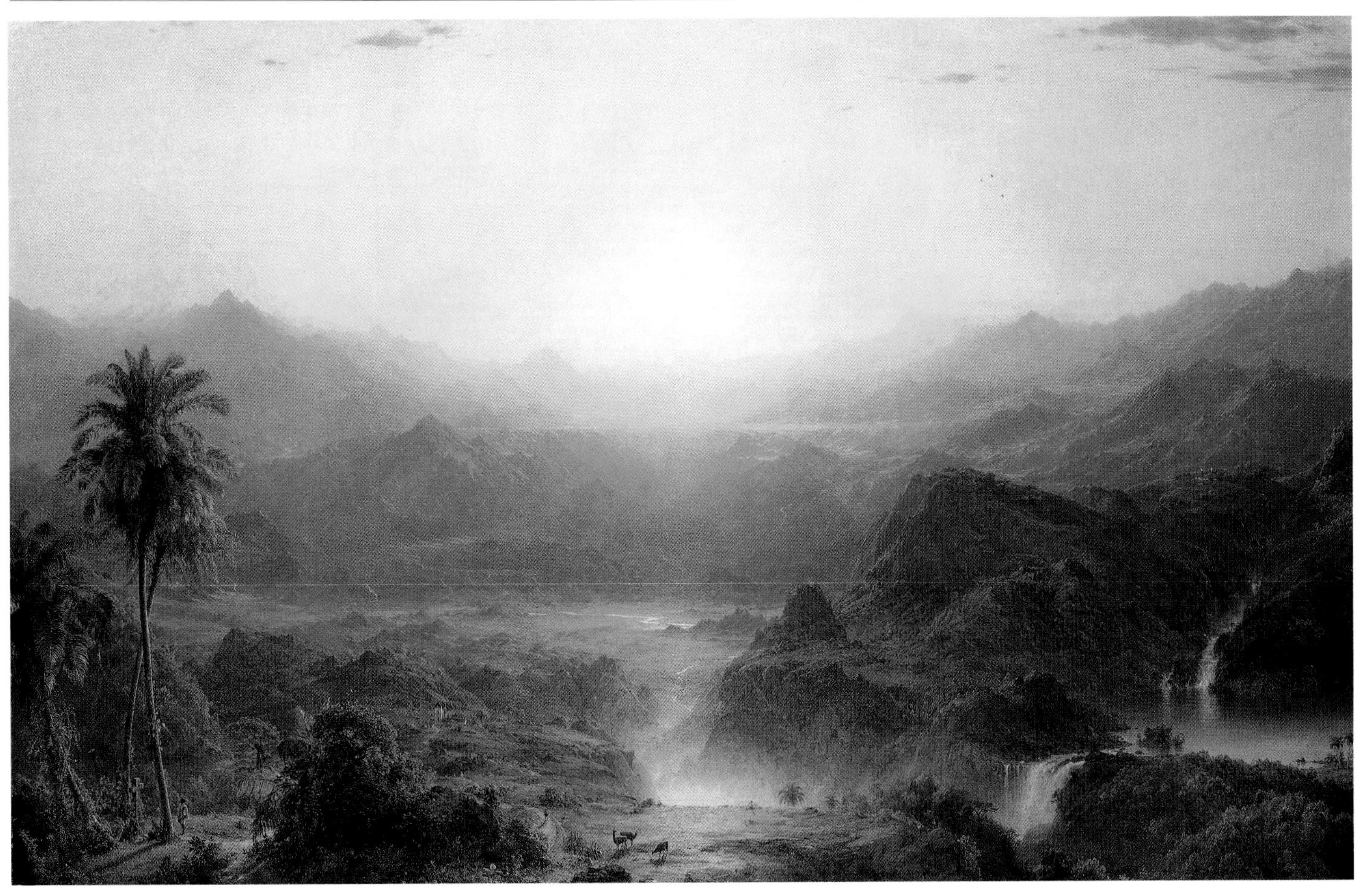

12

Oil on canvas, 48 x 75 in. (121.9 x 190.5 cm)
Signed and dated at lower center: F. E. CHURCH/-1855-
Original purchase fund from the Mary Reynolds Babcock
Foundation, Z. Smith Reynolds Foundation,
Area Foundation, and Anne Cannon Forsyth

offers a precedent to paintings with a centrally located sun. Like Turner, Church had been influenced by the paintings of the seventeenth-century French landscapist Claude Lorrain, who was the first to use this device. American artists, however, had a predilection for conveying light in a different manner than their European forebears; they imbued their paintings with a stillness and all-pervasive illumination that suggest divine presence and inspire a sense of transcendence. The light-filled radiance designates *The Andes of Ecuador* Church's luminist masterpiece. Luminism is generally considered the visual counterpart of Emerson's transcendentalism, but Church's casting of the central sunbeam, as it bisects the reflecting surface of the plateau, into the form of a cross supports an orthodox Christian interpretation. Crosses and chapels scattered throughout the landscape supply symbols of the divinity of Christ and the promise of redemption. These details reinforce the suggestion that *The Andes of Ecuador* stands today as "the first painting to declare the distinctive unity of light and faith."[7]

NOTES

1. Alexander von Humboldt, *Cosmos: A Sketch or A Physical Description of the Universe*, vol. 2 (New York: Harper & Brothers Publishers, 1855), 93.
2. *Crayon* 1 (April 25, 1855): 268.
3. William James Stillman, *The Autobiography of a Journalist*, vol. 1 (Boston and New York: Houghton, Mifflin, and Co., 1901), 114.
4. Nicholas Millhouse has identified this peak unquestionably as Tungurahua, situated south of Quito near Banos. Manthorne, *Creation and Renewal: Views of Cotopaxi by Frederic E. Church* (Washington, D.C.: Smithsonian Institution Press, 1985), 14, states that Church explored Tungurahua from Riobamba. He must have taken the eastern route from Ambato to Riobamba, passing through Banos and within view of both Tungurahua and Cotopaxi. This area also abounds in the high, narrow waterfalls that he painted into the background.
5. Humboldt, *Cosmos*, vol. 1, 33.
6. *Crayon* 1 (May 9, 1855): 291, reported that in 1834 the National Academy of Design exhibited Cole's work beneath the work of Turner.
7. David C. Huntington, "Church and Luminism: Light for America's Elect," in *American Light: The Luminist Movement, 1850–1875* (Washington, D.C.: National Gallery of Art, 1980), 180–81.

Detail of *The Andes of Ecuador*

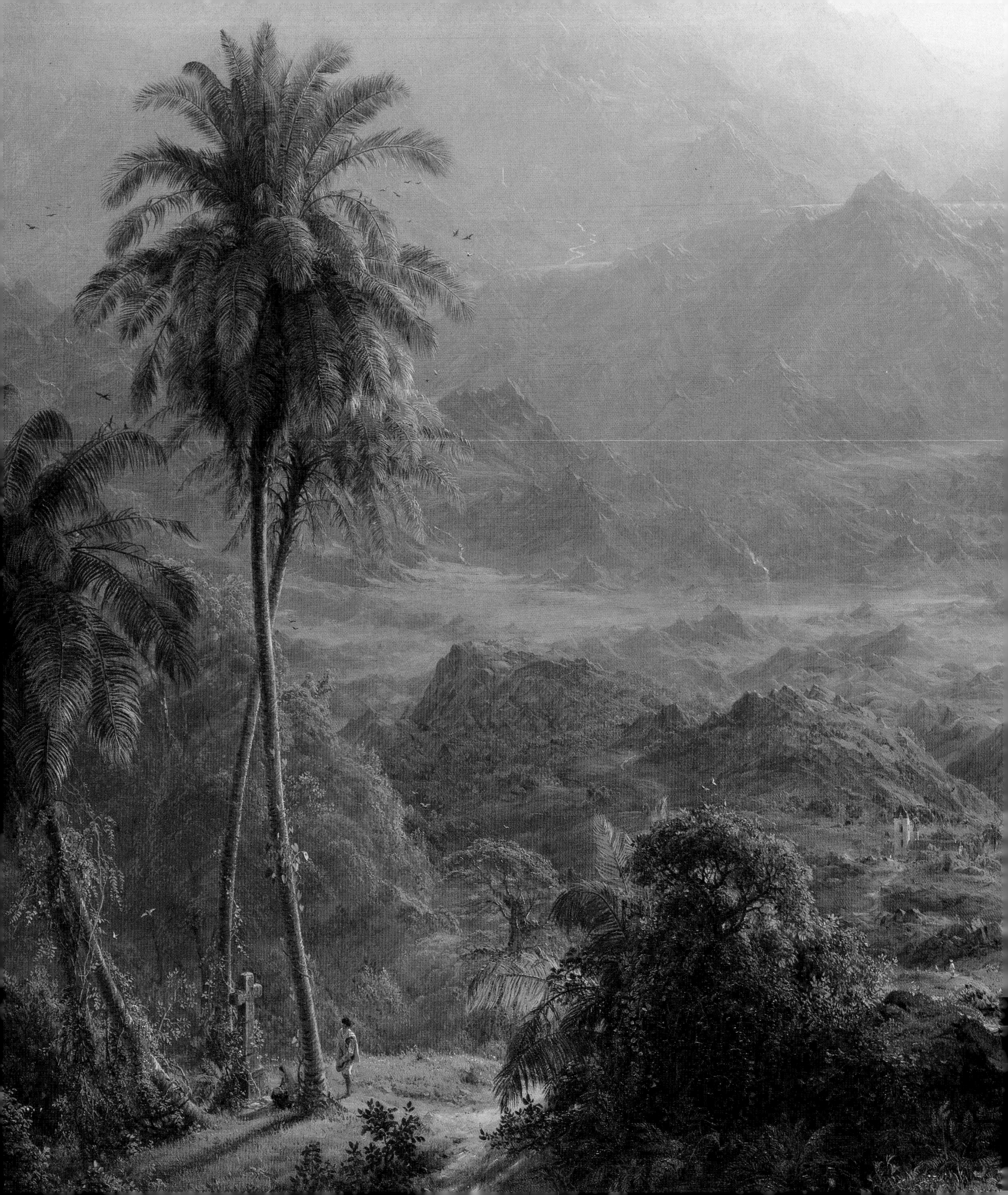

ROCKY CLIFF, c. 1860
ASHER B. DURAND
1796–1886

In this painting Asher B. Durand explores at close hand a rock outcropping that supports an array of lichens, mosses, and plant life. He has cast the scene in the lackluster uniformity of a cloudy day, deriving dramatic effects not from theatrical variations of weather but from the viewer's confrontation with a massive granite wall part way up a steep mountain incline. At the far right a glimpse of a distant mountainside discloses that this ledge is located at a considerable elevation. The leafless trees in the background offer a traditional Romantic contrast between their transitory, frail appearance and the solid, enduring quality of the geological formation.

This particular rock, however, does not seem to be chosen so much as a traditional symbol of permanence than as an up-to-date example of geological processes. Durand's intense interest in its well-defined stratification and the peculiar effects of erosion that shaped the mushroomlike rock on the right evokes a suspicion that he, like so many people of his generation, might be grappling with the astounding data that rock strata were yielding at this time. With the publication of Charles Lyell's *Principles of Geology* in 1830, the most advanced geological discoveries were brought to a large public, and their impact on biblical authority began to be widely disputed. The magnitude of the newly discovered geological time scale was unfathomable to many nineteenth-century minds accustomed to dating Creation at 4004 B.C. The subject of *Rocky Cliff*, therefore, suggested far-reaching associations that were forecast a hundred years earlier by the pioneer of modern geology, James Hutton (1726–1797), when he wrote, "in the beveled edges of folded strata" we view "the ruins of an older world."

With rocks central to a rapidly changing worldview, it is not surprising that this subject found its way into the paintings of the leading New York artists.[1] Yet aesthetic considerations also enter prominently into the dynamics that created *Rocky Cliff*. In the 1850s converts to John Ruskin's view that the imitation of nature was the principal function of art were growing at such a rate that the English art critic's book *Modern Painters* became the mainstay of nearly every landscape painter. Durand expressed his agreement with Ruskinian aesthetics through a series of letters he wrote in 1855 for the art journal *Crayon*. In 1863 a short-lived publication called *The New Path* took up Ruskin's challenge to imitate nature so enthusiastically that a writer warned that the artist must copy nature or "be lost to art."[2] Although Durand was not a member of the American Pre-Raphaelites who sponsored this journal, their theories led Durand to a closer observation of nature reflected in paintings such as *Rocky Cliff*.

NOTES

1. In Benjamin Champney's *Sixty Years' Memories of Art and Artists* (Woburn, Mass., 1900), 104, he reports that he joined a group of artists at North Conway, New Hampshire, "to make close studies" of "a group of boulders." Although this statement is not dated and the artists are not named, this description follows his mention of finding there in 1851 the New York contingent headed by John Casilear and including David Johnson, John Williamson, and a nephew of Asher B. Durand.
2. Linda S. Ferber and William H. Gerdts, *The New Path: Ruskin and the American Pre-Raphaelites* (Brooklyn, N.Y.: Brooklyn Museum, 1985), 25.

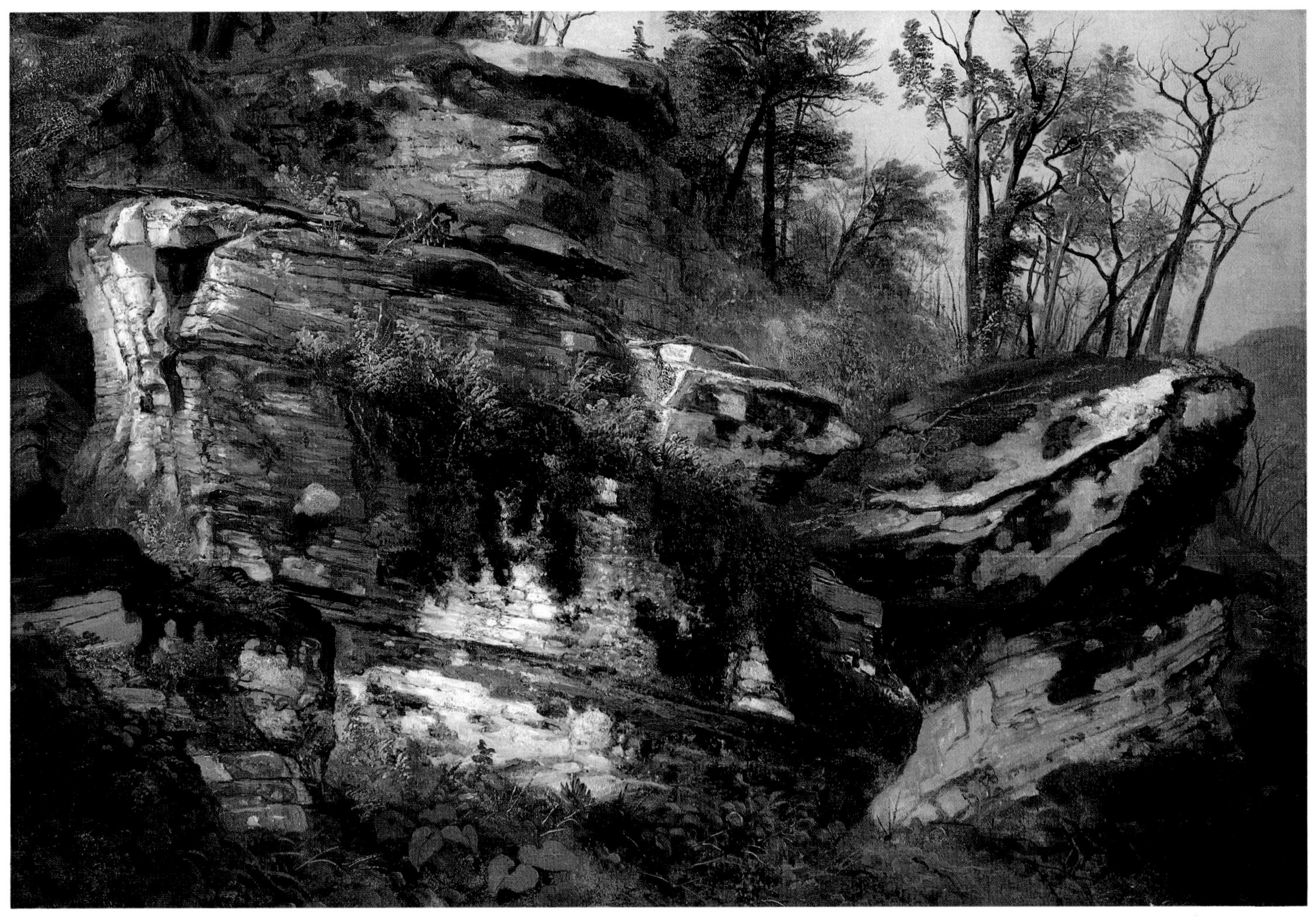

13

Oil on canvas, 16½ x 24 in. (41.9 x 61 cm)
Signed at lower right: ABD

Natural Bridge, Virginia, 1860

David Johnson

1827–1908

In the late eighteenth and the nineteenth centuries in both Europe and America, the Natural Bridge in Virginia was considered a rival to Niagara Falls in its power to evoke the sublime. Thomas Jefferson, who owned the Natural Bridge and described it in his *Notes on the State of Virginia* (1784), believed that "It is impossible for emotions arising from the sublime to be felt beyond what they are here [at Natural Bridge]." If viewed from below it was "delightful," but from above it was "painful and intolerable." Its extraordinary impact was magnified when a traveler approached from the wagon road that ran over the arch. The chasm was hidden so well by trees, brush, and rocks, which formed a natural parapet, that travelers could pass over the bridge without being aware of the two-hundred-foot drop on both sides. Moreover, this natural causeway so conveniently connected two mountains that writers had to assure their readers that it was "entirely the work of God."[1]

With the formation of the bridge through erosion still a matter of speculation, the mystery and terror of the sight was heightened by the popular belief that it had been created by a cataclysmic event. Jefferson himself had written that it "seems to have been cloven through its length by some great convulsion."[2] But in 1816 the amateur scientist Francis W. Gilmer opposed Jefferson's theory, stating more accurately: "It is probable that the waters of Cedar Creek originally found a subterranean passage beneath the arch of the present bridge. . . . The stream has gradually widened and deepened this ravine to its present situation."[3] Despite this perceptive analysis, not until mid-century were the effects of erosion widely accepted.

Although this geological spectacle evoked elevated language in literary descriptions, David Johnson was commited to depicting it exactly as he saw it without superimposition of artful or dramatic effects. One of the few references to Johnson during his lifetime, recorded in Benjamin Champney's *Sixty Years' Memories of Art and Artists*, indicates his commitment to depicting the exact contours and coloration of nature. Champney finds Johnson in the 1850s pursuing his favorite and challenging subject—rock painting in North Conway, New Hampshire—as part of the "New York contingent" under the leadership of the artist John Casilear. The group set out to spend the day painting close-up studies of a pile of boulders. During lunchtime, when the artists were silently pondering this difficult and complex task, Champney reports that David Johnson broke forth with, "It's purple by thunder!"[4] Johnson thought he had discovered the true color of the rocks.

Johnson's trip to Natural Bridge may well have been prompted by a travel account that appeared in 1857 in *Virginia Illustrated*, a book by Porte Crayon. The author challenges artists by declaring that he never saw an illustration "that conveyed, even in a remote degree, any idea of the majestic grandeur of the original." He then states: "One of the most satisfactory views is obtained from a hillside about half a mile below the bridge."[5] The book contains an illustration, taken from this location, which is closely related to the view Johnson selected in this painting.

From his 1860 trip to Natural Bridge, Johnson produced three paintings of this subject—two close-up and one from afar. To prepare for this panoramic view he first made a sketch in pencil, leaving the foreground empty.[6] This area was reserved for the most characteristic elements of the Blue Ridge Mountains: the split rail fence, winding dirt road, and grazing sheep. Modern tourist facilities held no pictorial interest and, accordingly, the huge hotel that stood on the right of the bridge was eliminated from both the sketch and the final painting.[7]

Very little is known about David Johnson's life. He probably received his early training from his brother, who was a portrait painter. In 1850, when he took a few lessons from Jasper Francis Cropsey, he was already an accomplished artist. He exhibited frequently at the National Academy of Design, and lived and painted in New York City during most of his career. He produced paintings of high quality based on locations in the Catskills, the White Mountains, New Hampshire, Virginia, and Warwick, New York, where Cropsey lived, and in 1876 he was awarded a first-class medal at the Centennial Exposition in Philadelphia.

Notes

1. E. P. Thompkins, *The Natural Bridge and Its Historical Surroundings* (Natural Bridge, Va.: The Natural Bridge Inc., 1939), 17, 29.
2. Thomas Jefferson, *Notes on the State of Virginia* (1784; reprint, New York: W. W. Norton and Co., 1982).
3. Francis W. Gilmer, "On Geological Formation of the Natural Bridge of Virginia," *Publications of the American Philosophical Society*, n.s., 1 (no. 13): 187–192.
4. John I. H. Baur, " '. . . the exact brushwork of Mr. David Johnson,' An American Landscape Painter, 1827–1908," *American Art Journal* 7 (Autumn 1980): 39.
5. Porte Crayon (pseudonym of David Hunter Strother), *Virginia Illustrated* (New York: Harper Brothers, 1857), 195.
6. Johnson's close-up view from below is in the collection of Jo Ann and Julian Ganz., Jr. A miniature oval of the subject belongs to Mr. and Mrs. Wilbur L. Ross, Jr. The sketch for this painting is in the Ganz collection.
7. The Natural Bridge Hotel is clearly visible in the illustration in Crayon's *Virginia Illustrated*, 195.

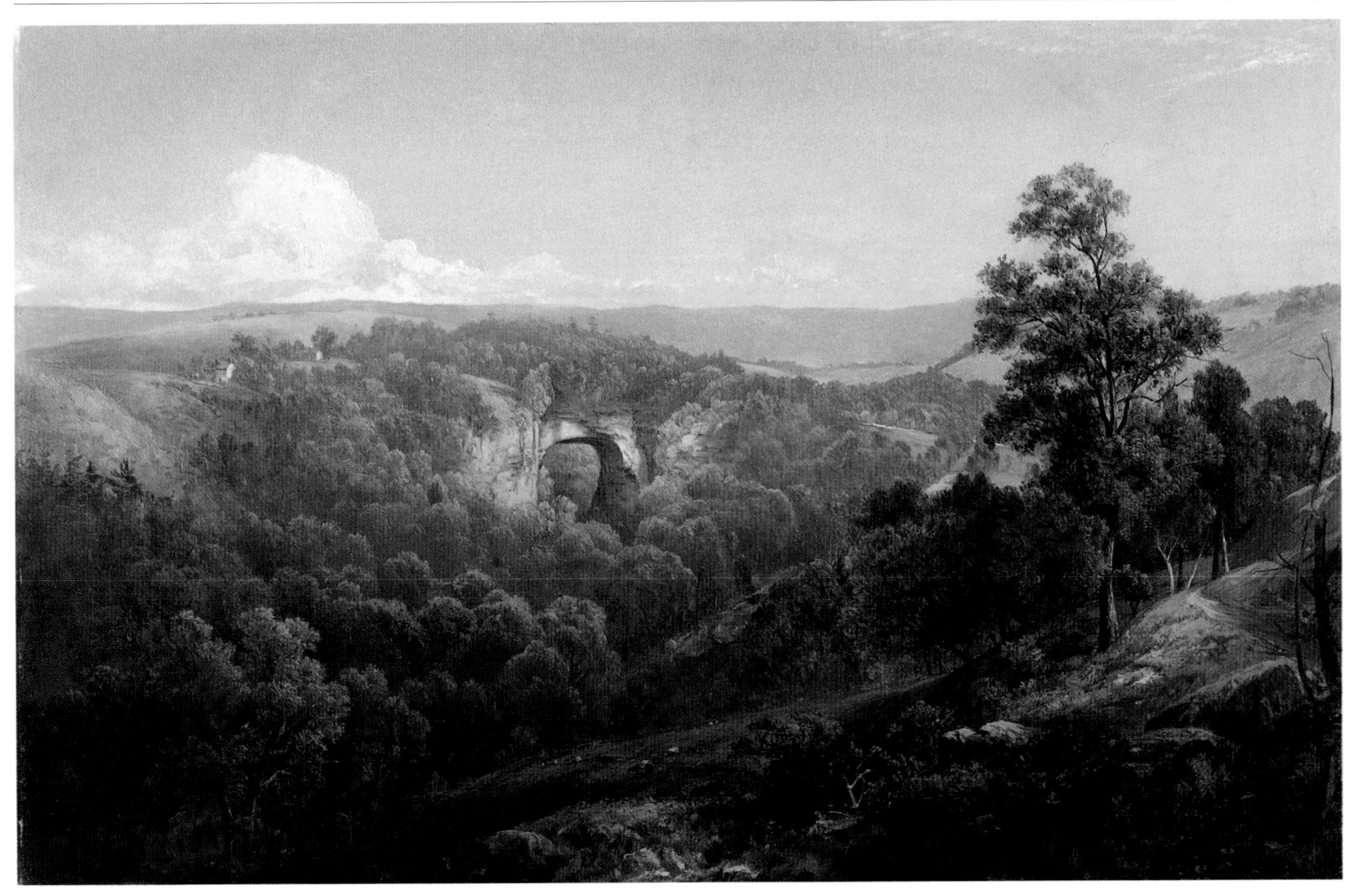

14

Oil on canvas, 14¼ x 22¼ in. (36.2 x 56.5 cm)
Signed and dated at lower right: D. J./1860
Gift of Philip Hanes in honor of Charles H. Babcock, Sr.

The Storyteller of the Camp (Maple Sugar Camp), c. 1861–66

Eastman Johnson

1824–1906

After returning from Düsseldorf, where he acquired his artistic training, Eastman Johnson made his reputation in New York City in 1859 with *Old Kentucky Home: Life in the South,* a painting depicting slaves at leisure in the backyard of his parents' house in Washington, D.C. Following this success he began an ambitious project to make a large-scale painting of the people of Maine harvesting maple sap and celebrating the end of a long, cold winter.

In the spring of each year between 1861 and 1866 Johnson returned to the scene of his early boyhood in Fryeburg, Maine, to paint studies of the people who gathered at caldrons of boiling maple sap to gossip, tell stories, fiddle, and dance.[1] From a mobile, heated studio, Johnson moved about the camps making detailed studies of the individual features and colorful attire of the inhabitants. Johnson apparently intended to create a genre painting on a scale that could compete in size and complexity with the popular landscapes by Frederic Church and Albert Bierstadt.[2] Just as these scenic painters gathered numerous natural details from various locations into panoramic views, so too, it seems, Johnson intended to combine multiple human activities into a panorama of life in the maple sugar camps. Although Johnson could not find a patron for the final painting and, therefore, did not complete this ambitious project, the existing finished studies are considered his most vital and significant work of the 1860s.

The figures in *The Storyteller of the Camp*—one of thirty oil studies made in preparation for the large composition[3]—occupy a central foreground position in the full study *Sugaring Off at the Camp, Fryeburg, Maine.* This elaborate but unfinished composition, which includes a number of groupings for which Johnson had made completed studies, reveals that he intended to place the storyteller amid a crowd of people gathered in a forest clearing where the sap is boiling in a huge caldron. *The Storyteller of the Camp* focuses on a tall, rosy-cheeked male seeking the attention of two young women in order to begin a story. They, however, seem fixed upon their own conversation. A beguiling youth in a blue velvet cap seems to be contending for the attention of the females. The wizened face and knowing smirk of the old hag listening to the pretty young ladies inject the scene with a moralistic warning that time will ravage their beauty, too.

With Johnson's extensive art school training in the Hague, he was well equipped to devote to this subject the expert treatment required to create a masterpiece. Drawn to the maple sugar camps for their nostalgic appeal, Johnson demonstrates in these paintings his commitment to preserving the unique rural customs of the Northeast. Twenty years after Johnson's maple sugar series, the modern evaporator replaced this picturesque method of boiling sap over wood fires and with the introduction of the more efficient process the attendant merrymaking vanished.[4]

Notes

1. A few American artists preceded Johnson's attempt to capture these picturesque festivities. In 1845 New York history and genre painter Tompkin Harrison Matteson (1813–1884) painted a work entitled *Sugaring Off,* and a folio print by Nathaniel Currier of Arthur Fitzwilliam Tait's *American Forest Scene-Maple Sugaring* was published in 1856, but neither artist had the training to create the masterpiece that Johnson intended.
2. Patricia Schulze Hills, "Eastman Johnson: The Sources and Development of His Style and Themes, vol. 1 (Ph.D. diss., New York University, 1973), 104.
3. Ibid., 103.
4. "The evaporator came in use after 1880," Arthur Davenport, unidentified newspaper article, Jefferson, N.Y.

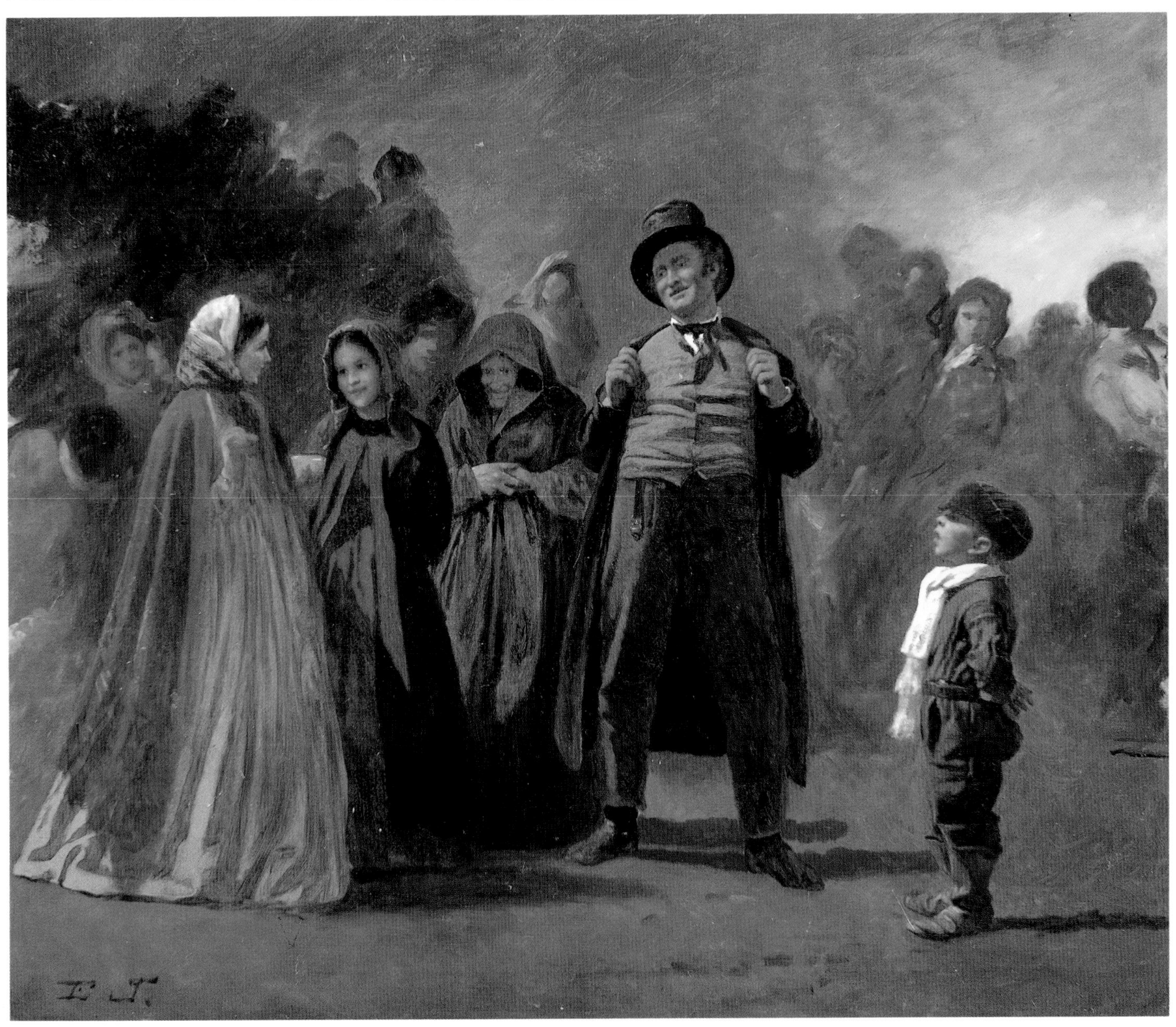

15

Oil on board, 22¾ x 26¾ in. (57.8 x 67.9 cm)
Signed at lower left: E. J.
Signed on back: MAPLE SUGAR CAMP E. J.
Original purchase fund from the Mary Reynolds Babcock Foundation, Z. Smith Reynolds Foundation, Area Foundation, and Anne Cannon Forsyth

The Old Hunting Grounds, 1864

Worthington Whittredge

1820–1910

Having spent ten years pursuing his artistic studies in Düsseldorf and Rome, Ohio-born Worthington Whittredge knew firsthand that endless, undisturbed wilderness no longer existed in Europe. Soon after his return to this country in 1859, therefore, he sought out the secluded wooded regions of the Catskill mountains for his first American subjects. His European training was inadequate for organizing a harmonious composition out of the chaotic scenery, but within five years he had mastered the depiction of the disarray and denseness of the American wilderness, as evidenced in this masterpiece, *The Old Hunting Grounds*. The importance of this painting in its own time can be

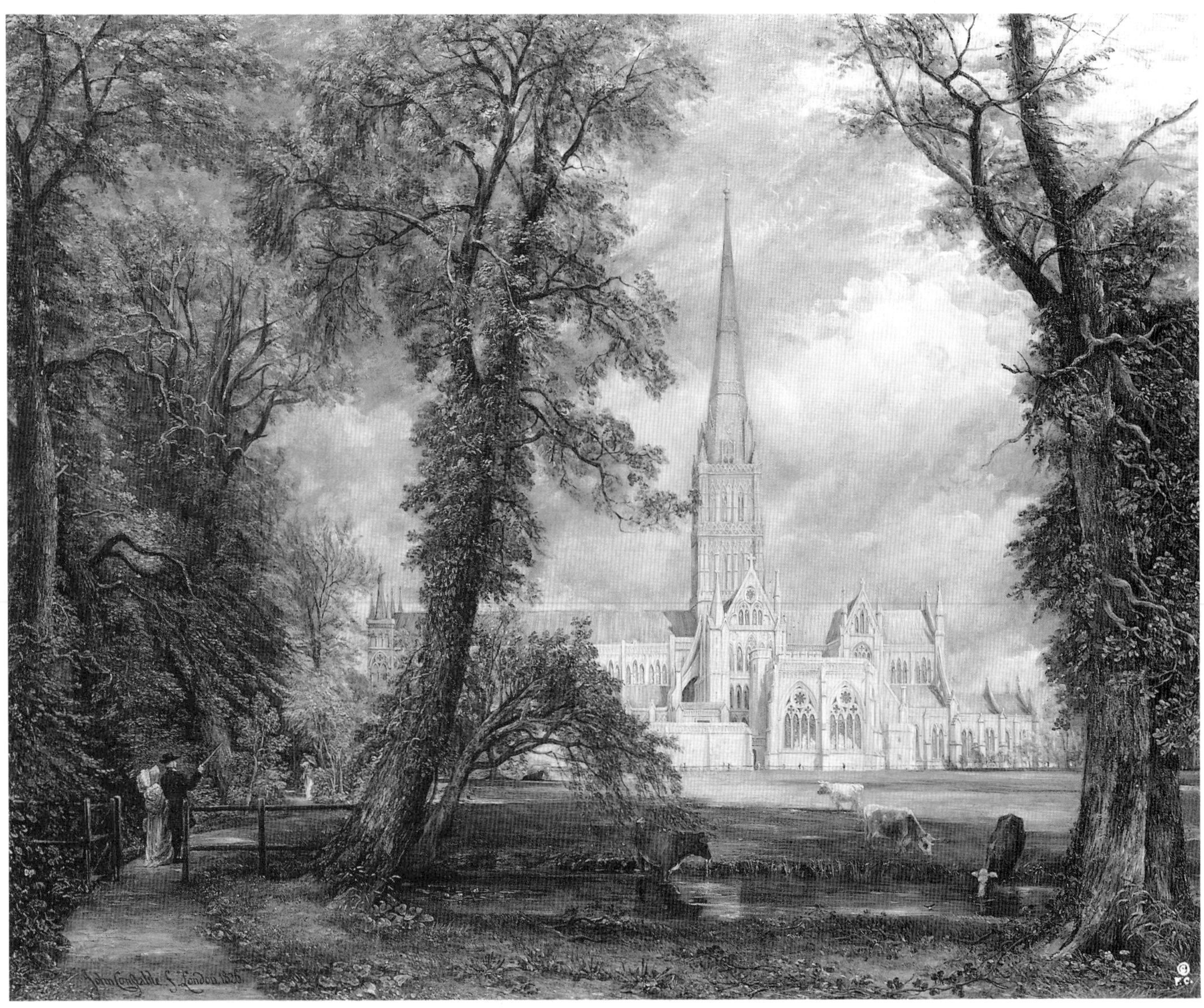

Figure 8 JOHN CONSTABLE, *Salisbury Cathedral*, 1826. The Frick Collection, New York, A563

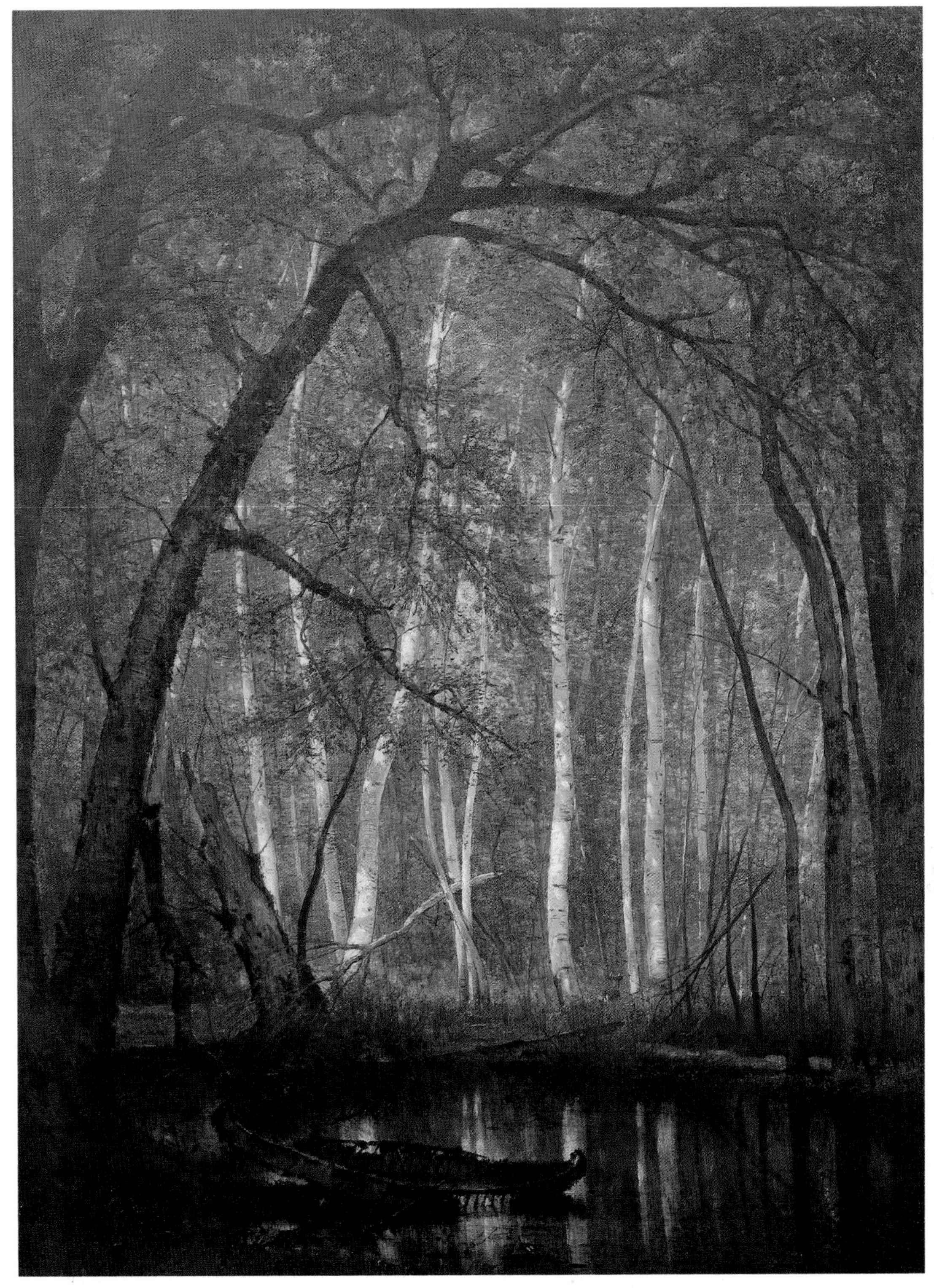

16

Oil on canvas, 36 x 27 in. (91.4 x 68.6 cm)
Signed at lower right: W. WHITTREDGE
Gift of Barbara B. Millhouse

surmised by its exhibition in the Paris Exposition of 1866 and from the lengthy description written by the art historian Henry T. Tuckerman in his well-known *Book of the Artists* in 1867.[1]

The title of this painting and the disintegrating birchbark canoe establish the theme of nostalgic reminiscence of the Indian tribes who once hunted in the forests of the Catskill region of New York State. Contemporary historians interpret the sentimentalization of the departed Indians as a nineteenth-century affectation camouflaging the carnage that was actually occurring. A passage from *Godey's Ladies Book* of 1858 expresses the popular sentiment that inspired a painting such as this: "The red men of America are rapidly becoming extinct. . . . Those children of the forest, whose places we have usurped, are passing away; but they leave behind them many a history and tradition of self-sacrificing generosity and thrilling romance, which may fitly serve to paint a moral or adorn a tale."[2]

The ancient black birches in the foreground offer the traditional regenerative polarity to the glowing cluster of young white birches in the background, with the dead, split stump marking the transition between them. The comforting belief that nature functions in continuous cycles of renewal and decay supported the notion that white people usurping the place of the Indian is as inevitable and irreversible as the young birches replacing the old gnarled trees.

A precedent to *The Old Hunting Grounds* can be found in American art in the woodland interiors of Asher B. Durand. Although he achieved some powerful effects, he did not develop the capability of making the viewer feel remote from civilization. With only fragments of sky filtering through the dense foliage and no path or stream to serve as a guide out of the forest, Whittredge, unlike his predecessor, has succeeded in presenting a forest interior fully equipped with the remoteness, boundlessness, and immersion that inform the descriptive passages of James Fenimore Cooper, Washington Irving, and William Cullen Bryant.

The configuration of trees echoing the vaulted ceiling of a Gothic cathedral harks back to the German Romantic artist Caspar David Friedrich, whose paintings frequently reveal parallels between nature and the Gothic.[3] This recurrent metaphor appears closer to home in a well-known poem by the American writer, editor, and poet William Cullen Bryant, whose "Forest Hymn" refers to the forest as "These dim vaults." Striking compositional similarities also exist between *The Old Hunting Grounds* and John Constable's *Salisbury Cathedral* (1826; fig. 8), which suggest that Whittredge may have consciously modeled his painting on this widely known and admired masterpiece. Both compositions are framed by a nave of trees and both contain a pool from which an animal is drinking. In the background Whittredge seems to make a further analogy by bending two white birch trees into the shape of the cathedral's spire. Whittredge's selection of a famous view of a cathedral as his compositional model perhaps suggests his belief that the American forest is a worthy alternative to God's traditional dwelling place.

NOTES

1. Henry T. Tuckerman, *Book of the Artists* (New York: James F. Carr, 1966), 518.
2. "An Indian Tale Founded on Fact," *Godey's Ladies Book* 56 (1858): 45 ff, cited in Patricia Schulze Hills, "Eastman Johnson: The Sources and Development of His Style and Themes (Ph.D. diss., New York University, 1973), 50.
3. David B. Lewall, "Asher Brown Durand: His Art and Art Theory in Relation to His Times," vol. 2 (Ph.D. diss., Princeton University, 1966), 481. Whittredge had probably not seen Friedrich's paintings but undoubtedly saw his influence in a painting exhibited at the American Art Union in 1849, Joseph Vollmering's *Red Rock Eherbergh, Germany*.

Detail of *The Old Hunting Grounds*

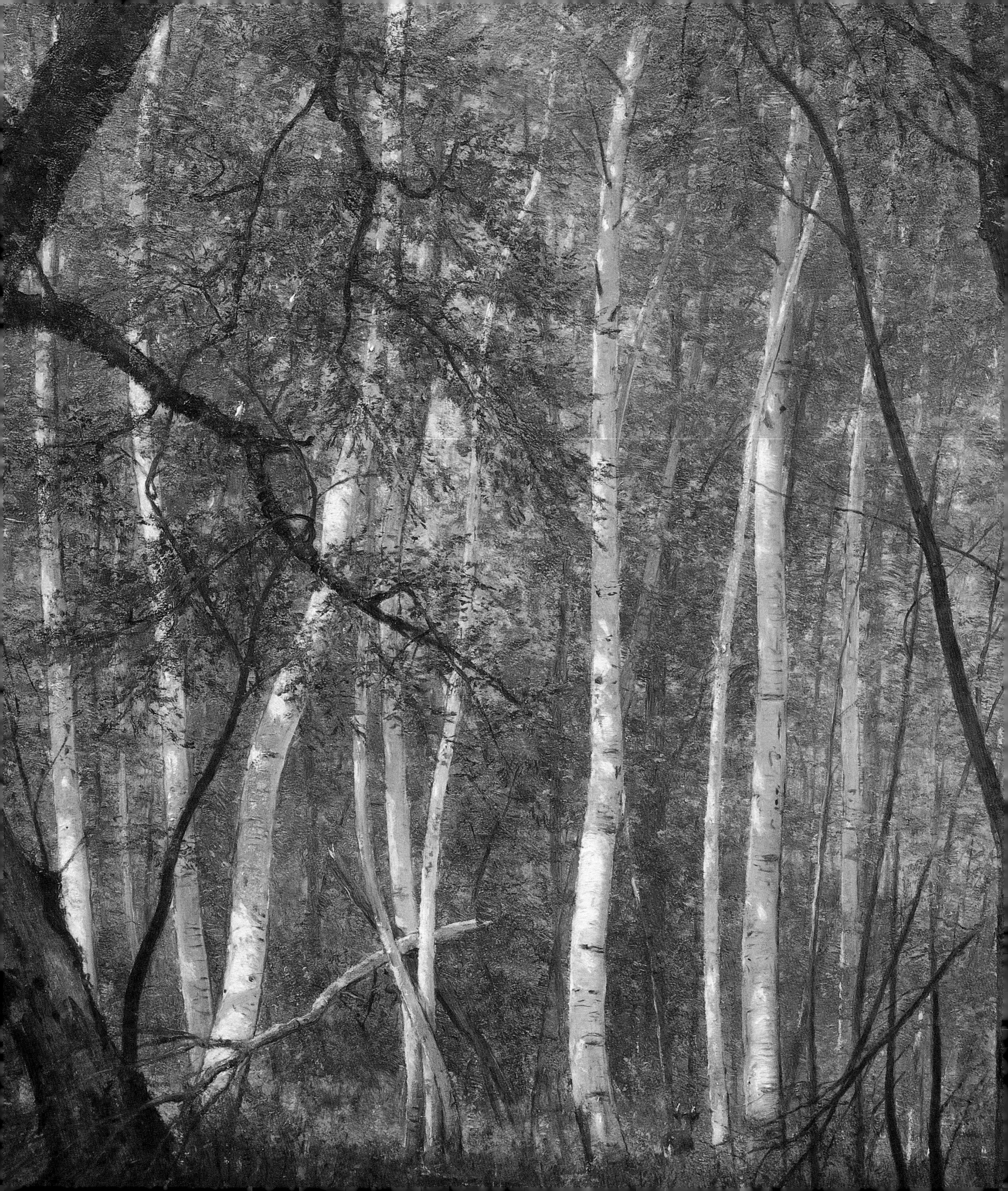

Worthington Whittredge in His Tenth Street Studio, 1865

Emanuel Leutze

1816–1868

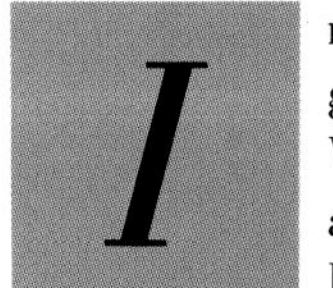

n this painting Emanuel Leutze provides a glimpse of the Hudson River School artist Worthington Whittredge at work in his well-appointed room in the famous Tenth Street Studio Building. With the exception of the chalice on top of the bookcase, the room is empty of ornament. Only the articles associated with the artist's work—sketches, oil studies, open books—are visible.[1] The pink cherry blossoms seen through the open window designate the season and may indicate that Whittredge is completing a painting for the National Academy of Design, which opened its annual exhibition each April.

This painting is a rare and significant record of an artist's working habits during this period, as well as of the interior of the first building in the country designed specially for artists. James Boorman Johnston, a New York businessman whose brother served as the first president of the Metropolitan Museum of Art, understood the importance of providing artists with suitable working rooms at reasonable rents, as well as a congenial atmosphere where they could exchange ideas. When Johnston commissioned the well-trained but unproven architect Richard Morris Hunt (1827–1895) to design this building in 1857, he made a courageous and intelligent choice. Hunt was to become famous for designing Beaux-Arts mansions, most notably the Vanderbilt estates—the Biltmore near Asheville, North Carolina, and the Breakers in Newport, Rhode Island.

The Tenth Street Studio Building was located just off Fifth Avenue on the north side of Tenth Street. The three-story brick building contained about twenty-three studios surrounding a glass-roofed court that initially served as an exhibition room, and later as the studio of William Merritt Chase. In 1858 the first artists moved in, and the following year the building became the site of the most sensational exhibition of a single landscape in the history of the country, Frederic E. Church's *Heart of the Andes*. The success of this painting brought Whittredge back from a ten-year stay in Europe and Leutze soon followed. Both artists rented quarters in the newly proclaimed center of the New York art world.

Leutze's friendship with Whittredge began in 1849 when Whittredge arrived in Düsseldorf as a student during the time Leutze was combing the streets for an American to pose for the figure of George Washington in his large historical piece *George Washington Crossing the Delaware*. Although Leutze was born in Germany, he had lived in the United States from age nine to age twenty-five before returning to Düsseldorf. By 1841 his historical paintings had won him an international reputation. *George Washington Crossing the Delaware* became one of the best-known paintings of its time. Leutze was also an accomplished portrait painter, and produced a striking portrait of Whittredge in a Spanish outfit (1856; Metropolitan Museum of Art, New York).

Note

1. Another painting in the Reynolda House collection, *In the Studio* (c. 1884) by William Merritt Chase, shows an interior in the same building, twenty years later. A comparison of these two paintings reveals a shift in attitudes toward the artist's studio.

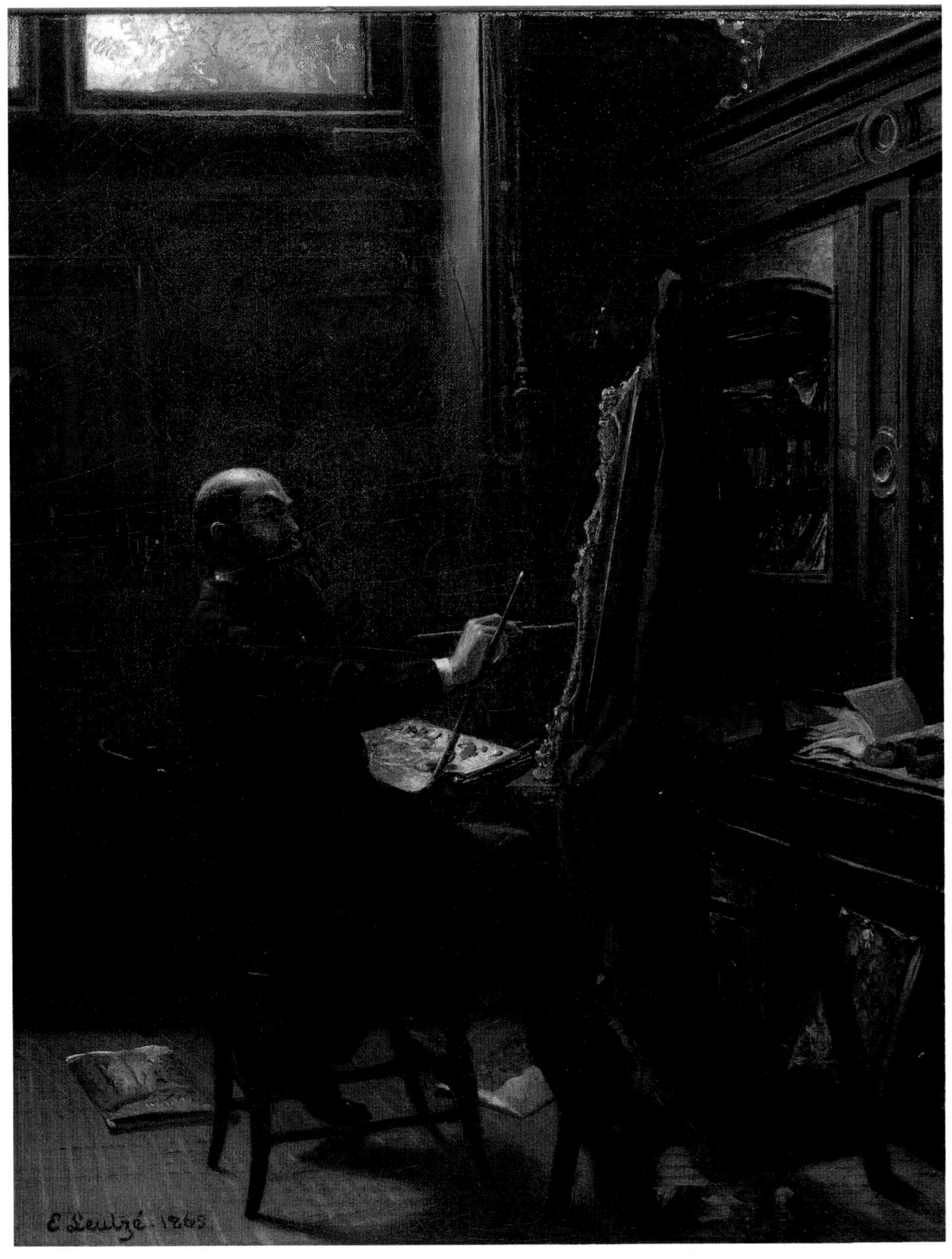

17 Oil on canvas, 15 x 12 in. (38.1 x 30.5 cm)
Signed and dated at lower left: E LEUTZE. 1865
Gift of Barbara B. Millhouse

Orchid with Two Hummingbirds, 1871

Martin Johnson Heade

1819–1904

Born in Pennsylvania, Martin Johnson Heade began his artistic training around 1837 with the folk artist Edward Hicks. He sent his first paintings to the National Academy of Design in 1843 and continued to exhibit there throughout his life. In 1859 he was drawn to the Tenth Street Studio Building where Heade made a lifelong friend of Frederic E. Church. Heade exhibited with his Hudson River School colleagues but his subjects differ considerably from theirs; he painted marshlands, coastal scenes, and still lifes rather than mountainous panoramas. Although little recognized in his lifetime, his paintings are now considered among the most original of the period.

Heade visited Brazil in 1863–64 to paint the many varieties of hummingbirds that had long fascinated him. He intended to have the paintings made into chromolithographs but the project failed, and he abandoned the subject for a few years. He took up the hummingbird theme again in 1871, combining it with the orchid, which was the object of considerable interest at this time.[1] The hummingbird and flower motif had been used in English botanical illustrations,[2] but when Heade translated the subject from a documentary to a Romantic style he created "an image unprecedented in American art."[3] *Orchid with Two Hummingbirds* is one of Heade's first ventures into this new genre, which he repeated in many variations until his death in 1904.[4]

The drama of this painting is derived from the inaccessibility of its setting in the forest canopy far above the visibility of man. Yet its sureness of execution and atmospheric plausibility persuade the viewer that the artist painted this engaging interaction exactly as he saw it. Heade, an amateur ornithologist and naturalist, depicted each hummingbird so accurately that the bird with the long red tail and green throat can be identified as a male red-tailed comet. To achieve this authenticity Heade used "skins" as models, but he believed that because he had the opportunity to study the hummingbirds in their native habitat, he could portray them more accurately and more convincingly than John Gould, who was famed for his portfolio of botanical prints.[5]

The orchid in this painting has an unusually frisky demeanor. Its sprightliness is not a misrepresentation but rather an authentic interpretation of the current attitude toward these captivating epiphytes. The naturalist C. M. Tracy found the shapes of orchids so bizarre that he was "tempted sometimes to believe they are animated creatures under some strange disguise of enchantment."[6] Tracy continues with a vivid description that might easily excite the artistic imagination: "All through the dense forests of Brazil . . . these plants are found in myriads . . . [with] roots that seem quite as much like rope-yarns, and with green leaves starting freshly in such curious situations, pushing out long swinging stems of flowers, that dangle hither and thither like strings beset with white or red or bronzy butterflies." The orchid seemed to display endless ingenuity: "Varied with an excess that is perfectly reckless and prodigal," continues Tracy, "a new form meets the observer at every turn."

Heade made a radical departure in this painting from Gould's earlier botanical prints by showing the orchid not as a cut flower against a plain background, but as a complete plant growing on a mossy limb high in the treetops of a Brazilian rain forest. This change occurred in part because aesthetic journals of the period were advocating the depiction of "a free, vigorous plant as it grows," advice that can be traced to the influential English art critic John Ruskin, as well as to the larger, revolutionary world view that was being set forth by Charles Darwin.

Only nine years earlier Darwin had chosen the orchid to demonstrate evolutionary anatomy in *The Various Contrivances by Which Orchids are Fertilised by Insects* (1862).[7] He astonished the world by describing the orchid not as a static specimen made perfect by God at creation but as part of a family of plants exhibiting ingenious devices that had been modified over time to ensure cross-fertilization. By including the leaves, pods, and pseudo-bulbs of the orchid, the moisture-filled air that nourishes it, and the hummingbirds that provide a means of fertilization, Heade was responding to Darwin's integrated worldview.

Notes

1. C. M. Tracy, "The Orchids," *American Naturalist* 2 (September 1868): 349. In the 1860s orchids were grown in hot houses, sold in florist shops, and written about in horticultural magazines.
2. Dr. John Thornton's aquatint *Mimosa*, from *Temple of Flora* (London, 1799–1807), combines hummingbirds and mimosa in a mountainous setting, but the setting is arranged as a backdrop rather than an environment.
3. Ella M. Foshay, *Reflections in Nature: Flowers in American Art* (New York: Alfred A. Knopf, 1984), 314. Annette Blaugrund, "The Tenth Street Studio Building" (Ph.D. diss., Columbia University, 1987), 187–88, mentions that another Tenth Street Studio artist, William J. Hays, began painting orchids about the same time as Heade.
4. *Cattleya Orchid and Three Brazilian Hummingbirds* (National Gallery, Washington, D.C.) is also dated 1871. This and *Orchid with Two Hummingbirds* are both painted on the same size panel. Another painting of the same size and date is *Apple Blossoms and Hummingbird* (Addison Gallery of American Art, Andover, Massachusetts).
5. According to Heade, Gould did not see a live hummingbird until 1857.
6. C. M. Tracy, "The Orchids."
7. Theodore E. Stebbins, Jr., *The Life and Works of Martin Johnson Heade* (New Haven and London: Yale University Press, 1975), 238.

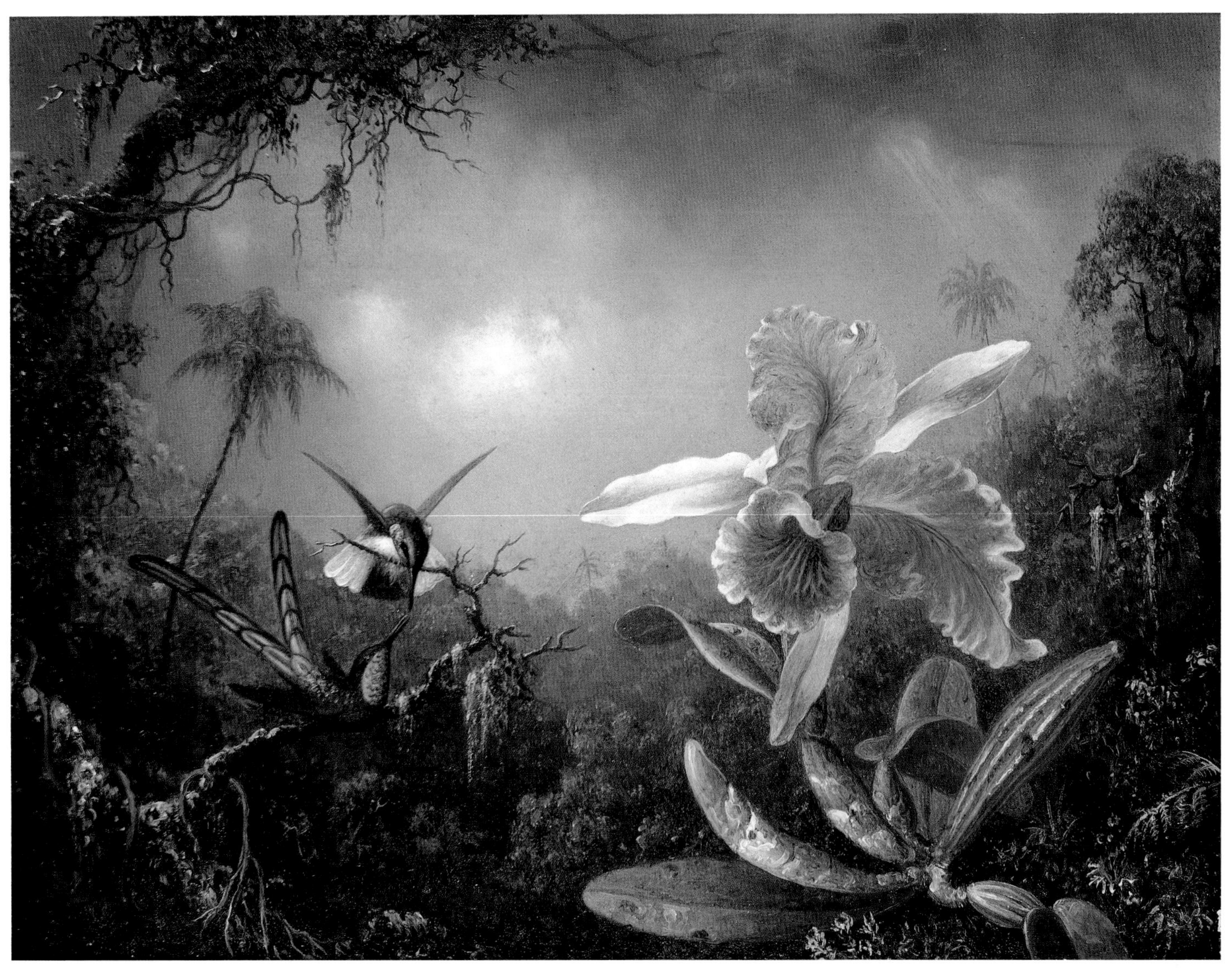

18

Oil on prepared panel with Winsor & Newton label,
13¾ x 18 in. (34.9 x 45.7 cm)
Signed and dated at lower center: M. J. HEADE/1871

Dancing Girl (La Regina), 1871

Elihu Vedder

1836–1923

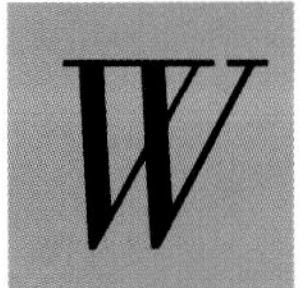

With her loosely parted lips and languid facial expression, this alluring model imparts a sensuality associated with Moorish dancers, who were often featured in the popular orientalist paintings of the period.[1] The tambourine and juggling instruments also refer to the entertainments of North African harems, while the trousers and slippers are of Turkish origin. With her fair northern European complexion, however, the model lacks authenticity as an exotic type. The artist also seems to cast doubt upon the designation as a dancing girl by dressing her incongruously in a heavily draped Renaissance-style dress and by casting her in a pose reminiscent of Greek sculpture.[2] Vedder's intentions may at first seem muddled, yet the incongruities achieve a new artistic intent that directs the viewer away from a historical or anecdotal reading toward a strictly aesthetic appreciation. The intensely patterned surface, which echoes the richness both of palatial Islamic interiors and the domestic interiors of the Aesthetic style, reminds us that decoration held dominance over narrative during this period.

Raised in New York City and Havana, Cuba, Vedder made Rome his lifetime headquarters after 1869 and won a reputation in the United States as an important expatriate artist. In 1884 he became widely known for his illustrations for the *Rubaiyat of Omar Khayyam,* and in the 1890s his reputation was further enhanced when he won a number of mural commissions, including five panels for the Library of Congress.

The presentation of a single standing figure viewed from below with objects at her feet can be traced to James Abbott McNeill Whistler's *The White Girl* of 1862. *Dancing Girl,* however, shares more pronounced stylistic affinities with the work of Whistler's friend Sir Albert Moore, whose paintings Vedder could have seen in London in 1870. As the decade proceeded London art exhibitions became saturated with this female prototype, but in 1871, when Vedder painted *Dancing Girl,* he was at the forefront of the Aesthetic Movement, which was described that very year in the *London Art Journal* as a "new school" rejecting "common realism and vulgar naturalism."

Adhering to the Aesthetic Movement credo of "art for art's sake," Vedder has placed emphasis upon the woman as an artist's model and the setting as an artist's studio. But he also reveals his American heritage by not entirely rejecting art's traditional moralizing purpose. Interested in the occult and haunted by death since childhood, Vedder included in the left corner a wheel of fortune with its pointer stopped dangerously close to an image of a skull. Thus the painting can be read not simply as a beautifully colored surface but as a warning on the whimsical nature of fate.

Notes

1. The French writer Theophile Gautier visited Algeria in 1845 and described a Moorish dancer: "languid facial expressions, eyelids fluttering, eyes flashing or swooning, nostrils quivering, lips parted, bosoms heaving, necks bent like the throats of love-sick doves." See Lynne Thorton, "Women as Portrayed in Orientalist Painting," in *The Orientalists*, vol. 3 (Paris: ACR Edition Internationale Courbevoie, 1985), 136.
2. See, for example, *Attic Grave Stele of a Woman* (the *Radeke Stele*) in the collection of the Rhode Island School of Design, Providence.

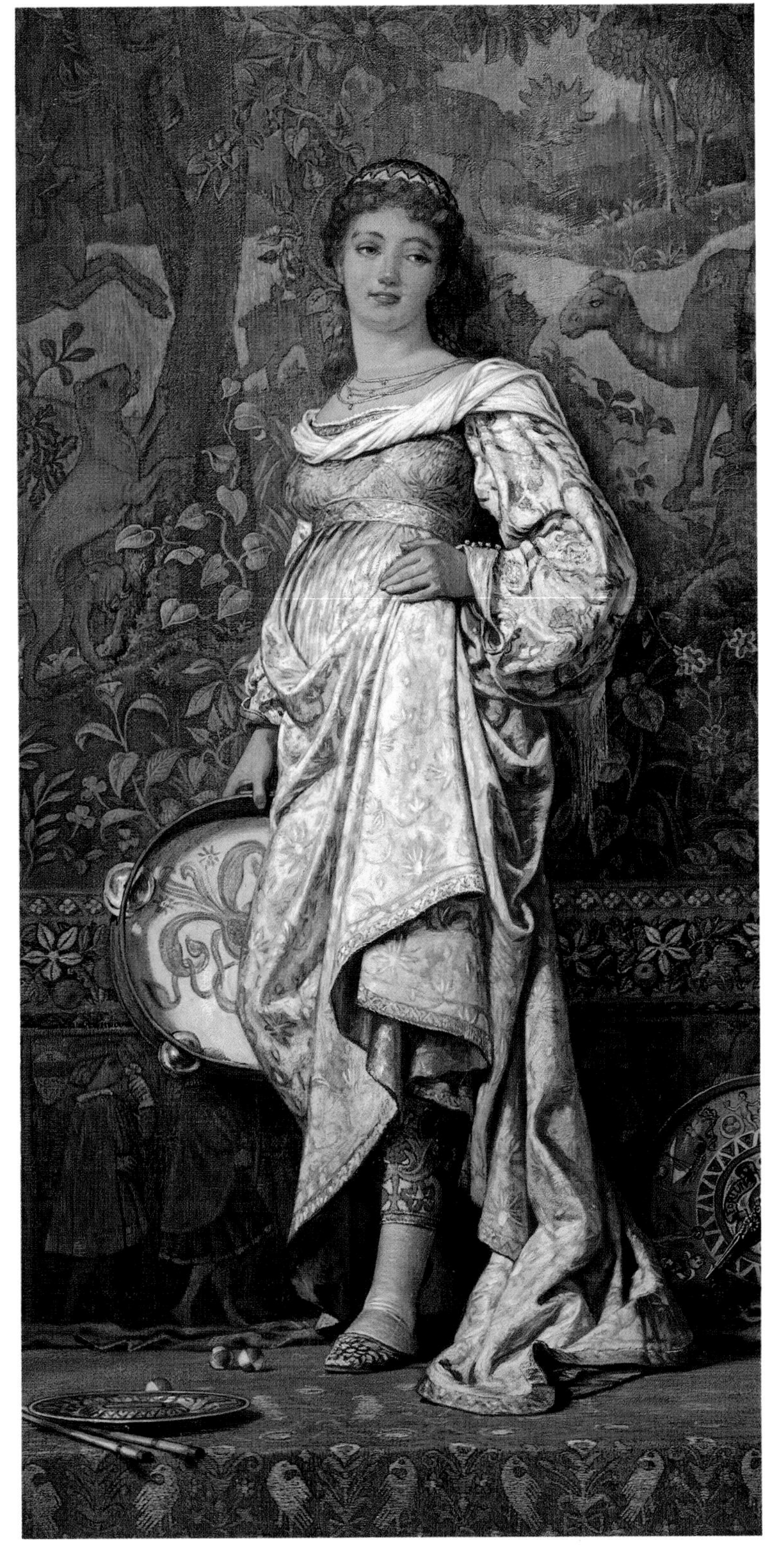

19 Oil on canvas, 39 x 20 in. (99.1 x 50.8 cm)
Gift of Barbara B. Millhouse

SIERRA NEVADA, c. 1871–73

ALBERT BIERSTADT

1830–1902

Born in Germany and raised in Massachusetts, Albert Bierstadt was the principal proponent of grand panoramic landscapes celebrating the expansiveness of the American West. Educated in art in the rigorous academic tradition of the Düsseldorf Academy, Bierstadt showed an early passion for spectacular landscapes while sketching vistas in the Alps as a student. Upon his return to New England and an unsuccessful attempt to establish himself in his hometown, Bierstadt joined an expedition west along the Old Oregon Trail. Over the course of five subsequent trips west during a thirty-year period, Bierstadt developed a tremendous visual resource from sketches that were to provide the inspiration for dozens of grandiloquent canvases.

The remote Mount Whitney region in the imposing Sierra Nevada range had been causing great excitement since 1864 when a surveying party discovered the tremendous heights of the peaks in the Kings-Kern district. In 1871 (the year Bierstadt arrived in California) the summit of Mount Whitney was thought to have been reached by a member of the surveying group, but by 1873 it was learned that he had mistakenly climbed a lower peak since Mount Whitney was hidden by storm clouds. While the controversy raged over whether the elusive peak had been climbed and who was the first to reach the summit, Bierstadt returned to his New York studio and turned out some of his most impressive canvases of the highest mountain yet discovered in the United States.

Sierra Nevada is composed primarily of the sketches

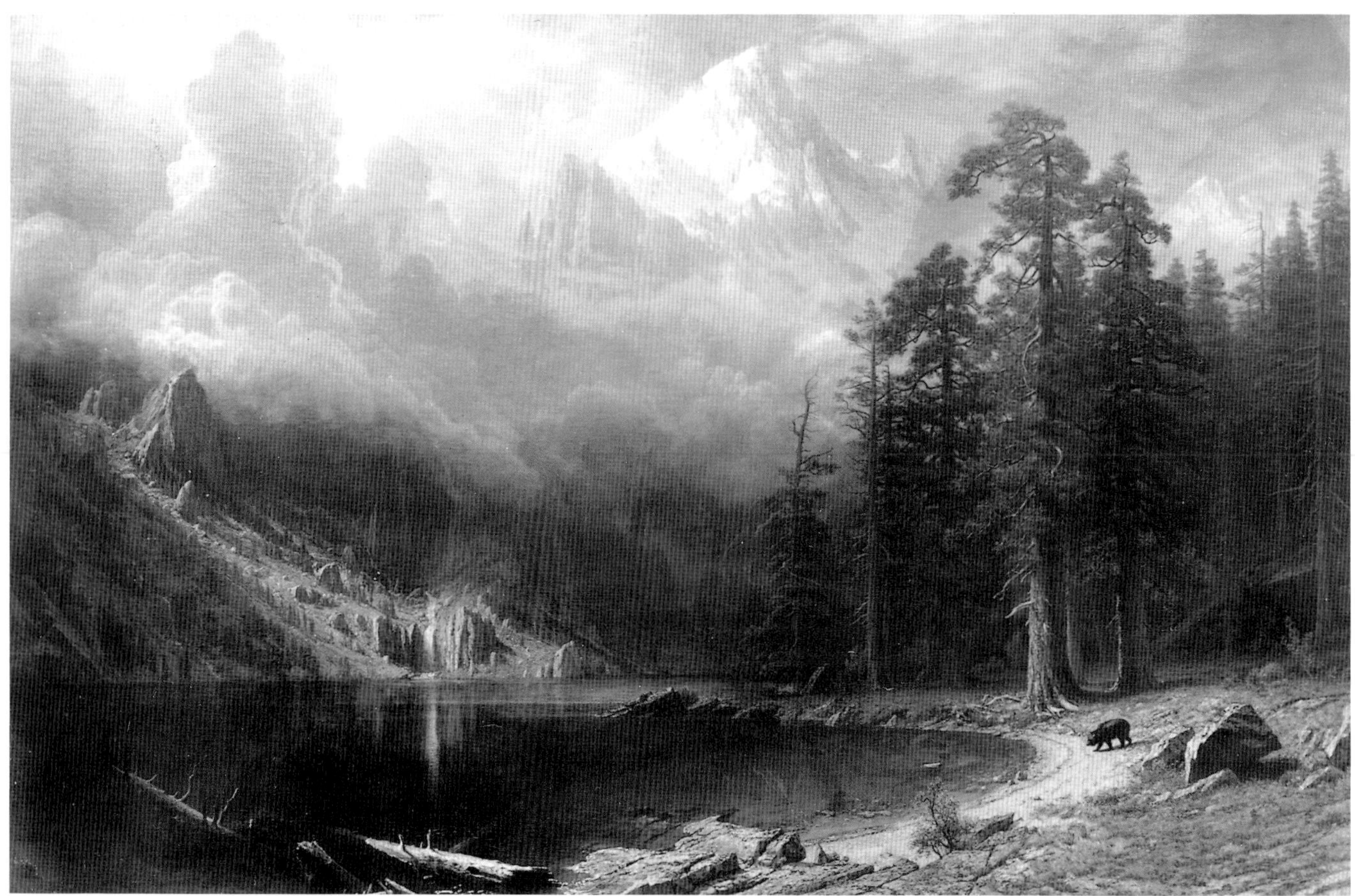

Figure 9 ALBERT BIERSTADT, *Mount Corcoran*, 1877. The Corcoran Gallery of Art, Museum Purchase, 78.1

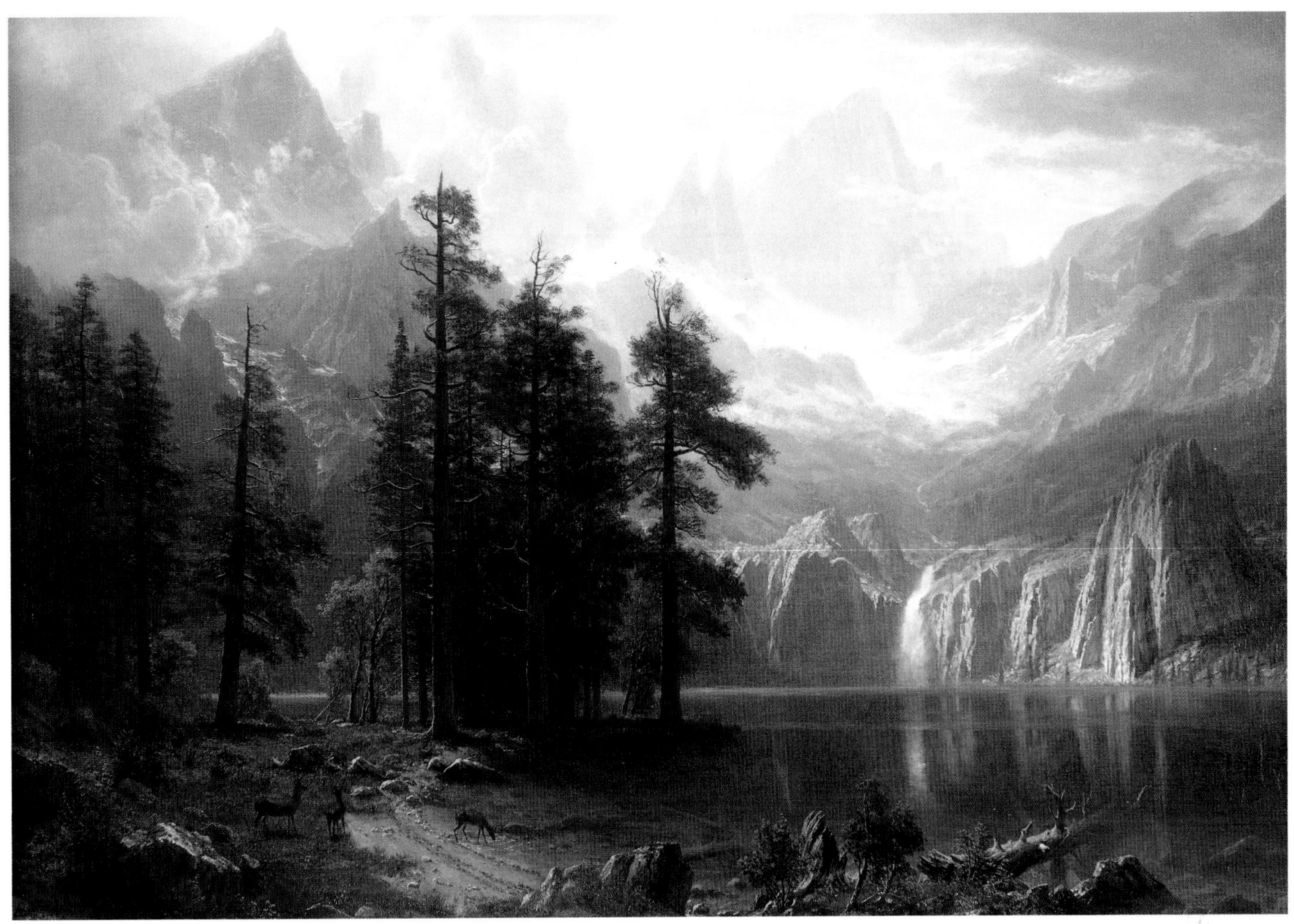

20 Oil on canvas, 38½ x 56½ in. (97.8 x 143.5 cm)
Signed at lower left: ABIERSTADT
Original purchase fund from the Mary Reynolds Babcock Foundation, Z. Smith Reynolds Foundation, Area Foundation, and Anne Cannon Forsyth

Bierstadt made in the Mount Whitney area during his visits there in 1872 and 1873.[1] The central mountain peak in the painting is similar to the peak identified as a spur of Mount Whitney in Bierstadt's famous painting *Mount Corcoran* (fig. 9), named after the buyer, Colonel William Corcoran.

Though often praised for his topographical accuracy, Bierstadt was willing to take license with the scenery to create the maximum effect.[2] He habitually produced compositional variations to please his clients, who enjoyed choosing what they liked best from the sketches that lined the walls of his thirty-five-room mansion overlooking the Hudson River. The impact of his dark middle ground and spotlighted sunlight lend a theatricality to his work that dramatizes the spectacular scenery. And because Bierstadt looked upon the Rockies and Sierras with Germanic eyes, his exaggerations often take on a suspiciously alpine flavor.

Particularly notable in Bierstadt's art is the acute sense of proportion with which he communicated to an eager public the tremendous heights and distances of western scenery. He applied the most sensitive talent to the relative size and placement of these natural beauties, thus conveying with accurate scale, rather than with figures, the impressive 14,495-foot height of Mount Whitney. The tiny trees on the distant shore, actually giant sequoias like those in the middle ground, indicate the immense height of the dazzling falls. The crystal-clear lake appears small due to the giant heights above it, but at the same time paradoxially conveys its vastness. Bierstadt achieved this optical illusion of dimension, typical of western scenery, with a skill few artists of his time attained.

The clear atmosphere and sparkling color make *Sierra Nevada* one of Bierstadt's finest works. The middle ground is not obscured in shadow, nor are the peaks smothered in mists, as is sometimes the case in his work. A shoreline of blooming fireflowers vividly accents the icy blues of water, rock, and mist. Infrared photographs reveal Bierstadt originally intended to show additional stones and stumps on the lake bottom, and *pentimenti* (visible evidences of changes in the composition) indicate he was undecided on the number of deer to include in the foreground.

During the 1860s and '70s the public so loved Bierstadt's extravagant depictions of the West that they were willing to pay more for his paintings than had ever before been paid for the work of an American artist. Perhaps a victim of his own popularity, Bierstadt's paintings grew increasingly formulaic and his later works lost the fresh vision and awesome impact of his earliest images.

When the first transcontinental railroad was completed in 1869, people could travel with ease and comfort and see the sights for themselves. Consequently, the function of the artist-explorer began to diminish. Uninterested in new developments in landscape painting such as the intimate views of the French Barbizon painters, Bierstadt lived to see his fame vanish as the vitality of the Hudson River School declined at the end of the nineteenth century.

NOTES

1. The *San Fransisco Daily Evening Bulletin* of September 4, 1872, reported on Bierstadt's travels: "lately returned temporarily to the city from a long field experience in the King's River country, under the shadow of Mount Whitney. He will go back there shortly."
2. Accurate topographical identification of this image has proved difficult. In a letter of April 15, 1970, from Vernon Pascal to Barbara Millhouse (Reynolda House Curatorial Files), Pascal identified this and others of the Sierra series that "ostensibly represent the western slope of Mt. Whitney and Mt. Brewer, near the head of Kings River, in the southern portion of the Sierra Nevada range." This view would have necessitated an arduous trek through the higher elevations of the mountains. It has been suggested that the spires in the center of the composition represent Keeler Needle and its twin pinnacle, Day Needle. Their placement in front of Mt. Whitney, however, suggests a view from the more accessible eastern slope. If the identification of the twin needles is correct, this adds support to the theory that the work is an amalgam of various sketches arranged to create the most dramatic effects.

Detail of *Sierra Nevada*

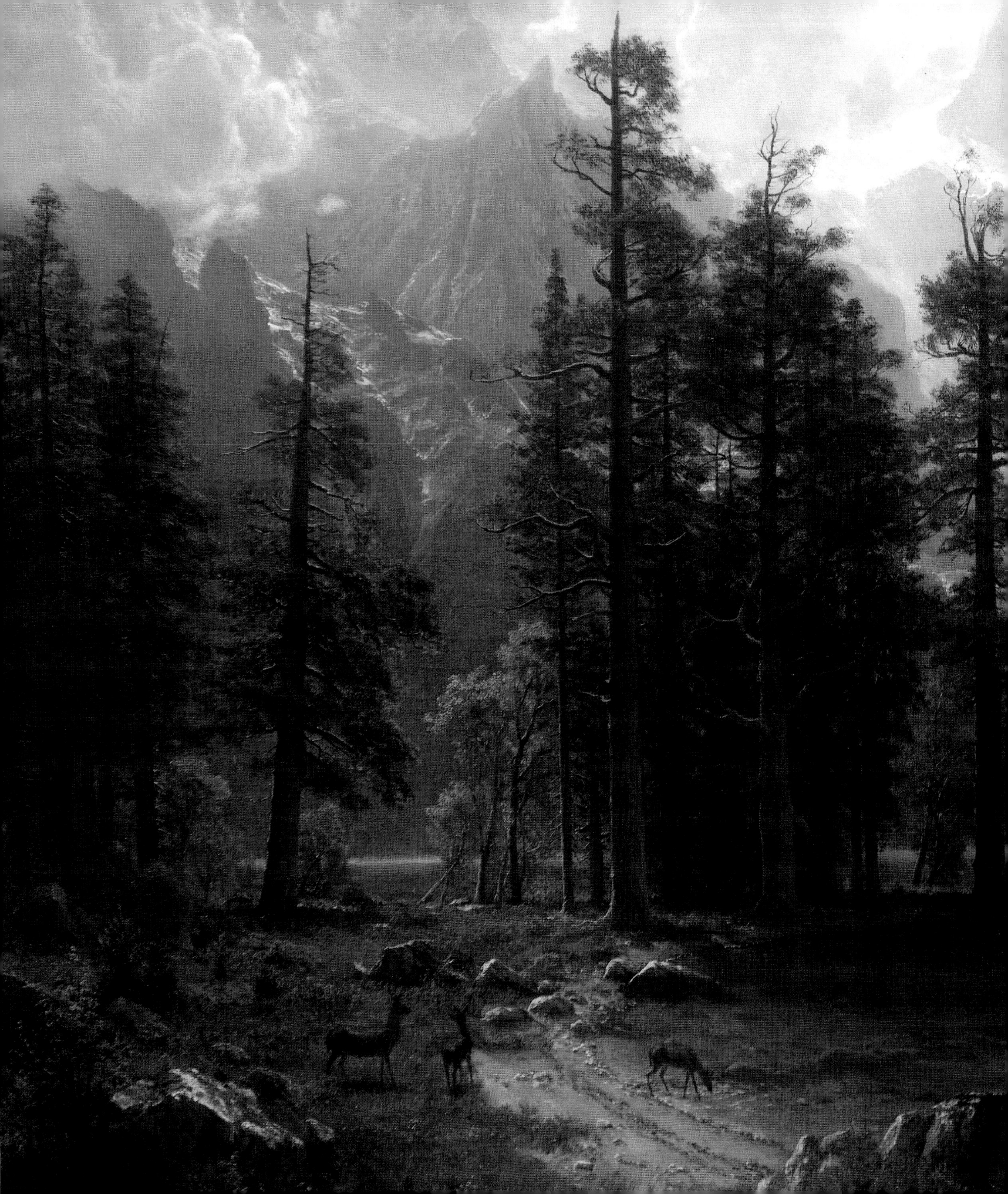

Mounts Adam and Eve, 1872

Jasper Francis Cropsey

1823–1900

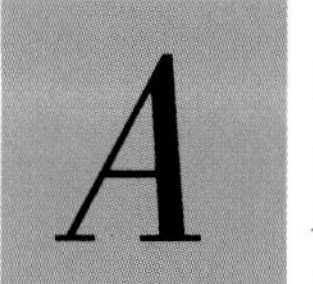

A native of Staten Island, New York, Jasper Francis Cropsey made his reputation in London in 1860 with a large, glowing landscape entitled *Autumn—on the Hudson River.* The British, unfamiliar with the brilliant array of northeastern United States foliage, accused Cropsey of being untrue to nature—a heresy at a time when the John Ruskin's truth-to-nature credo was paramount. In response to the public controversy Cropsey hung some real autumn leaves next to his painting.[1] The mounting publicity introduced the British to American autumnal splendor, and Cropsey's reputation as a first-rank landscape artist was established. Cropsey returned to New York in 1863, and two years later he built a summer home in Warwick, New York. The view depicted in *Mounts Adam and Eve* was taken from this site.[2]

Although Cropsey painted landscapes in all seasons, in his later years he turned more frequently to autumn scenes. His growing preoccupation with this season can be explained partly as a means to display his talent as a colorist and partly as a way to imbue his work with symbolic meaning. In the nineteenth century it was widely believed that America's autumnal splendor, unknown in Europe and Asia, represented God's blessing on this nation. In addition to its nationalistic significance, it also represented the last stage of life when spiritual illumination, embodied by autumn brilliance, was supposed to supplant diminishing physical powers.[3]

Cropsey's debt to Thomas Cole, the founder of the Hudson River School, is widely recognized, especially in their shared interest in allegorical landscapes. Although *Mounts Adam and Eve* is a realistic view, certain additions and adjustments suggest that Cropsey also intended it to convey a message about Christian life corresponding to Cole's renowned four-part series, *Voyage of Life.* The tree with exposed roots on the right, for example, is a common reminder of the fragility of life. The nearly imperceptible brook, which dances across the foreground beneath the ancient maple, widens into a calm river, then transforms into rapids before vanishing, seems to represent life's passage from the innocence of childhood to the dangers of manhood.[4] The church spire, strategically located before the twin mountain peaks rising like temple gates to eternity, offers a last moment's opportunity for redemption.

Notes

1. William S. Talbot, *Jasper F. Cropsey, 1823–1900* (Washington, D.C.: Smithsonian Institution Press, 1970), 33–34.
2. Ibid., 97–98.
3. Edward Hitchcock, "The Euthanasia of Autumn," in *Religious Lectures on Peculiar Phenomena in the Four Seasons* (1853), 85.
4. See Alan Wallach, "The Voyage of Life as Popular Art," *Art Bulletin* 59 (June 1977): 239. The widely read "Farewell Sermon" (1823) by Reverend Reginald Heber (1783–1826) is purported to have inspired the subject of Cole's *Voyage of Life*. It begins with the lines: "Life bears us on like the stream of a mighty river."

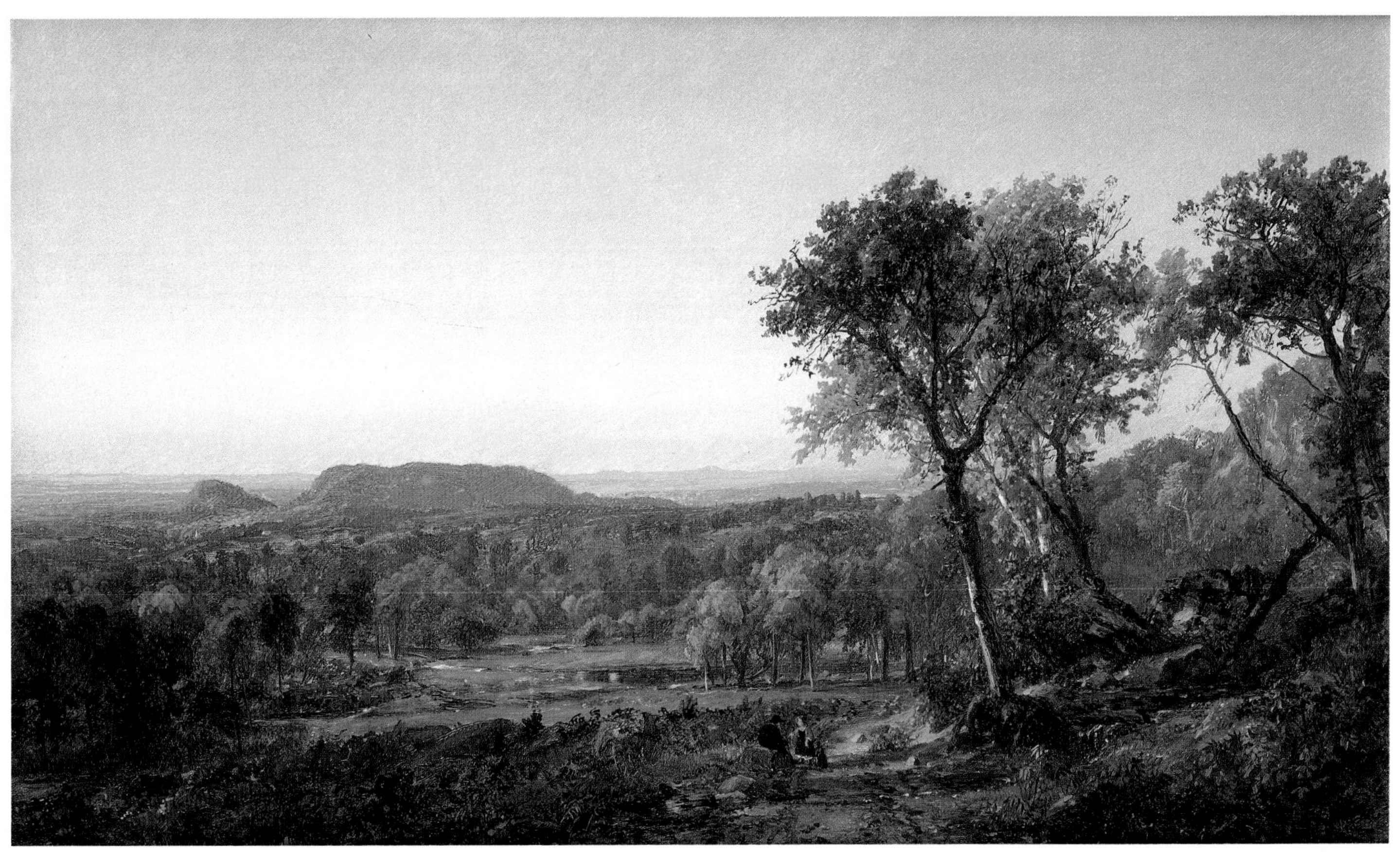

21

Oil on canvas, 12⅛ x 20⅛ in. (30.8 x 51.1 cm)
Signed and dated at lower right: J. F. CROPSEY/1872
Gift of Barbara B. Millhouse

Lion in the Arena, c. 1873–76

William Rimmer

1816–1879

The continual struggle between man's animal and spiritual selves occupies a central place in William Rimmer's art and writings and attests to his preoccupation with the psychic division between the higher and lower nature of man, a popular nineteenth-century theme. Although extremely poor throughout his lifetime, Rimmer was an educated man who first practiced as a self-taught physician and later conducted drawing classes in Boston. The precision with which Rimmer delineated the muscles, tendons, and veins of the figures confirms his reputation as the finest anatomical draftsman in this country up to that time.

Lion in the Arena is complex and ambiguous in its iconography.[1] Rather than exemplifying the heroic man, the gladiator represents sheer physical power[2] and demonstrates the attributes of brute described by Rimmer in *Art Anatomy*: "the hips wide; the thighs short; the knees coarse or thick."[3] The features of the lion, on the other hand, suggest certain human qualities.[4] In contrast to the gladiator's hidden face and animal strength, the lion's expression is so anguished that it elicits human sympathy.

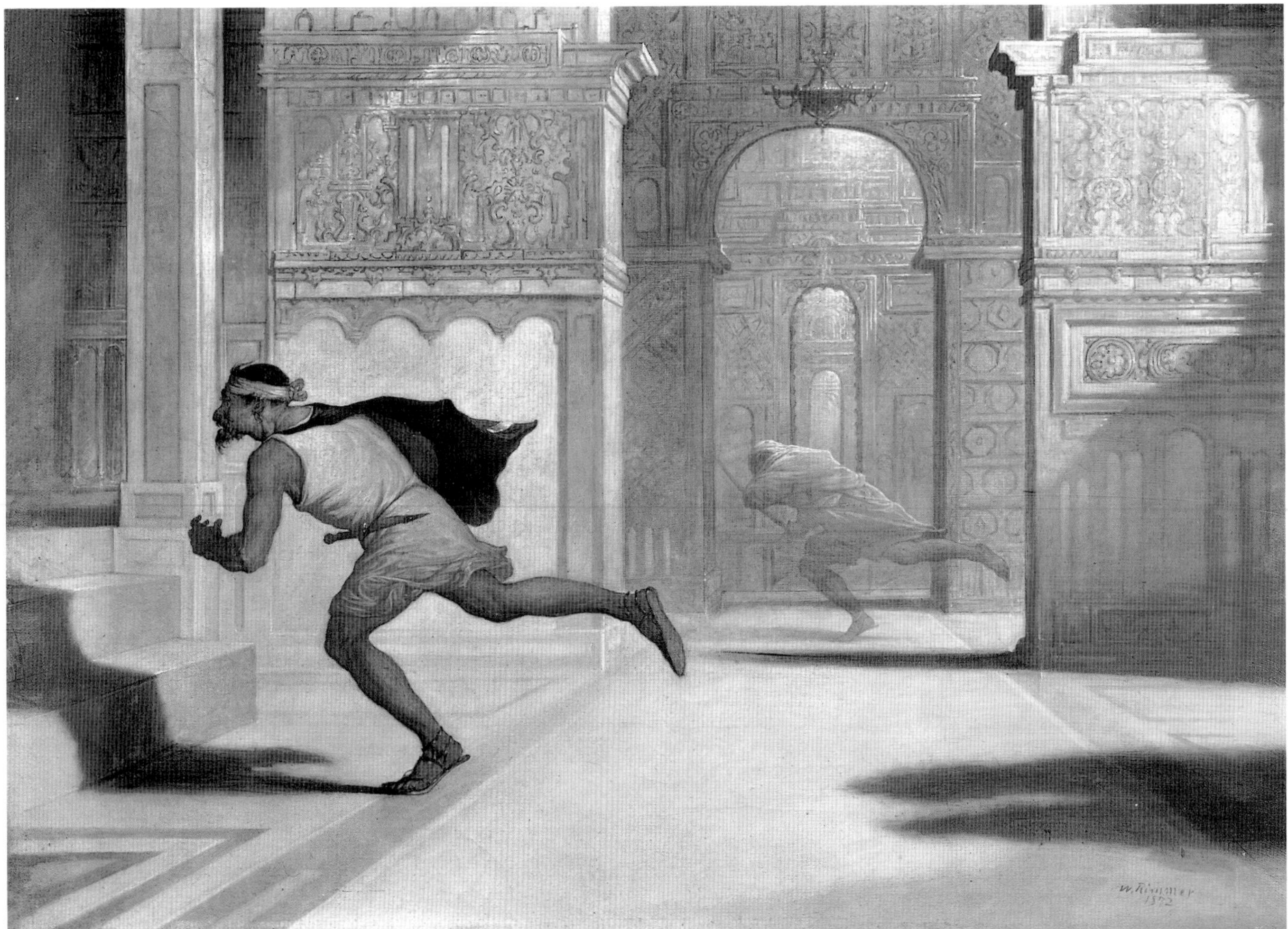

Figure 10 WILLIAM RIMMER, *Flight and Pursuit*, 1872. Museum of Fine Arts, Boston, Bequest of Miss Edith Nichols, 56.119

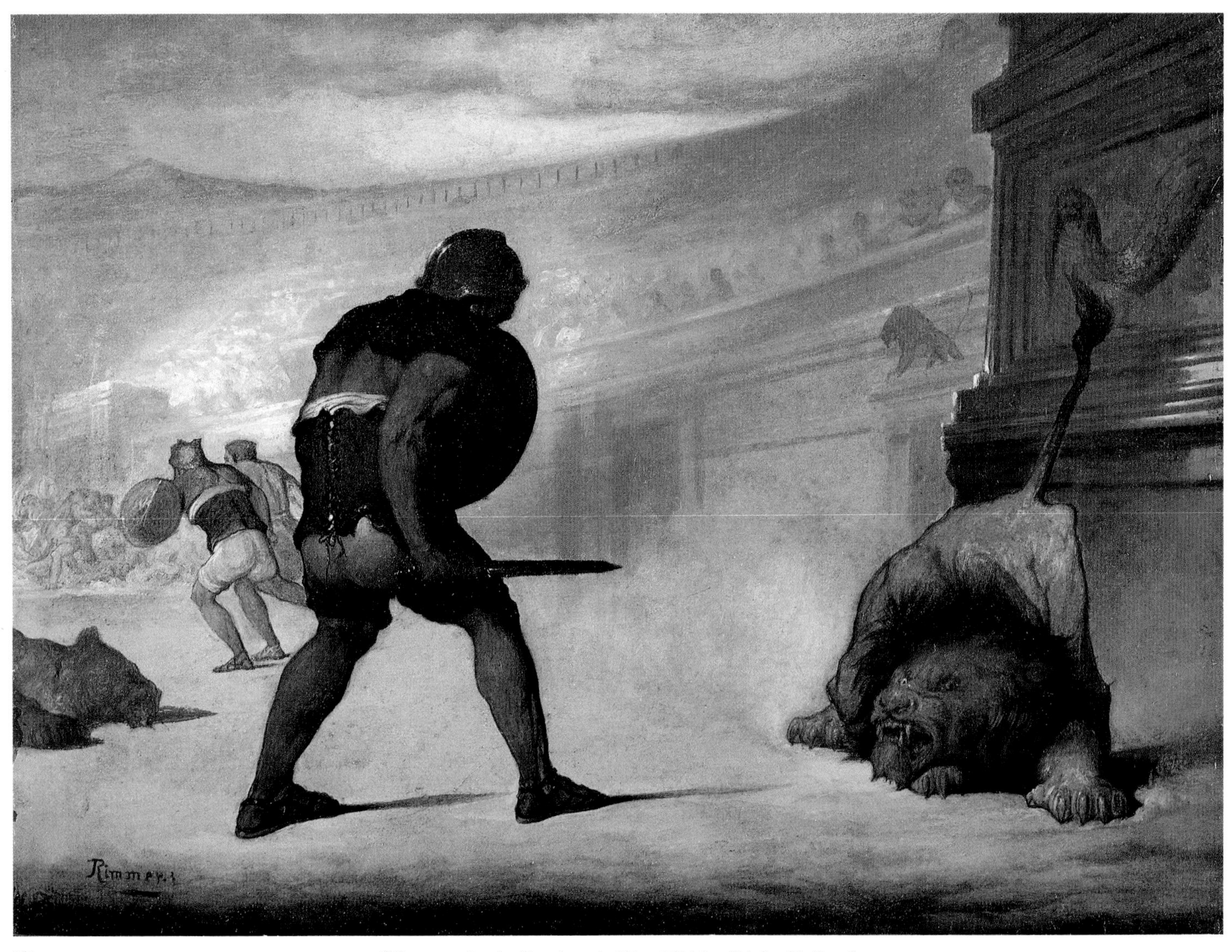

22

Oil on wood pulp fiber board, 9½ x 12½ in. (24.1 x 31.8 cm)
Signed at lower left: RIMMER.
Gift of Barbara B. Millhouse

The lion appears frequently in Rimmer's work, and seems to carry a personal symbolism associated with his father's claim to royal inheritance. Rimmer's deranged father propagated a family myth, which his son also believed, that he was the French Dauphin, the son of Marie Antoinette and Louis XVI.[5] This belief may help explain Rimmer's curious placement of a phantom king of beasts atop a pillar in the background of *Lion in the Arena*. Located in a commanding position generally reserved for the emperor's loge, this ghostlike lion appears to function as an agent controlling the fate of the combatants.

In 1872 Rimmer painted *Flight and Pursuit* (fig. 10), a haunting image into which he injected his split personality. Both *Flight and Pursuit* and *Lion in the Arena* illustrate the archetypal dopplegänger theme. In *Flight and Pursuit*, for example, the villain flees his shadow, and in *Lion in the Arena* the gladiator confronts his shadow self in the guise of a lion. In both paintings, however, an apparitionlike third party is introduced—the phantom villain running down a parallel hallway in one and the phantom lion perched on top of a pillar in the other. The addition of these enigmatic beings suggests psychic depictions not just of one self divided in two, but of several selves that dominate, oppose, and shadow each other.

Notes

1. Jeffrey Weidman, "William Rimmer: Critical Catalogue Raisonné" (Ph.D. diss., Indiana University, 1981), 632–33. When it was exhibited in 1876 at the Boston Art Club, and in 1880 at the Boston Museum of Fine Arts, *Lion in the Arena* was selected from the exhibitions by several critics for special attention. It was praised for "its finish," "correctness of detail," and "originality of subject." Few other works by Rimmer received positive criticism in the press.
2. Weidman, "William Rimmer," 632–33. An anonymous writer in 1880 noted: "The man is perhaps unlike a human being if it be examined in detail, the animal is certainly unlike the flesh and blood of the menageries, but both man and lion are impressive types of physical strength and courage on the one hand, and fiendish ferocity and cruelty on the other." No mention is made of the psychological theme.
3. William Rimmer, *Art Anatomy* (reprint; New York: Dover Publications, 1962), 132.
4. Weidman identifies the model for the pyramidal body of the lion as an illustration in James Ridley's *Tales of the Genii*, 2 vols. (London: J. Adlard, 1810), vol. 1, 149. Rimmer's lion, however, differs considerably, especially in the shape and expression of the head, the position of the tail, and the delineation of the muscles.
5. Lincoln Kirstein, "Who was Dr. Rimmer?" *Town and Country* 100 (July 1946).

Detail of *Lion in the Arena*

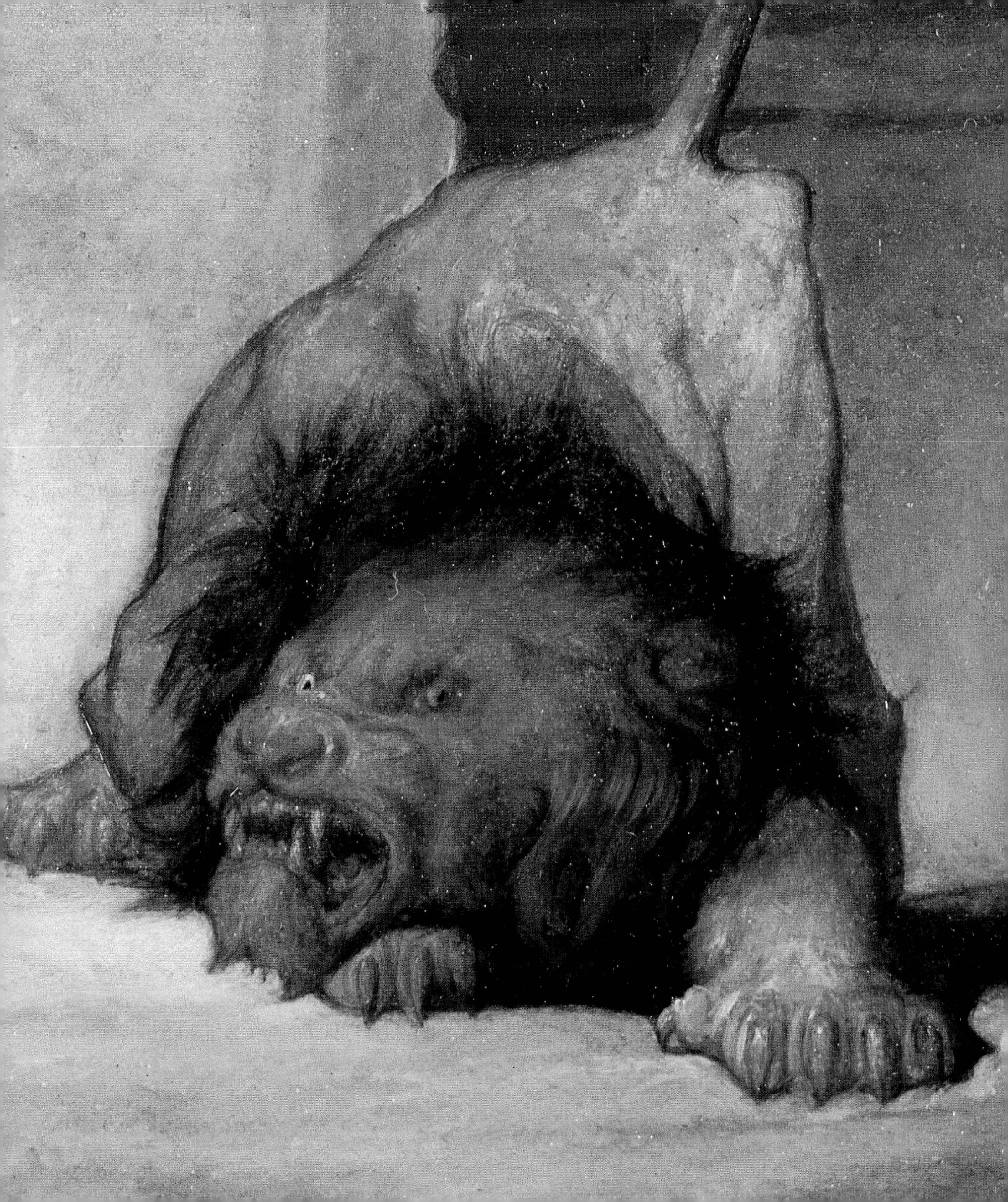

JOB LOT CHEAP, 1878

WILLIAM M. HARNETT

1848–1892

In the late nineteenth century Harnett's highly illusionistic style attracted enthralled crowds to the places of business where his paintings frequently hung. Textile manufacturers in particular became avid collectors, and two days after Harnett's death an article appeared in the *Dry Goods Economist* stating that "B. Nugent of B. Nugent and Bros., the well-known St. Louis dry goods jobbers, owns his celebrated book picture entitled *Job Lot*."[1] No information exists to explain this reference to the notoriety of *Job Lot Cheap*, but it probably rested on its trompe l'oeil effects, of which Harnett was the leading American master.

Harnett, whose family had immigrated from Ireland to Philadelphia around 1849, supported himself as an engraver in his early years while he took night courses at the Pennsylvania Academy of the Fine Arts. Around 1871 he moved to New York

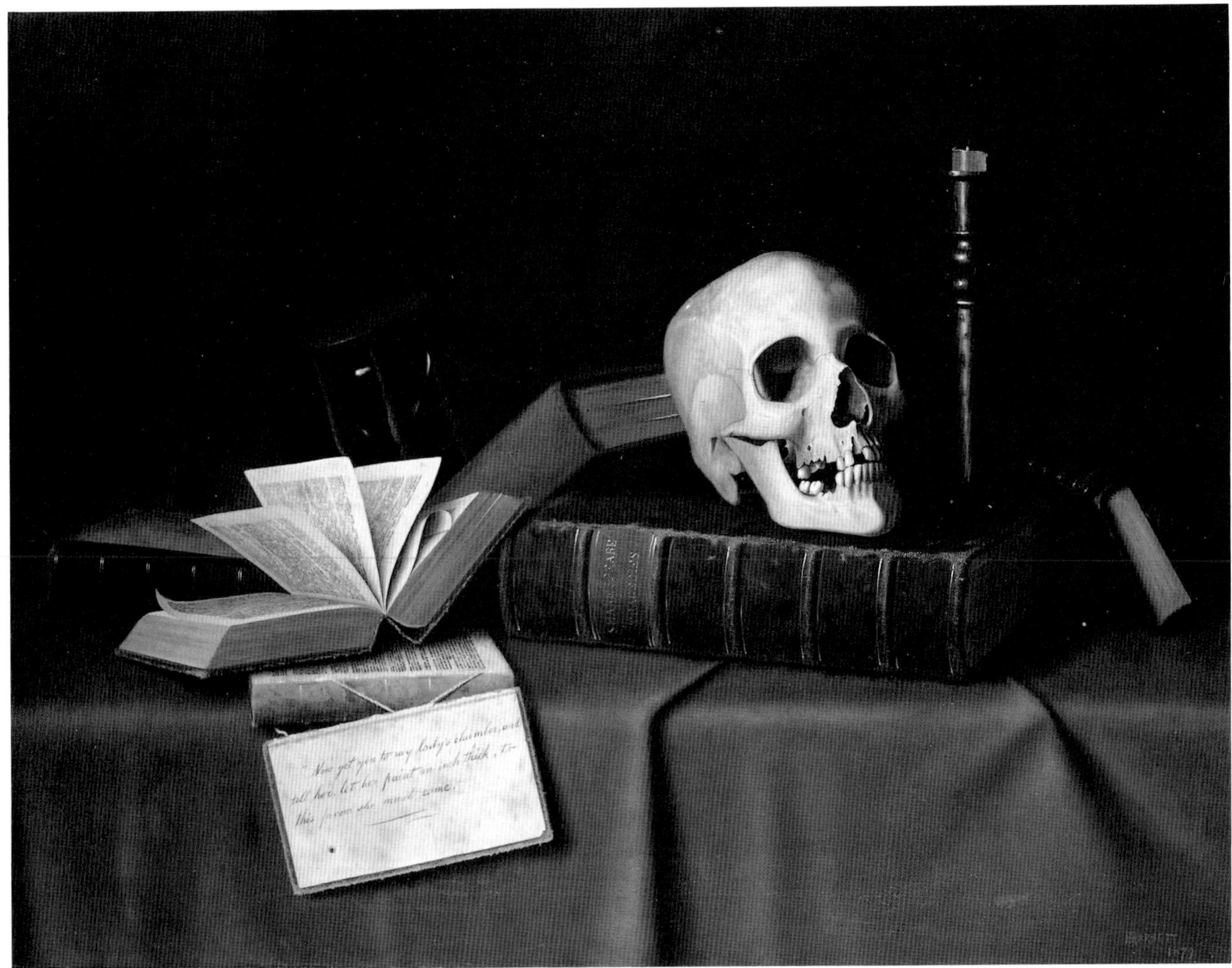

Figure 11 WILLIAM HARNETT *Memento Mori—"To This Favour,"* 1879. The Cleveland Museum of Art, Mr. and Mrs. William H. Marlatt Fund, 65.235

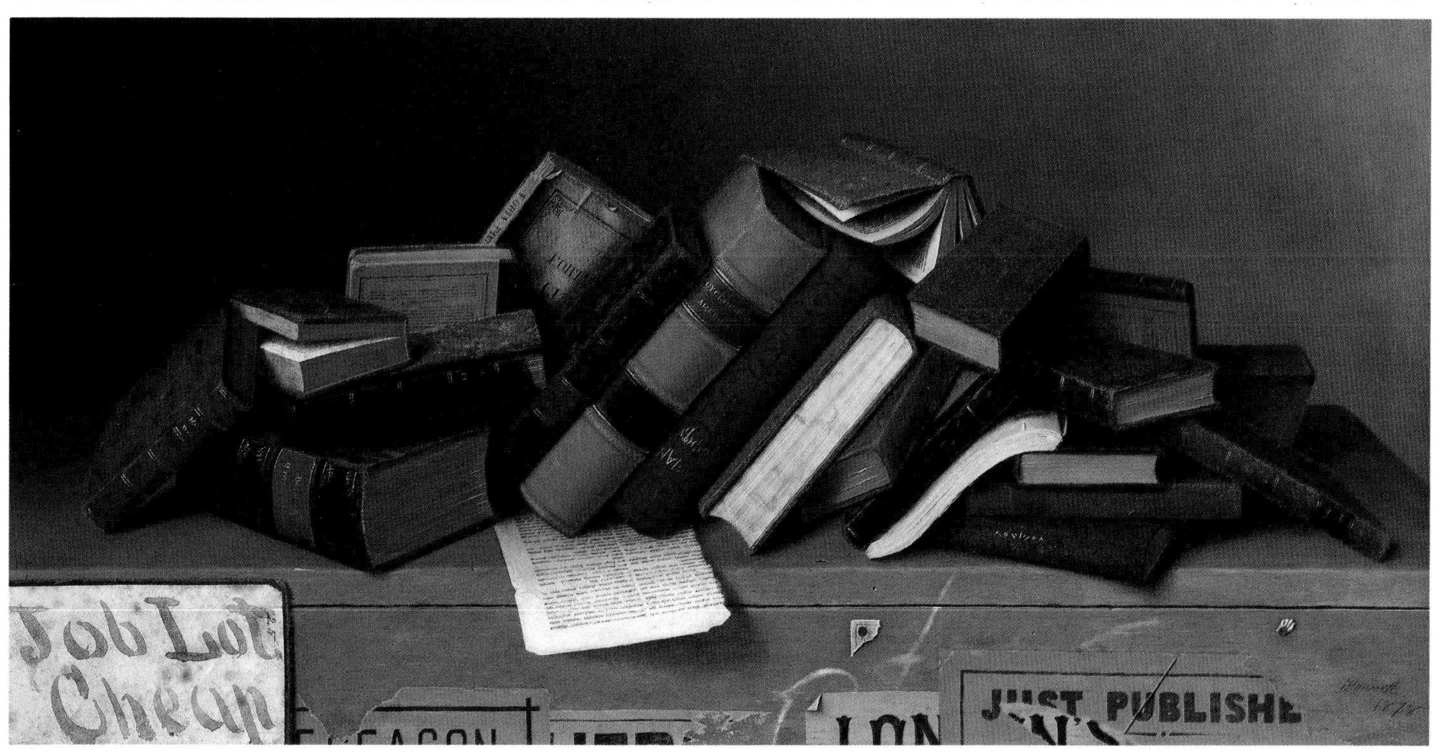

23

Oil on canvas, 18 x 36 in. (45.7 x 91.4 cm)
Signed and dated at lower right:
WMH [monogram] ARNETT/1878
Original purchase fund from the Mary Reynolds Babcock
Foundation, Z. Smith Reynolds Foundation,
Area Foundation, and Anne Cannon Forsyth

for five years, continuing his studies at Cooper Union and the National Academy of Design. His first oil paintings date from 1874, and soon thereafter appeared in exhibitions. By 1878, the year *Job Lot Cheap* was painted, he received his first mention in the press.

An important example of his early period, *Job Lot Cheap* reveals his full mastery of illusionistic devices without the benefit of European training. The placement of the books close to the picture plane, the projection of a printed page seemingly into the viewer's space, and the careful differentiation of textures evoke a compelling tactile response. In addition the manipulation of paint to mimic mottled leather, marbleized papers, gilt edging, printed pages, wood graining, and a variety of other materials reinforces the deception that is elicited even by the signature shaded to appear as though it is pressed into soft wood with a hard pencil.

Although *Job Lot Cheap* achieves a heightened aesthetic based on technique alone, an inscription in Harnett's handwriting on the reverse of a photograph of this painting thanks his friend E. T. Snow for the "idea"—presumably the idea upon which the painting is based.[2] Later, in a biographical statement, he supports a narrative intent when he admits, "I endeavor to make the composition tell a story."[3] Three paintings from the late 1870s reveal that at the time Harnett painted *Job Lot Cheap* he was preoccupied with the age-old theme of *memento mori*—mementos of death.[4] In these still life paintings he used books in conjunction with traditional symbols of mortality—a skull, burnt-out candle, hourglass, or faded rose. In *Job Lot Cheap,* however, he piles together twenty-two books unrelieved by paraphernalia associated with the brevity of life, which is an unconventional idea, unprecedented in American art. The torn bindings, worn corners, and rumpled cloth covers indicate Harnett's preoccupation with the age of these discarded books. They have been placed not on a tabletop but on a packing case with a partly legible label that reads "Just Published." With the new books in the crate waiting to replace the old, worn-out ones, Harnett has discovered an innovative means of communicating the Romantic lament over the passing of time.

A surprising number of book titles are legible. The partly visible blue paperback with a torn and rippled cover, which reads *The Forty-Five Gu——*, is possibly a songbook. On the far right *Mo . . . r's Works* props open an untitled book and leans against a thick brown volume whose title begins with a *B* and appears to be in German. It is difficult to draw any conclusion about the significance of these titles, but the central grouping of the *Cyclopedia Americana* flanked by two upside down books, *The Arabian Nights* and Homer's *Odyssey,* evoke speculations that may support a number of themes. Each book carries an association with a continent—Europe, America, and Asia. The placement of the American book right side up may have patriotic overtones.

The inclusion of these two ancient classics as cheap sale items—worthless and no longer read—seems to confirm a musing on time's erosions parallel to those in Washington Irving's popular essay of 1819, *The Mutability of Literature.*[5] Irving debates whether all books eventually become antiquated and obsolete or whether certain authors, especially poets, whose thoughts are "rooted in the unchanging principles of human nature" will defy the encroachment of time. Barbara Groseclose reads a similar meaning in Harnett's *Mortality and Immortality* painted two years earlier: She suggests that this still life indicates that "man's creative achievements, like his mortal existence, come to nothing."[6] It is probable, therefore, that the message contained in *Job Lot Cheap* is the same as Irving's essay: a questioning of the longevity of man's works.

NOTES

1. Alfred Frankenstein, *After the Hunt: William Harnett and Other American Still Life Painters, 1870–1900* (Los Angeles: University of California Press, 1953), 45.
2. Edward Taylor Snow (1844–1913) was a landscape painter, writer, collector, and prominent figure in the Philadelphia art world. He had close associations with the Pennsylvania Academy of the Fine Arts, and in 1904 his portrait was painted by his friend Thomas Eakins. The photograph with this notation is in the Archives of American Art, New York.
3. Frankenstein, *After the Hunt,* 55.
4. Harnett's *memento mori* paintings are *Mortality and Immortality* (1876, Roland P. Murdock Collection, Wichita, Kansas), *Memento Mori—"To This Favour"* (1879, fig. 11), and *To This Favor—A Thought from Shakespeare* (1879, private collection). These are discussed by Barbara S. Groseclose in "Vanity and the Artist: Some Still Life Paintings by William Harnett," *American Art Journal* 19 (no. 1): 53.
5. I am indebted to Dr. Richard Rust, Professor of English and Adjunct Professor of American Studies, University of North Carolina, Chapel Hill, for this observation.
6. Groseclose, "Vanity and the Artist," 54.

Detail of *Job Lot Cheap*

In the Studio, c. 1884

William Merritt Chase

1849–1916

Returning to New York in 1878 from his studies in Munich, William Merritt Chase leased a studio (figs. 12, 13) in the Tenth Street Studio Building, which twenty years earlier had become famous as the headquarters of the Hudson River School. As one of the earliest interiors in New York City decorated in the Aesthetic style, Chase's studio attracted considerable attention, and was described in the press as "a shrine" to be "entered with bated breath and deep humility."[1] Placing the utmost importance on style in every aspect of his life, Chase outfitted himself daily in a cutaway with a carnation in the lapel and strolled down New York avenues with two Russian wolfhounds on leashes. His luxurious studio, flamboyant personality, remarkable paintings, and influential teaching (Joseph Stella, Charles Sheeler, and Georgia O'Keeffe were among his pupils) placed Chase at the center of the New York art world for the next two decades.

In the Studio provides a glimpse of the sumptuous interior that became the subject of some of Chase's finest paintings. The

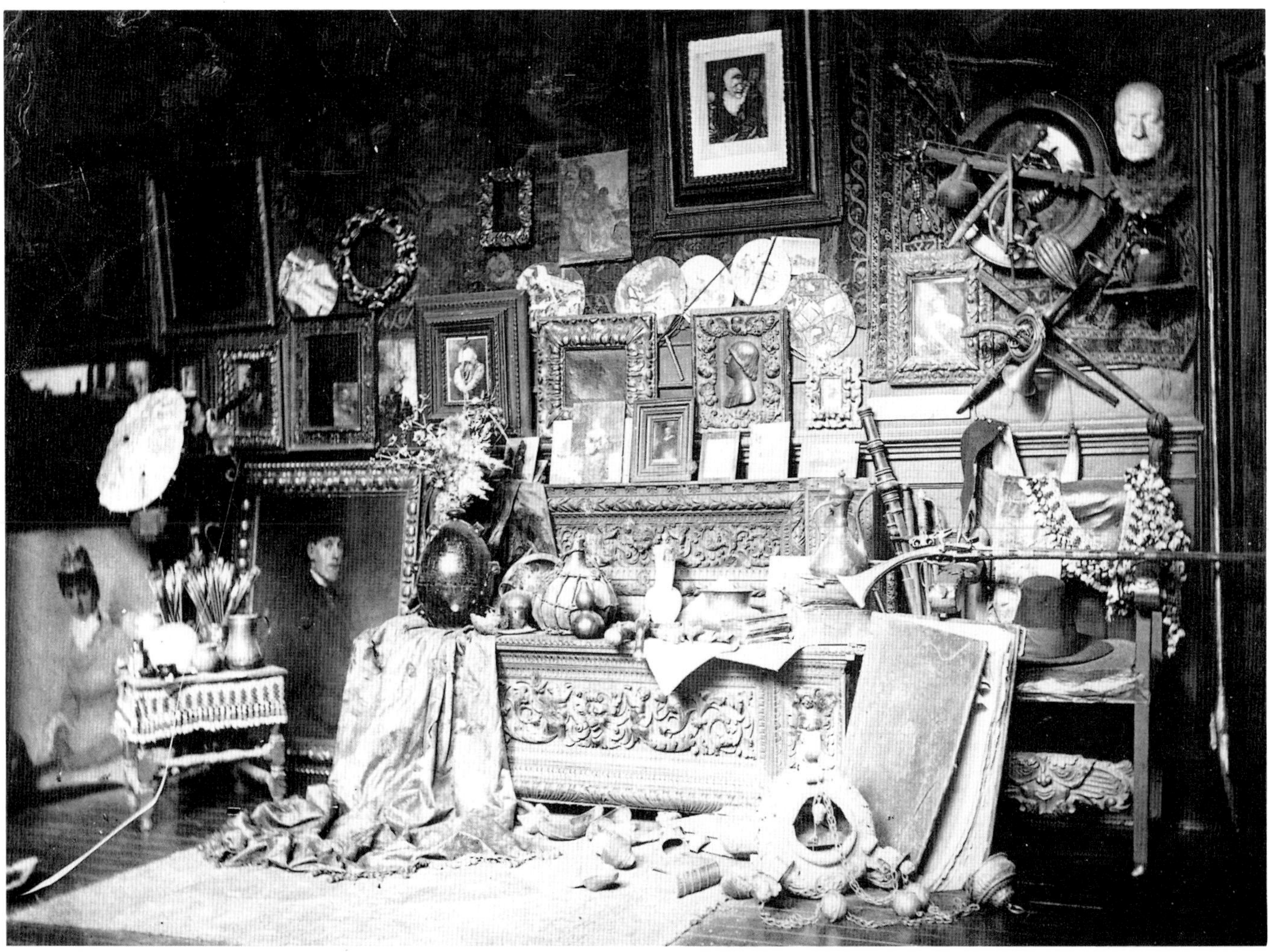

Figure 12 *William Merritt Chase's Studio*, c. 1890. The William Merritt Chase Papers, Archives of American Art, Smithsonian Institution

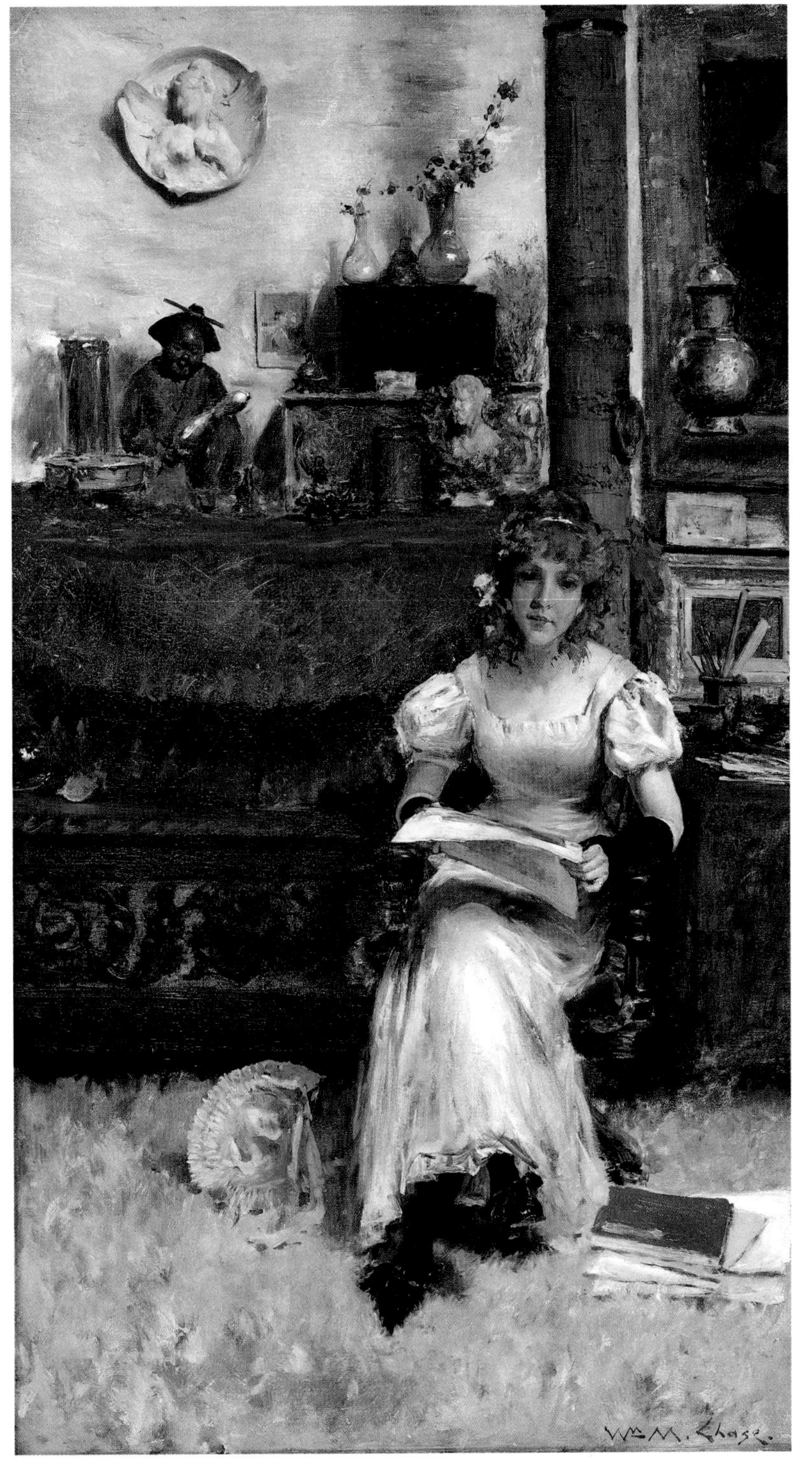

24 Oil on canvas, 39 x 22 in. (99.1 x 55.9 cm)
Signed at lower right: WM M. CHASE-
Original purchase fund from the Mary Reynolds Babcock
Foundation, Z. Smith Reynolds Foundation,
Area Foundation, and Anne Cannon Forsyth

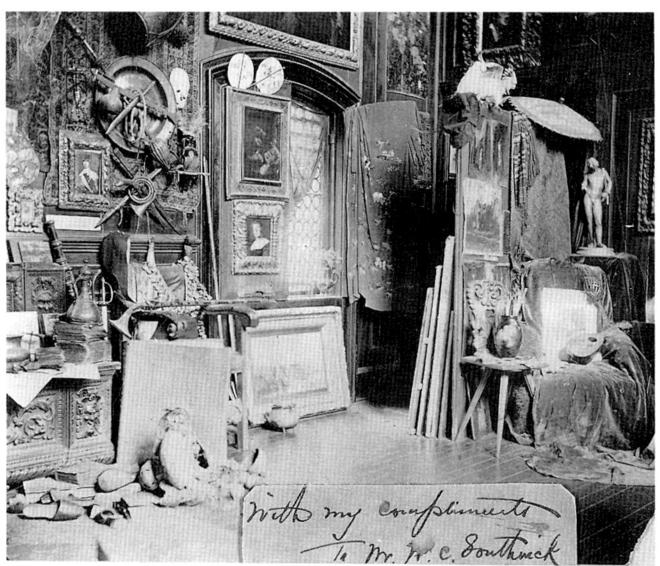

Figure 13 *William Merritt Chase's Studio, West 10th Street, New York*, c. 1890
The William Merritt Chase Papers, Archives of American Art, Smithsonian Institution

attractive young woman seated in the swivel chair resembles one of the Gerson sisters, who posed for him frequently at this time. In 1886 Alice Gerson became Chase's wife, but the sitter here is more likely to be her sister Virginia, who is the subject of a related pastel with the same date and title.[2] The simple white satin dress seems to have been one of the artist's numerous props, appearing on other models in Chase's paintings. Like Whistler, a leader of the Aesthetic Movement, Chase intended to create a pleasing painting without moral content, a revolutionary aim in the United States in the 1880s.

Carefully and compactly arranged on the red textile is a group of curios that exhibit a variety of textures—wood, marble, pewter, lacquer, inlay, and glass. Chase loved the varied surface qualities of these objects, yet in his paintings his interest lies less in duplicating their specific textures than in creating an exciting overall painting surface. Chase's acquisitiveness represents an entirely new phenomenon. The Oriental figure, classical relic, small Japanese print, Turkish brass incense burner, and various other decorative objects bring a microcosm of world cultures into artistic unity. These objects contribute at once to the elegance of his studio decor, and reflect as well the burgeoning capitalism that was creating the first generation of American consumers.

Contrary to the sentimental paintings of the previous decades, Chase does not use the female model to evoke tender feelings. She represents instead a fresh, independent young woman whose expression excites no emotion. He imbues her pearly flesh, limpid eyes, and delicate ringlets with the same sensuous treatment applied to her soft suede mitts, shiny satin dress, and black patent-leather shoes. The flamboyant and masterful brushwork in the feathery area around the shoes demonstrates Chase's premium on effortlessness and supports his contention that a successful painting ought to look as if it had been "blown on the canvas with one puff."[3]

Notes

1. Doreen Bolger Burke, "Painters and Sculptors in a Decorative Age," in *In Pursuit of Beauty: Americans and the Aesthetic Movement* (New York: Metropolitan Museum of Art, 1986), 322.
2. *In the Studio (Virginia Gerson)* (c. 1884, Hirschl & Adler Galleries) is reproduced in Ronald G. Pisano, *A Leading Spirit in American Art: William Merritt Chase, 1849–1916* (Seattle: University of Washington Press, 1983), 73. A portrait of her c. 1880 is reproduced on page 47. Mr. and Mrs. Julius Gerson had three daughters, Virginia, Minnie, and Alice. Alice and Virginia, who was a writer and costume designer, frequently posed for artists.
3. Katharine Metcalf Roof, *The Life and Art of William Merritt Chase* (New York: Charles Scribner's Sons, 1917), 321.

Detail of *In the Studio*

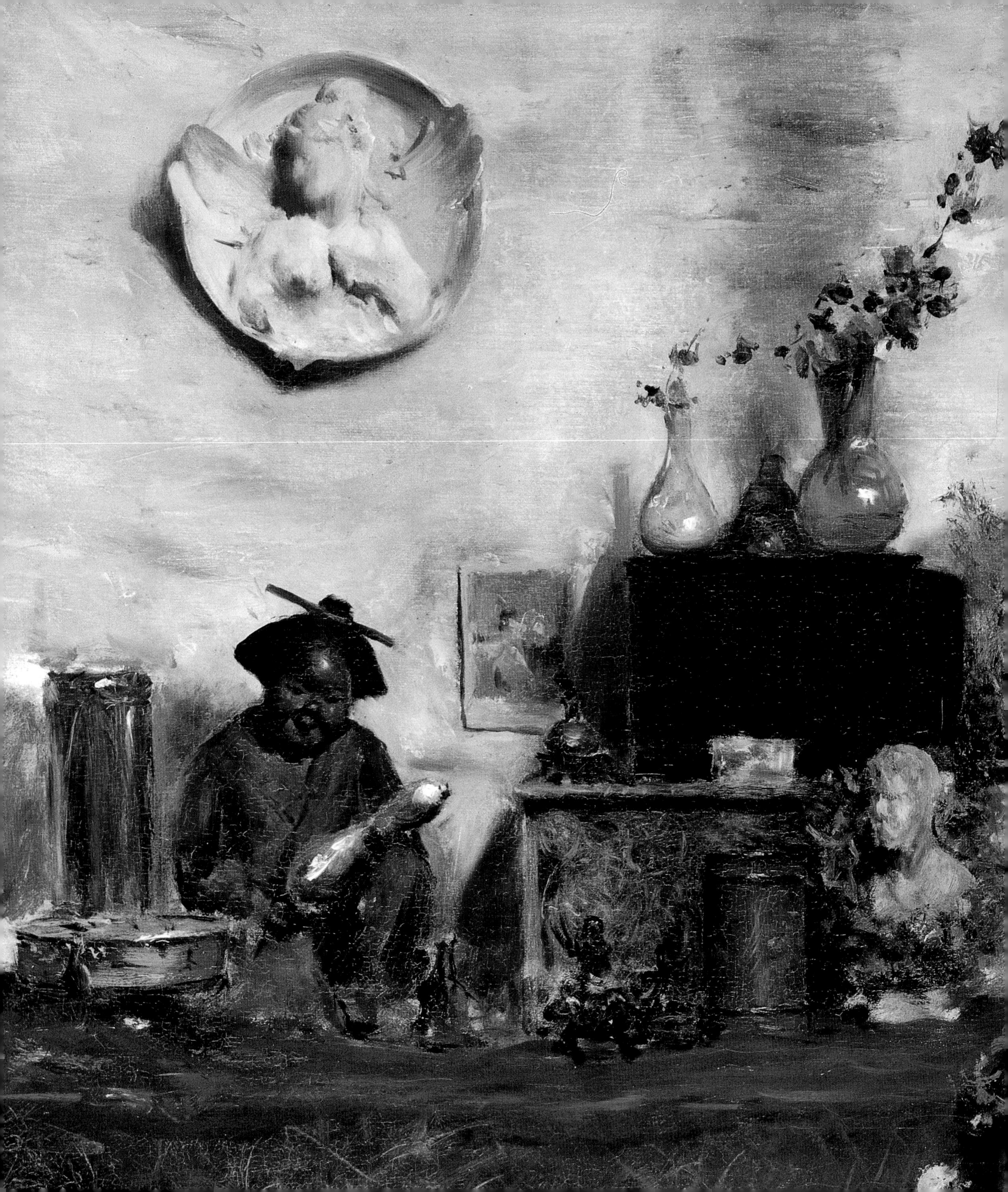

THE STORM, 1885
GEORGE INNESS
1825–1894

A work of art does not appeal to the intellect," declared George Inness in 1878. "It does not appeal to the moral sense. Its aim is not to instruct, not to edify, but to awaken an emotion."[1] He thus advocated a radical new artistic concept that was to change the appearance of American landscape painting in the last two decades of the nineteenth century. During the years when the public waited eagerly for each imposing panorama by Frederic E. Church and Albert Bierstadt, Inness was quietly studying the art of the French Barbizon school to learn how "to touch the soul with a mere thicket."[2] Overshadowed by these highly celebrated artists for much of his career, Inness experienced a turn of events in 1884 when he was given a large retrospective in New York at the American Art Galleries. The public finally responded to Inness's genius, and during the last decade of his life he enjoyed enormous fame.

Inness painted landscapes depicting all kinds of weather, but in the late 1870s he exhibited a preference for approaching storms. This work, the last of the important paintings in his storm series,[3] shows green meadowlands typical of New Jersey farms in 1885. A dark, rich tonality pervades most of the painting, with the lightest area reserved for the background. The low vantage point and virtually unobstructed foreground invite the viewer to immerse himself in the soft grass. The heavy dark clouds set the mood to which all other elements contribute, most noticeably the line of trees that twist and bend in response to a sudden burst of wind. The storm's imminent approach has scattered the birds and sent the farmer, wrapped in private thought, heading for shelter. Rejecting the melodramatic freak storms of nature favored by the Romantic painters, Inness depicts this storm as a recurrent thunder shower common to hot summer afternoons. Although Inness was living in Montclair, New Jersey, when he painted this scene, it is probably not a specific place but an imaginative recreation.

The impact of this painting rests upon the artist's skill in rendering color and form to convey a single, harmonious mood. To achieve what Inness and his critics described as poetic effect, it was necessary to subordinate detail during a period when laborious delineation was regarded as an essential part of pictorial expression. Minute detail served the goals of Church and his colleagues in evoking scientific enquiry and veneration of nature, but broad masses and subtle tonalities were better suited for the evocation of a personal mood. Inness enlivened his surfaces with free brushwork and with glazes and scumbling—methods of paint application that allow one tint to emerge through another to imbue the color with a luminosity that cannot be obtained by direct application of paint.

His encounter with Barbizon painting taught Inness to place the center of interest in the middle ground rather than the foreground, which had been the practice of the Hudson River School. The hollow stump, twisted sapling, and full-leafed mature trees demonstrate an age range that harks back to the Romantic preoccupation with the passing of time and the cycles of life. Perhaps he was recalling the trees he had seen in Italy, those "odd-looking trees that had been used or tortured or twisted—all telling something about humanity."[4] Inness "seldom painted a group of trees as effective as this one. Arranged like parts of a friezelike composition, they embody the scale of reactions to the imminently impending storm. . . . In a repertory of poses and gesticulating movements, they make this drama of nature legible in terms of human action and feeling."[5]

NOTES

1. Elizabeth McCausland, *George Inness, An American Landscape Painter, 1825–1894* (Springfield, Mass.: George Walter Vincent Smith Museum, 1946), 65.
2. John Sillevis and Hans Kraan, *The Barbizon School* (The Hague, Netherlands: Haags Gemeentemuseum, 1985), 33.
3. Nicolai Cikousky and Michael Quick, *George Inness* (Los Angeles: Los Angeles County Museum, 1985), 166, no. 45.
4. Cikousky and Quick, *George Inness*, 209.
5. Ibid, 166, no. 45.

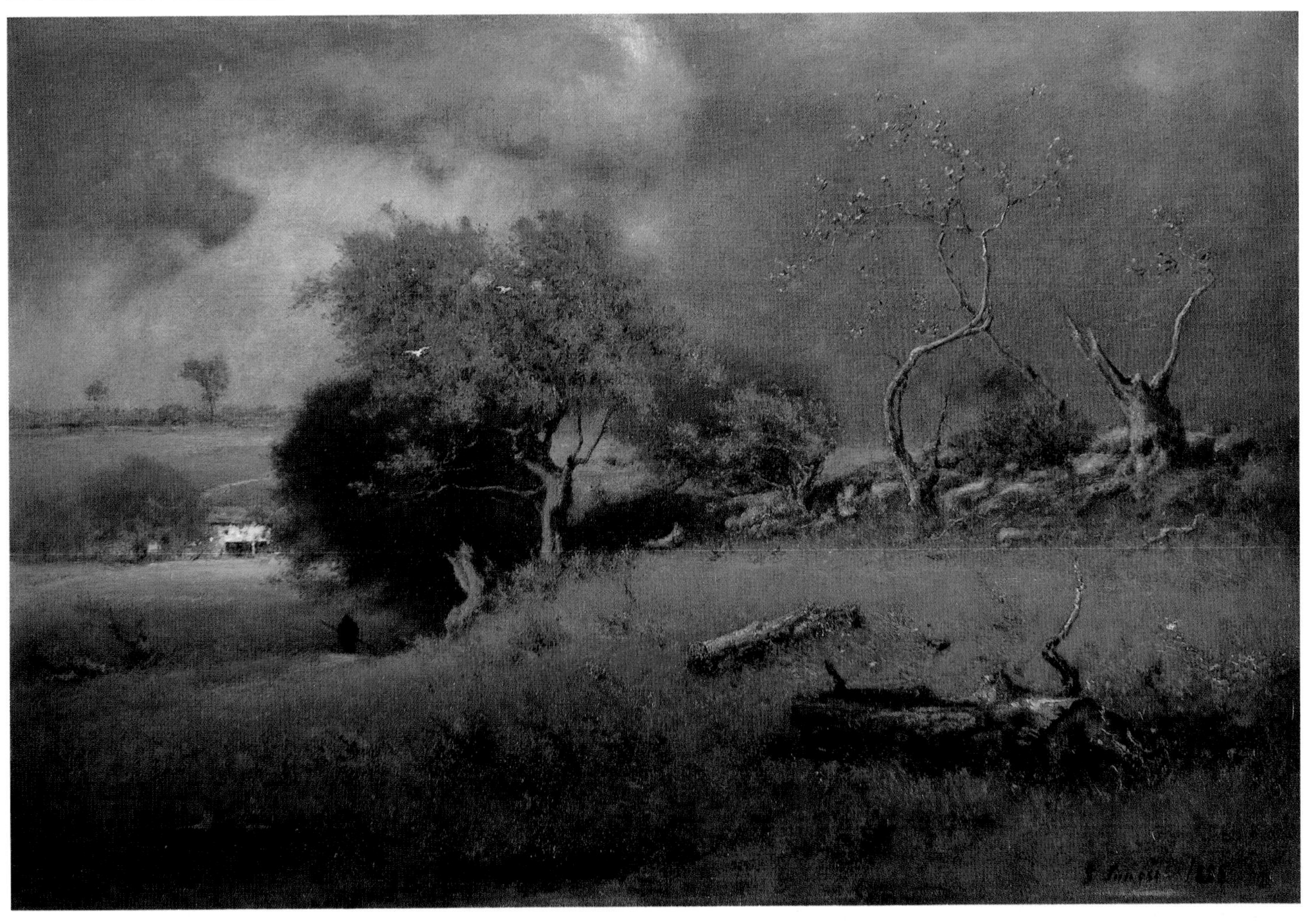

25

Oil on canvas, 20 x 30 in. (50.8 x 76.2 cm)
Signed and dated at lower right: G INNESS 1885
Gift of Barbara B. Millhouse

PHLOX, 1886

DAVID JOHNSON

1827–1908

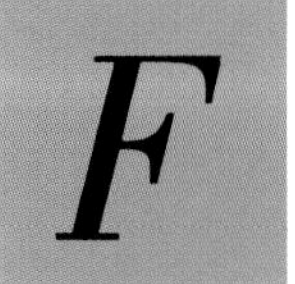

ew nineteenth-century American painters produced an oeuvre with a greater variety of subject and style than did David Johnson. Predominantly remembered as a landscape painter of the American northeast wilderness, Johnson also produced still lifes, portraits, and an occasional genre subject. His art evolved from the traditional selected observation of nature as transformed by the Hudson River School artists' notion of the ideal, to an art that incorporates the precise clarity of vision as practiced by the American Pre-Raphaelites. Later in his career Johnson employed the diffused suggestions of nature developed by the Barbizon artists in France. Partly as a result of Johnson's stylistic fluctuations, his career has only recently been reexamined and the full richness of his abilities more accurately defined.[1]

Little is known about Johnson's early career. He spent one month studying with Jasper Cropsey in his native New York City,[2] perhaps enrolled for two sessions in the antique class at the National Academy of Design, and at an early age knew and traveled with leading landscape painters, including John Kensett, John Casilear, and Benjamin Champney. Johnson owned several European paintings, but there is no specific evidence to suggest he ever traveled abroad.

Johnson was clearly an artist acutely aware of his surroundings, both in the natural world that was his subject as well as the art of his colleagues and the newest European works sold and exhibited in New York City. *Phlox* is first a detailed, accurately rendered representation of this species of flower. Johnson renders the blossoms and foliage as knowledgeably as a botanist might describe them. In his role as an interpreter of nature, Johnson balances this scientific clarity with the subjective beauty of a hidden corner of nature revealed to the viewer. Johnson transforms specific elements of nature into immediately accessible expressions of aesthetic beauty. *Phlox* suggests a familiarity with contemporary French flower painting, particularly in its diffused background and the monumentality of the rich textured blossoms.

Johnson demonstrated a remarkable consistency in his approach to still-life subjects. *Phlox*, painted in 1886, compares stylistically to *Three Pears and an Apple* (1857) and *Sketch of Apple Blossoms with May Flowers* (1873). All these works treat the still life as a perfect specimen, devoid of the blemishes of wear that natural forces can bestow.

NOTES

1. The two most recent studies of David Johnson's art are John I. H. Baur and Margaret Conrads, *The Drawings of David Johnson* (Yonkers, N.Y.: Hudson River Museum, 1988), and Gwendolyn Owens, *Nature Transcibed: The Landscapes and Still Lifes of David Johnson* (Ithaca, N.Y.: Herbert J. Johnson Museum of Art, Cornell University, 1988).
2. Jasper Cropsey's account books indicate that David Johnson paid for lessons in 1850; Owens, *Nature Transcribed*, 17.

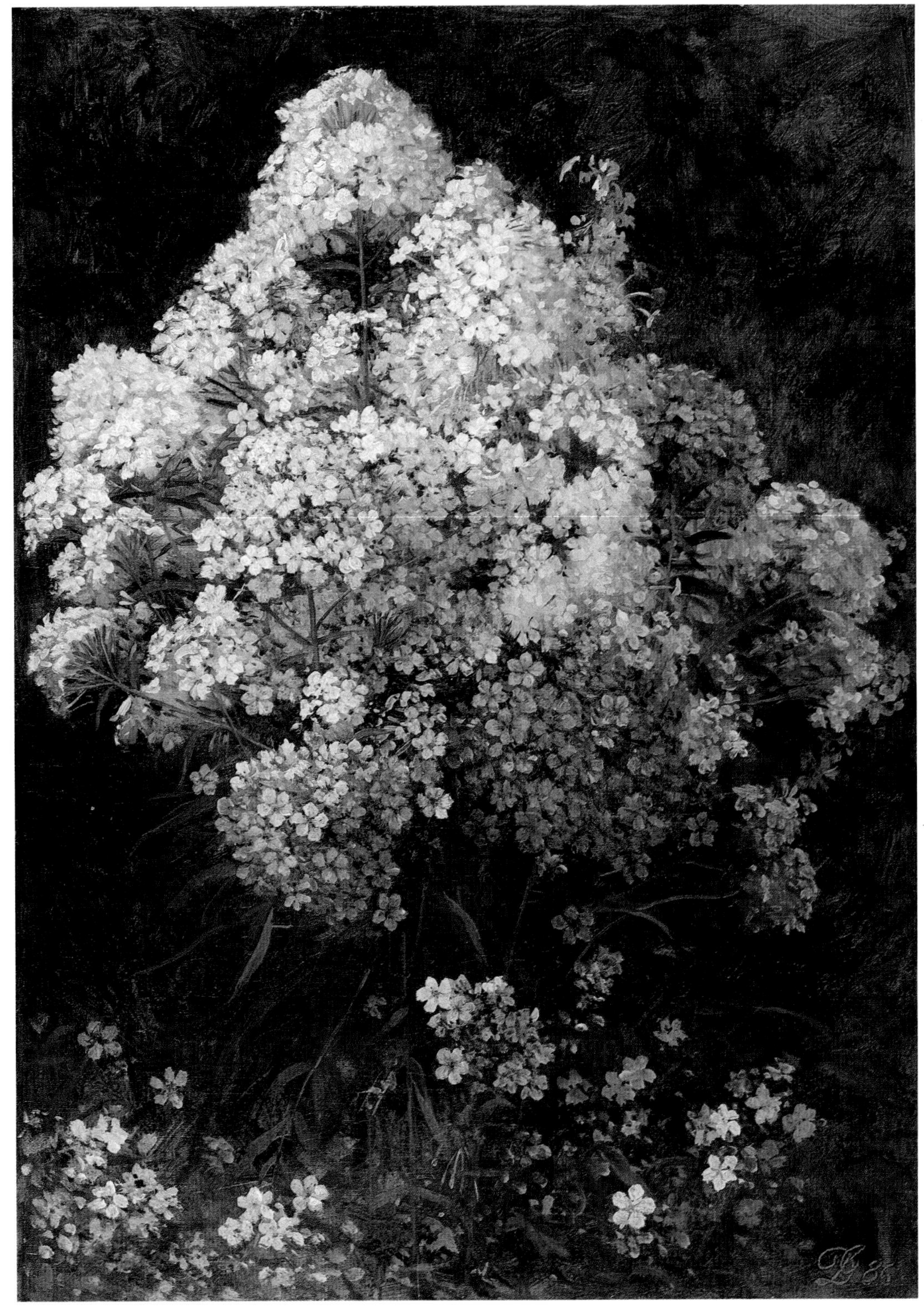

26 Oil on canvas, 19¼ x 14½ in. (48.9 x 36.8 cm)
Signed and dated at lower right: DJ '86
Gift of Lawrence A. Fleischman in honor of Charles H. Babcock, Sr.

MADAME MEERSON AND HER DAUGHTER, c. 1899

MARY CASSATT

1844–1926

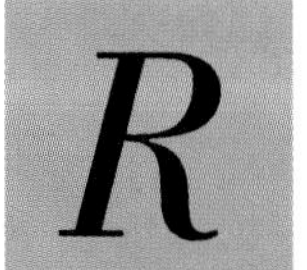

Recruited by Edgar Degas, who had been favorably impressed by her paintings when they were exhibited in the Paris Salon of 1874, Mary Cassatt joined the Impressionists in 1879 for their fourth exhibition. Her affiliation with this radical group brought her immediate notoriety, prompting her father to write to her brother that "she is now known to the art world as well as to the general public in such a way as not to be forgotten again so long as she continues to paint."[1] She exhibited with the Paris Salon from 1872 to 1876, joining the Impressionists exhibitions from 1879 until 1886, the year of their final exhibition. Not until the 1890s, however, did she receive her first solo exhibitions: in 1893 in Paris and two years later in New York, at which time her reputation was established in her native country. Today she maintains a special place in the history of art for the exceptionally high quality of her work and as the only American to be involved in the formative years of the Impressionist movement.

Mary Cassatt was born in Allegheny County, Pennsylvania, but she spent a large part of her girlhood with her family in Europe. After studying for four years at the Pennsylvania Academy of the Fine Arts, she returned to Europe to resume her artistic training and settled permanently in Paris in 1874. She drew her artistic subjects from her daily life, focusing for the most part on family and friends, occasionally employing models in her later work. Men outside her immediate family rarely enter her art, which she admitted was comprised of "women apart from their relations with men." During the 1880s, when she first began to combine women and children into a single format, she became recognized as a painter of motherhood—a reputation she maintained for the rest of her life.

From the first, Cassatt's innovative treatment of women and children exposed the public to the varied, satisfying, and fulfulling moments of motherhood, not as a single, recurrent experience but as diverse and poignant as other human relationships. Although she never married, she had a special sensitivity toward conveying the distinct personality of each child, no matter how young, and toward capturing the particular character of a momentary interaction with the mother.

In *Madame Meerson and Her Daughter* Cassatt seems intent upon the contrast between an attitude of physical closeness—emphasized by the merging of the two bodies into one black shape—and the particular variance in temperament between the subjects, evidenced by their strikingly dissimilar hair coloring and complexions. The close-up vantage point enforces a feeling of intimacy by thrusting the viewer into the parlor. Whereas the intense, solemn gaze of the girl makes contact with the viewer, the faraway, misty gaze of her mother seems fixed on thoughts of past times.

Degas was a primary force in reviving pastel as a major medium, and used it in most of his important work after 1885. Cassatt had started working in it around 1878 and by the decade of the 1890s it had become her preferred medium. In this work her deft application of colored chalk is calculated to describe with care and simultaneously create a decorative, vibrant surface appealing for its own sake. The black dresses are not composed of a single color, but vibrate with strokes of reds, yellows, and blues. The floating highlight on the daughter's puffed sleeve, which seems to adhere more to the picture plane than to the fabric, functions as a modernist device to create a dual reading between the flatness of the picture plane and the illusion of volume. This engaging double portrait, like so many of Cassatt's works, reveals her skill in combining innovative treatment with authentic emotion filtered through a sympathetic feminine sensibility.

NOTE

1. Nancy Mowll Mathews, "Mary Cassatt and the 'Modern Madonna' of the Nineteenth Century (Ph.D. diss., New York University, 1980), 57.

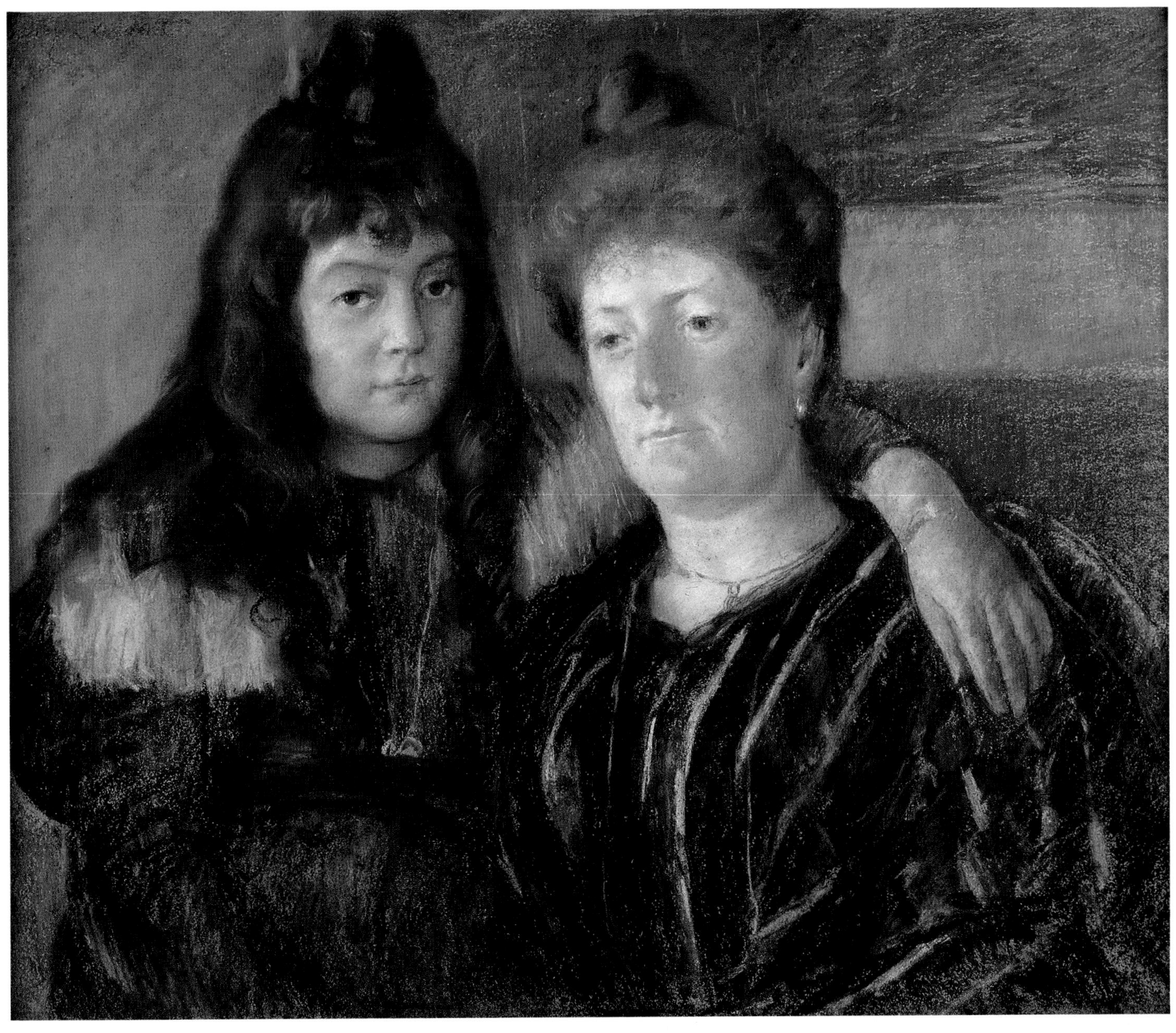

27

Pastel on paper, 23½ x 28¾ in. (59.7 x 73 cm)
Signed at upper left: MARY CASSATT
Gift of Barbara B. Millhouse

GIANT MAGNOLIAS, 1904
CHILDE HASSAM
1859–1935

In 1886 French Impressionist dealer Paul Durand-Ruel organized a major exhibition in New York of over three hundred paintings by the leading Impressionists. Over a decade after this radical movement appeared in Paris, it was greeted by the American public with genuine appreciation. Childe Hassam and many of the most talented younger American artists were eager to assimilate these new painting techniques. By 1897 Hassam, John Twachtman, J. Alden Weir, and seven other American Impressionists began to exhibit together. This group, known as the Ten, became so popular that they continued to hold exhibitions for the next twenty years, during which time Hassam produced a large body of outstanding work in which he applied the French Impressionist style to New York street scenes, New England landscapes, coastal scenes, figures in windows, and occasionally a still life such as *Giant Magnolias*.

The three large magnolia blossoms in this painting are arranged in a triangular configuration and their light coloration stands in abrupt contrast to the dark tonalities that pervade the rest of the painting. Comprised of energetic strokes that defy their natural sheen, the leaves display a lively texture that binds the arrangement to the background. The ample space given over to the polished table attests to an Impressionistic preoccupation with reflection.

In its rich, deep tonality *Giant Magnolias* is a departure from the light palette and full chromatic intensity of Hassam's outdoor scenes. It exhibits a characteristic that often distinguishes American from French Impressionism: the tendency to maintain well-rounded forms rather than dissolve them in an all-pervasive luminosity. The alternation between the loose, thin strokes that interact with the texture of the canvas and the tight, thick strokes that comprise the impasto highlights on the vase transforms this painting from a picture of objects to a dynamic, sensuous surface.

With the exception of Martin J. Heade, whose move to Florida in the 1880s precipitated his preoccupation with magnolia blossoms, and John La Farge, whose magnolia subjects were responses to the Oriental preference for large flowers, these magnificent blooms rarely found their way into American art. Native to southern climates, they must have held exotic appeal to Hassam, who painted in New York City and New England. In the nineteenth century, floral still life was often symbolic of womanly qualities. Although Hassam generally painted in a modernist vein without metaphorical overtones, it is tempting to relate the vigorous and robust quality of the *magnolia grandiflora* to the characteristics associated with the turn-of-the-century female type popularized by the famous illustrator Charles Dana Gibson (1867–1944).

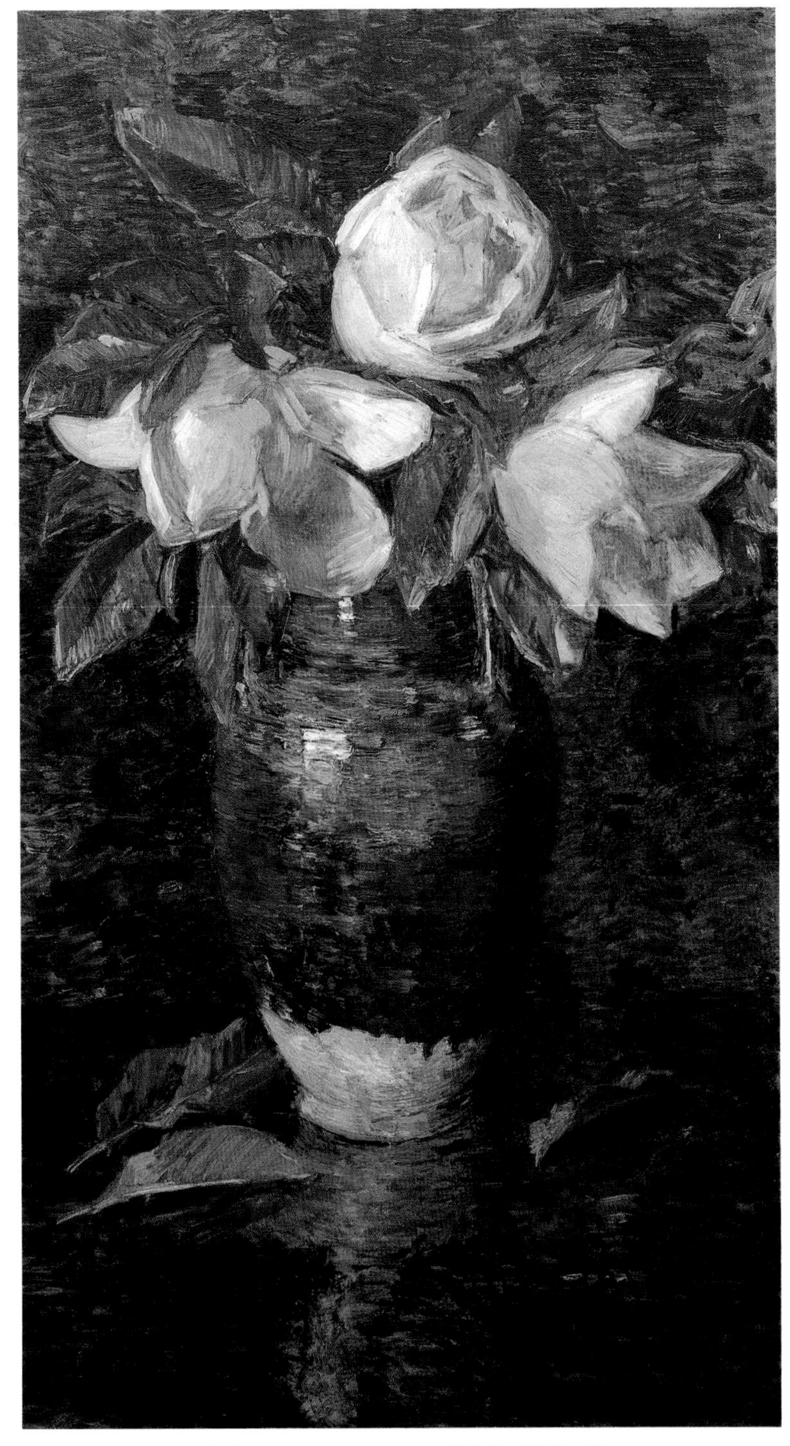

28 Oil on canvas, 35 x 20 in. (88.9 x 50.8 cm)
Signed and dated at lower left: CHILDE HASSAM 1904
Frame designed by the artist
Original purchase fund from the Mary Reynolds Babcock Foundation, Z. Smith Reynolds Foundation, Area Foundation, and Anne Cannon Forsyth

A. W. Lee, 1905
Thomas Eakins
1844–1916

After studying in Paris with the celebrated academician Jean-Léon Gérôme, Thomas Eakins returned to Philadelphia in 1870. Believing accurate scientific knowledge essential to his art, he took anatomy classes at Jefferson Medical College. In 1876 he outraged the public with *The Gross Clinic*, which depicts a famous surgeon as he operates on a patient and lectures to medical students in an amphitheater. Turning later to portraits, Eakins, like Courbet before him, projected the uncertainties and complexities of his age upon his sitters.

Ashbury Wright Lee (1841–1927) was the leading citizen of Clearfield, Pennsylvania. His descendents describe him as a tall man who walked with his hands clasped behind his back. He was punctual and kind and had a deep sympathy for human frailty.[1] A local obituary stated that his "remarkable powers of organization and detail" and "tireless energy" equipped him for founding many successful business enterprises. He was also active in philanthropy and in Democratic politics, serving several times as a delegate to the National Convention. The obituary described him as "one of the richest men in this part of the State."

Lee probably met Thomas Eakins around 1904 when Lee joined the Philadelphia Arts Club.[2] The first evidence that Eakins was to paint Lee's portrait is found in a letter of January 28, 1905, from Lee to Eakins. Lee writes: "I am sorry that I have been unable to give you a sitting. Am now going South and will return by your city in March, when I hope to be able to give you some time." Since Eakins was actively soliciting portraits at this time, this apology suggests that Eakins rather than Lee may have initiated the sitting. By September 18, 1905, Lee had seen the portrait, decided not to keep it, and asked his daughter to return it. His letter to Eakins reads: "You will receive the Painting back. . . . I may make a suggestion when I am down soon. While not accepted by me I send you a cheque for $200 anyway. In a general way my daughter liked it." Since Eakins' price at this time was $700 for a half-length portrait, Lee was making only a token payment.[3]

It is not surprising that Lee refused the portrait. This portrayal of him in a rumpled suit with red-rimmed eyes and opaque, sallow flesh robs him of any distinction. The skin of his cheek, which hangs loosely on the bone, seems more a display of Eakins's anatomical knowledge than a telling characteristic of the sitter. A Bachrach photograph taken within a few years of the portrait (fig. 14) shows Lee as a handsome, portly gentleman with a self-assuredness that reflects his accomplishments. In this portrait, however, Eakins, who was often praised for his scientific realism, has converted him into an apparently bitter and disagreeable man, thus projecting onto him his own regrets and failures.[4] This powerful work illustrates how portraits can reflect the artist's view of reality as much as the sitter's character.

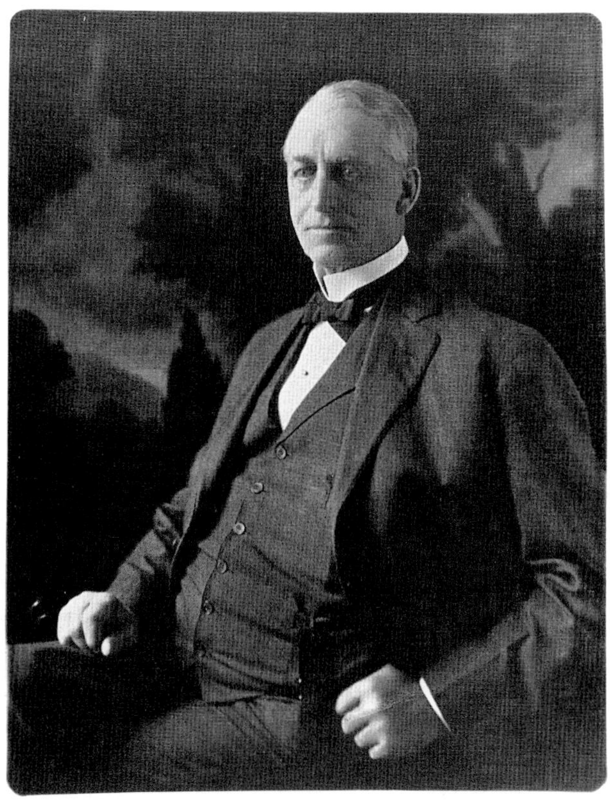

Figure 14 Bachrach
A. W. Lee, n.d.
Reynolda House, Museum of American Art,
Gift of Joseph A. Lee

Notes

1. Author's telephone conversation with Mrs. H. Rembrandt Woolridge of Clearfield, Pa., granddaughter of A. W. Lee.
2. Lloyd Goodrich, *Thomas Eakins*, vol. 2 (Cambridge, Mass.: Harvard University Press, 1982), 232.
3. Goodrich, *Thomas Eakins*, vol. 2, 234.
4. Goodrich, *Thomas Eakins*, vol. 2, 259. Mrs. Eakins said of her husband: "He was a silent man, not sad exactly, but disappointed—he has had blows . . . there was sadness underneath; he had not been able to do what he wanted to do."

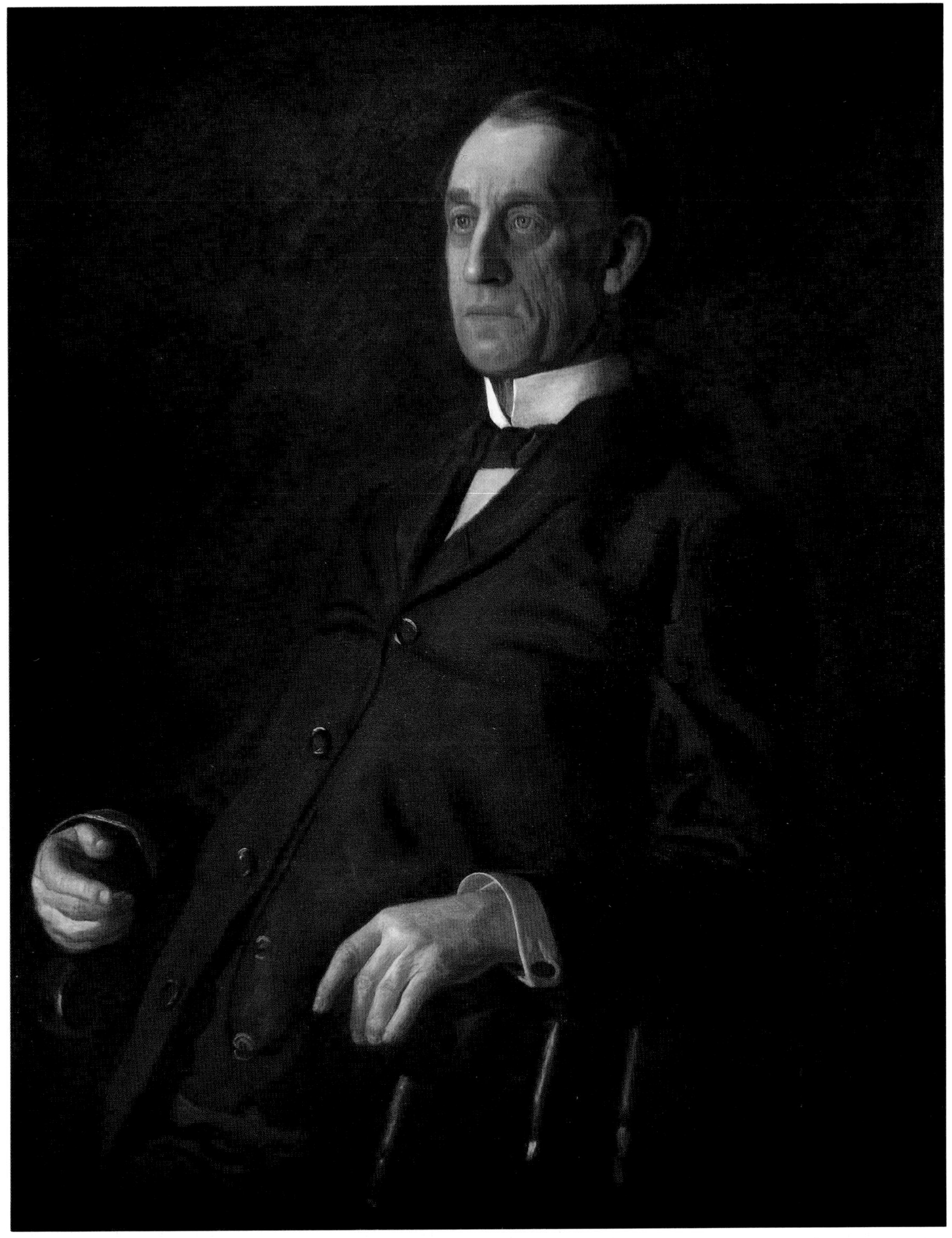

29 Oil on canvas, 40 x 32 in. (101.6 x 81.3 cm)
Gift of Nancy Susan Reynolds and Barbara B. Millhouse

The Spirit of the Storm, c. 1912
Elliott Daingerfield
1859–1932

In 1911 the Santa Fe Railroad Company commissioned Elliott Daingerfield to paint views of the Grand Canyon to promote its attraction as a tourist stop.[1] Although he produced a number of views that convey the canyon's scenic grandeur in a realistic manner, his aesthetic intentions are most apparent in works such as *The Spirit of the Storm*, which transforms the scenic attraction into an ethereal region inhabited by a mystic being.

The Spirit of the Storm shares an affinity with two other works inspired by his Grand Canyon trips, *Genius of the Canyon* (1913) and *The Sleepers* (1914). All three share a dreamlike, visionary approach related to the Symbolist aesthetic, which may have been inspired in part by the paintings of the influential American Symbolist Arthur B. Davies, who also used American landscape as the stage for nude figures enacting mystic rites. *The Sleepers*, which depicts dozing figures inhabiting a craggy precipice, is accompanied by a poem that concludes with the lines: "Gods are they!—as you and I—,/Who see in spirit what the eyes deny."[2] This notation proves Daingerfield's allegiance to the Symbolist belief that a full experience of beauty can be obtained only through dreams and trancelike states of consciousness.

Raised in Fayetteville, North Carolina, Daingerfield arrived in New York in 1880 to study at the Art Students League. Although New York remained his winter residence throughout his life, he maintained his ties to North Carolina by spending his summers in the mountain resort of Blowing Rock. In 1884, when he moved into the Holbein Studios, he developed a close friendship with George Inness, whose influence can be seen in Daingerfield's work of this period. In the 1890s he produced religious paintings, most notably a mural commission for the Lady Chapel of the Church of St. Mary the Virgin in New York City. *The Spirit of the Storm* represents a shift from Christian concerns to pagan rituals and reflects the impact of James Gordon Frazier's widely read *The Golden Bough*.

In this painting Daingerfield obscures the grandeur of the Grand Canyon—identified only by the reddish cliffs momentarily visible through a break in the clouds—to focus on the gesturing nude, who seems to be summoning up mysterious forces from the depth of the abyss. Her loose, whiplike hair, blown forward in an arabesque, suggests an aura of ensnarement. Frequently found in turn-of-the-century paintings and objets d'art, this seductive nude is a common Art Nouveau motif associated with sirens, the Lorelei, and various mythological creatures who were thought to lure men to their destruction.[3] An immediate precedent to Daingerfield's nymph occurs in a painting by Albert Pinkham Ryder, *Siegfried and the Rhine Maidens* (1888–91), which he admired and described in a booklet he wrote on that artist. In American art the sexual destructiveness associated with these creatures was generally reduced to innocent playfulness. Daingerfield, for instance, modestly conceals the nakedness of the figure with a ragged, windblown cloth. Critic James Gibbons Huneker wrote of the nudes that populated the canvases of Arthur B. Davies that they do not contain "the suggestion of decadent paganism"[4] that was found in European Symbolist art, and the same may be said of this nude figure depicted by Daingerfield.

Daingerfield shared with Arthur B. Davies a penchant to locate mythological beings at the edge of cliffs to make the viewer feel "the vertigo of them that skirt the edge of perilous ravines, or straddle the rim of finer issues." Through this imagery Daingerfield is attempting to recreate a state of mind in transition between dream and waking—a state of mind that Huneker wrote dwelled in the "equivocal twilights."[5]

Notes

1. Robert Hobbs, *Elliott Daingerfield* (Charlotte, N. C.: Mint Museum of Art, 1971).
2. Charles C. Eldredge, *American Imagination and Symbolist Painting* (New York: New York University, 1979), 145.
3. A similar figure can be found in carved ivory on the base of a candelabrum made by Egide Rombaux and Franz Hoosemans, c. 1900.
4. James Gibbons Huneker, *Unicorns* (New York, 1917), quoted in the Metropolitan Museum of Art Catalogue of American Paintings, 423.
5. Ibid.

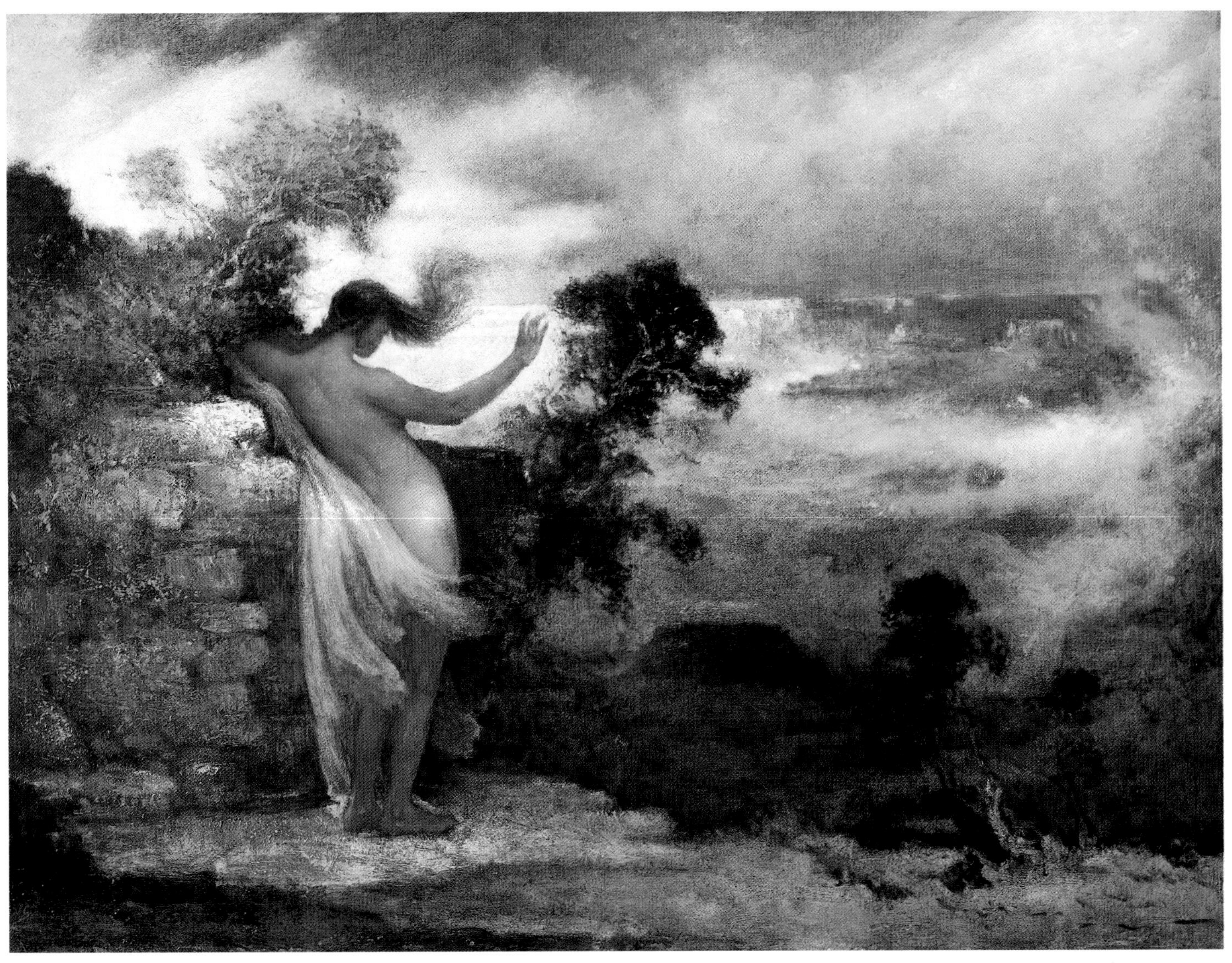

30

Oil on canvas, 36 x 48⅜ in. (91.4 x 122.9 cm)
Signed at lower left: ELLIOTT DAINGERFIELD
Gift of Barbara B. Millhouse

Landscape: Provence, c. 1912–22

Alfred Maurer

1868–1932

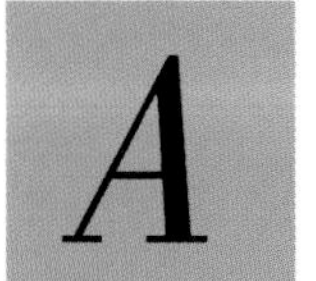

rriving in Paris as early as 1897, Alfred Maurer soon received considerable recognition with paintings of full-length female figures that related in their muted tones and Japanese-inspired compositions to the work of Whistler. Around 1904 he began to attend the salon of Gertrude and Leo Stein, where he became acquainted with avant-garde theories expounded by Matisse and Picasso. His conversion to the colorful style exemplified in *Landscape: Provence* occurred in 1905 in response to a Paris exhibition at the Salon d'Automne, where a group of young artists led by Matisse were exhibiting paintings with such wild color that they were given the name *Fauves*, which means wild beasts. Maurer soon permanently abandoned his traditional style in favor of the Fauves' style, in which he continued to work until after his return to the United States in 1914.

In Fauve paintings the traditional function of color to define form was superceded by the use of intense color for its emotional and decorative effects. The paint was applied brusquely, often straight from the tube, in widely spaced strokes leaving the unifying color of the support visible. The Fauves, like all modernists, adhered to the principle of maintaining two-dimensionality reinforced by flat strokes of paint that create colorful surface rhythms. Paintings of pure visual sensation like *Landscape: Provence* ensued, which in their time seemed primitive, abrasive, and entirely revolutionary.

Landscape: Provence contains clear, bright color that activates the entire surface. Released from the constraints of local color, Maurer painted the tree limbs mauve-pink and blue and the fields green, gold, and vermilion, relating the colors tonally to create a flat, decorative surface. Between the long, spontaneous strokes the support remains visible, giving the picture an unfinished appearance. Art critic Charles Caffin's description of Maurer's 1909 exhibition can be applied equally to this painting: "color notes of spiritual impressions received in the presence of nature."[1]

Between 1909, when Alfred Stieglitz gave Maurer his first solo exhibition, and 1913, Maurer received considerable attention in the New York press, although as with all avant-garde paintings many critics were offended by the art. In an essay accompanying the fifteen paintings all titled *Sketch in Oil* shown at Stieglitz's Photo Succession Gallery in New York, Charles Caffin explains Maurer's goal as "seeking an abstract expression through color harmonies somewhat as does the musical composer." He compares "the portions of ground apparent between the masses of color" to "the antique potters' method of applying colors and leaving parts of the biscuit of the vase in reserve." The newspaper reviewers, however, were more critical. James Gibbons Huneker, the *Sun*'s critic, seemed exasperated: "What is Maurer after? A Catherine Wheel at full tilt on the 4th of July night or an ordinary apoplectic aura."[2]

In 1913, the year of the famous Armory Show, at which Maurer exhibited four paintings, he was also showing at the Folsom Galleries in New York in his second solo exhibition. Still living in Paris, he had to return home hurriedly in 1914 at the outset of World War I. Many paintings from his Fauve period were left behind in his studio, and eventually they were dispersed, making this fine example a rarity. Because *Landscape: Provence* was part of his studio contents, it may have been sent to one of the 1913 exhibitions.[3]

Soon after his return to this country Maurer began to work in a Cubist-derived style, which he practiced until his suicide in 1932. His artistic fame had been at its height during his Paris years, and after his return to this country he was for the most part neglected. Maurer is appreciated today for the considerable talent he brought to all three styles in which he worked—his early traditional period, his Fauve period, and his late Cubist period.

Notes

1. Elizabeth McCausland, *A. H. Maurer* (Minneapolis: Walker Art Center, 1951), 108.
2. Ibid., 102.
3. Babcock Gallery purchased this painting from Hudson Walker, who bought the contents of Maurer's studio. Their records show a date of 1922, although the date on the bill is c. 1912.

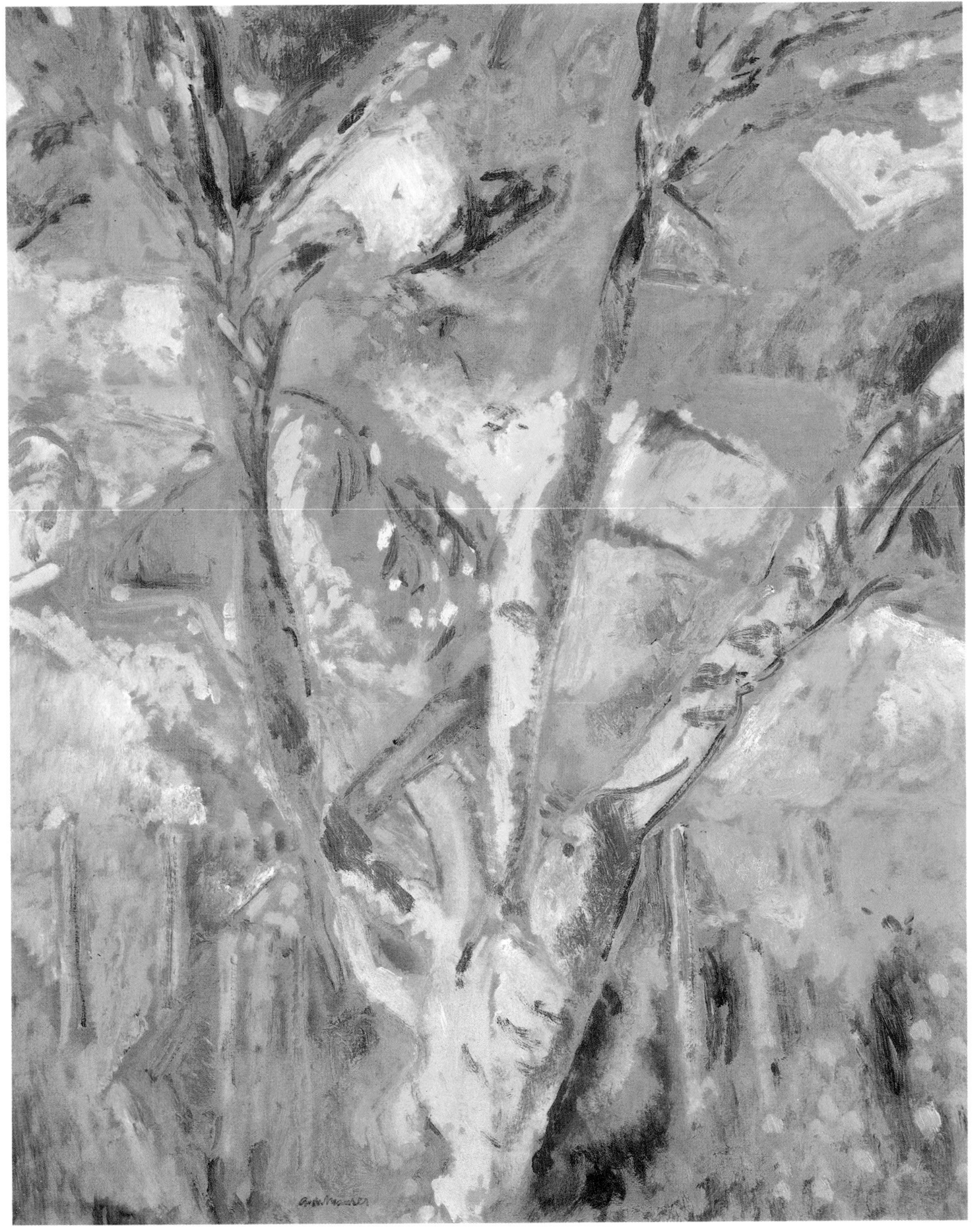

31

Oil on paper mounted on academy board, 21¾ x 18 in.
(55.2 x 45.7 cm)
Signed at lower left center: A. H. MAURER
Gift of Mr. and Mrs. Milton C. Rose

THE BATHING COVE, c. 1916–18

MAURICE PRENDERGAST

1859–1924

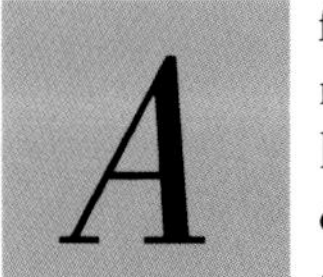

fter studying in Paris, Maurice Prendergast returned to Boston in 1894 and created colorful, loosely rendered watercolors and monotypes that established him as a successful artist who had assimilated modernist tendencies into a highly personal style. During the next two decades he traveled to Europe frequently, deepening his understanding of the avant-garde movements that were revolutionizing the art world. Around 1903 Prendergast began to translate the lively quality he had obtained in watercolor into the medium of oil paint. In a manner developed in the 1860s by Edouard Manet, he worked on several canvases simultaneously, building up layer upon layer of thick paint over long periods of time. Prendergast's paintings, however, maintain a strong, underlying structure apparent in the gridlike division of *The Bathing Cove* into vertical and horizontal bands.[1] He also maintains a Post-Impressionist tension between recession and surface by establishing an equilibrium between the receding tendency of the shoreline and the surface energy of the evenly distributed color values and textures.

After 1900 Prendergast's affiliation with the Macbeth Gallery brought him to New York frequently and he moved there permanently after the Armory Show of 1913. Although the idyllic content of Prendergast's art separates it from Robert Henri's Ashcan School, which focused on scenes of urban lowlife, Prendergast was invited, nonetheless, to exhibit with them in 1908 in the most radical exhibition of American art of the decade. He also exhibited in the notorious Armory Show, where he was able to study original paintings by Matisse. By 1913 he had perfected his late "tapestry style,"[2] of which *The Bathing Cove* is an example, and for the rest of his career he concentrated on oil paintings of crowds, in which the rich patterns of overlaid color are related to the technique of the French Nabis Edouard Vuillard and Pierre Bonnard.

An inveterate bather himself, Prendergast found anonymous vacationers an engaging subject. The festive mood of Prendergast's paintings echoes his expression of delight in the novel use of paint for its own sake as he shifts color and line to accommodate the general appearance of animated crowds. In *The Bathing Cove* arabesques representing linked arms and outlining frilly skirts mimic the playful rhythm of people enjoying a relaxed summer day at the beach. Muted tints of violet, green, turquoise, yellow, cream, and beige applied in patches of thick paint generate color sensations inconceivable fifty years earlier. The rich crusty texture creates a tactile response that replaces the traditional polished surface.

Matisse's Arcadian mood has been recreated in many Prendergast beach scenes, but in *The Bathing Cove* the distant shoreline, receding beach, and rocky promontory follow closely the shoreline of Matisse's Neo-Impressionist *Luxe, Calme, et Volupté* (1904).[3] A reference to Matisse also appears in the middle distance with the circle of figures that recall the central frolicking group in his Arcadian masterpeice *Joie de Vivre* (1906).[4] Prendergast, however, has transformed the European master's round of dancing bacchantes into the American idiom of innocent young girls playing a game of ring-around-the-rosy.

Although rejecting allusions to classical myth, Prendergast has concealed among the crowd unexpected biblical imagery. A pair of figures on the far right resembles a pietà. The three trees in the background represent the Trinity and the white animal in the foreground suggests the sacrificial lamb. Even the style of the sailing craft seems to partake in the biblical narrative. Although the intrusion of religious subjects into Prendergast's art is rare,[5] antecedents for the treatment of biblical imagery as a pictorial motif can be found in the work of one of the most admired French artists of the 1890s, Pierre Puvis de Chavannes.[6] Another precedent can be found in Paul Gauguin's *Ia Orana Maria* (Hail Mary) of 1891, in which the Virgin Mary appears as a native Tahitian wearing a *pareus* and holding the dark-skinned Christ child on her shoulder. Whatever the derivation of the intrusion of religious imagery into an otherwise secular painting, it testifies to the continued vigor of the Symbolist movement in America.

NOTES

1. The thrust of the distant shoreline is paralleled in the lower section by the intensity of the gaze that the standing figure on the right directs across the canvas.
2. Cecily Langdale, "Maurice Prendergast: An American Post-Impressionist," *Connoisseur* 202 (December 1979): 253.
3. The placement of the land in the lower right and the bay in the upper left is a traditional composition taken from earlier centuries. A similar composition can be found in Puvis de Chavannes's *The Pleasant Land* (1882, Yale University Art Gallery).
4. A reproduction of *Joie de Vivre* was exhibited at Stieglitz's Gallery 291 in 1910 during his exhibition of Matisee drawings. It was reproduced again in *Camera Work* as a full-page illustration in the August 1912 issue. Prendergast made a sketch of Matisse's *Dance II* (1912) when it was exhibited at the Armory Show.
5. Eleanor Green and Jeffrey R. Hayes, *Maurice Prendergast: Art of Impulse and Color* (College Park, Md.: University of Maryland Art Gallery, 1976), 65. According to Green, *Waterfall* is Prendergast's only known painting of a "traditional Christian subject." (It contains the figure of Eve.)
6. In *Summer* (1873, Musée d'Orsay, Paris) Puvis de Chavannes introduces Christian connotations by placing a woman on a donkey with a lamb nearby. Claudine Mitchells, "Time and the Idea of Patriarchy in the Pastorals of Puvis de Chavannes," *Art History* 10 (June 1987): 188.

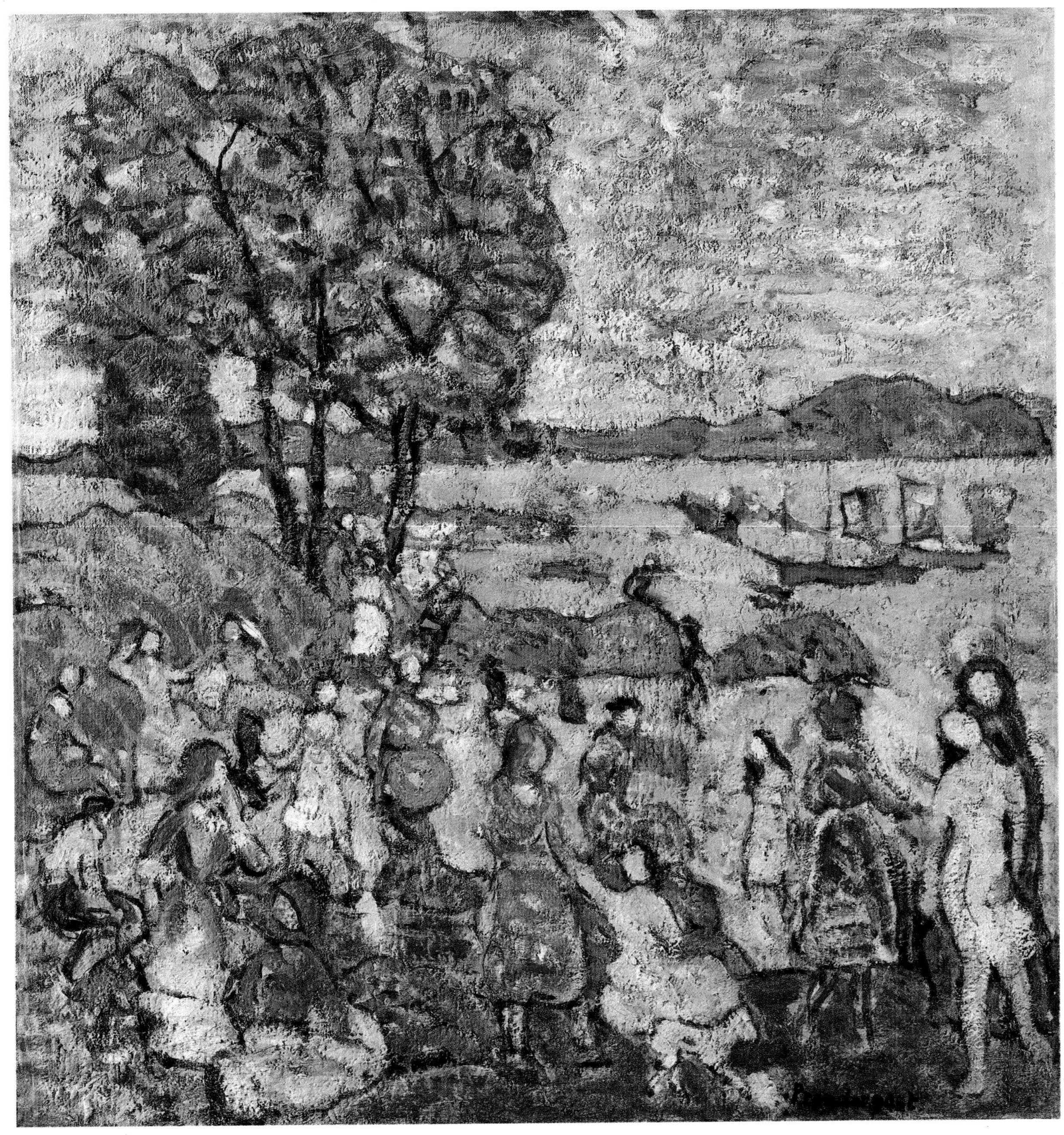

32

Oil on canvas, 27 x 26 in. (68.6 x 66 cm)
Signed at lower right: PRENDERGAST
Gift of Barbara B. Millhouse

Church of Heiligenhafen, 1922
Lyonel Feininger
1871–1956

In 1914 Lyonel Feininger wrote: "One thing I already know now: I shall give to mankind a new perspective of the world; I hope to live until I have formed it in a hundred pictures."[1] Feininger achieved his goal, for the body of over five hundred paintings he produced demonstrates a consistently progressive ability to formulate a unique style of abstracted realism.

Feininger, whose German parents were musicians, grew up in New York City. His childhood leisure was divided between his study of the violin and his fascination in watching the building of the city and the continual movement of boats on the rivers. At age sixteen, Feininger moved with his parents to Germany to continue his study of music. He abruptly abandoned music to formalize his study of art, training in the rigid German academies. For the next several years, until 1907, Feininger worked as a caricaturist for both German and American newspapers and periodicals. His career as a painter began when he was in his mid-thirties. He exhibited with Paul Klee, Wassily Kandinsky, and Franz Marc, but was never associated with the major trends in German art of the period—the violent color and heavy pigment of the Expressionists, the nihilistic spirit of the Dadaists, or the biting realism of the *Neue Sachlichkeit.* In contrast to the myriad of artistic experiments of the period, Feininger's subject matter, formal unity, and subjective coloration were unique. Teaching for a number of years at the Bauhaus, he remained in Germany until returning to the United States in 1937.

Architecture dominates much of Feininger's early paintings, and the church, either standing alone or embraced by a community, is a recurrent theme. From a formal perspective, the intersecting lines of the community, climaxing in the towering central structure of a church, fracture the space and its relation to the forms around it. The patterns thus established create motion and force and become visual metaphors for a romantic vision of man and nature. By using the church spire as the transitionary form between the material and the immaterial, the structure around which all form either ascends or descends, Feininger suggests universal questions about the illusive relationship between the known and the unknown.

In 1922 when Feininger painted this view of Heiligenhafen, a town on the Baltic Sea where he spent his summers, he was composing fugues inspired by Johann Sebastian Bach. *Church of Heiligenhafen* reveals some of the principles of polyphonic music in its overlapping and interpenetrating forms. The mirror effects of fugues are made visible in the steeple, which echoes its own shape in the glowing sky. The dark tonality of the painting equates with the sonorous organ sounds; at the same time, it evokes the natural effect of the low summer sun in the northern latitude of the Baltic Sea.

Feininger's controlled art reflects his belief that in the whole world, in *all* worlds, there can be nothing lawless, nothing accidental, nothing without *form* and *rhythm*, nor could there be.[2] Constructed of transparent planes like overlapping pieces of colored glass, his paintings create a new relationship whereby the viewer does not position himself outside the painting as in traditional work, but enters into the picture itself, a method Feininger shared with other artists of Cubist tendencies.

Notes

1. Letter to Julia Feininger, June 11, 1914, cited in Hans Hess, *Lyonel Feininger* (New York: Harry N. Abrams, 1961), 7.
2. Letter to Kubin, September 28, 1916, in ibid., 81.

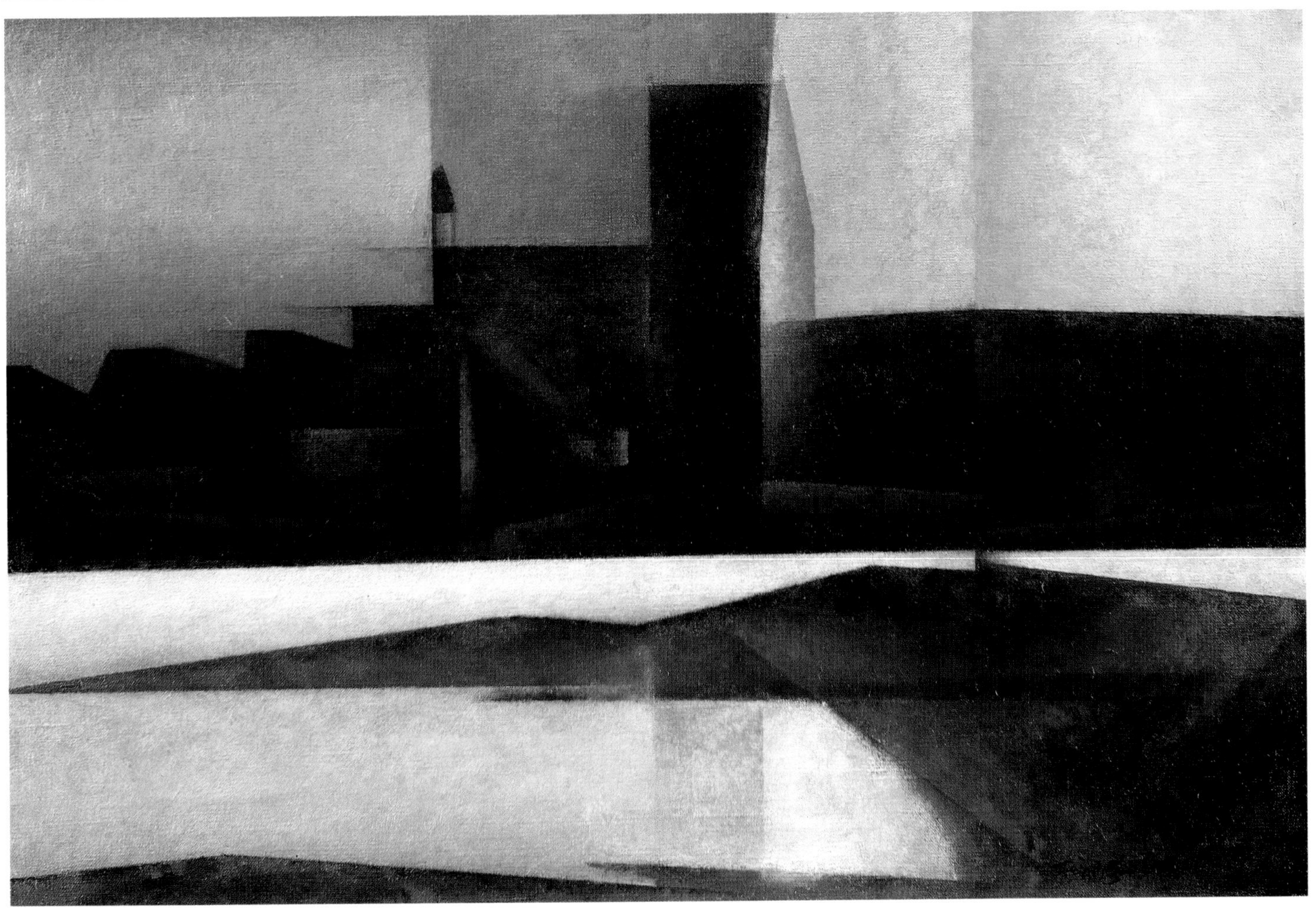

33

Oil on canvas, $15\frac{3}{4}$ x $23\frac{3}{4}$ in. (40 x 60.3 cm)
Signed and dated at lower right: FEININGER 1922
Written in crayon or charcoal on back of stretcher: L. FEININGER 1922/
KIRCHE AM WASSER 1922
Gift of Charles H. Babcock, Sr.

Pool in the Woods, Lake George, 1922
Georgia O'Keeffe
1887–1986

The prominence and immediacy of the dark, central cavity in *Pool in the Woods, Lake George* tap into unconscious forces that evoke sensations of secrecy and intimacy. Following concepts supplied primarily by the Russian artist Wassily Kandinsky and her teacher, Arthur Wesley Dow, Georgia O'Keeffe built her art on the creation of forms and colors as equivalents to her innermost feelings.[1] She succeeded so well that in an essay written for her 1928 exhibition at the Anderson Galleries, Lewis Mumford concluded: "she has opened up a whole area of human consciousness which has never, so far as I am aware, been so completely revealed in either literature or in graphic art."[2]

Pool in the Woods, Lake George was completed during O'Keeffe's most creative and productive period, one year before her first major exhibition. At the time she was spending summers at the Stieglitz family farm on Lake George in upstate New York. Since O'Keeffe's arrival in New York City in 1918 from a teaching job in Texas, she had been involved in a love affair with Alfred Stieglitz, one of the foremost photographers of his generation and a champion of modernism in the United States. In 1921 he took a series of daring photographs of O'Keeffe in the nude. Some of these were close-ups of various parts of her body, which critics interpreted as documenting her sexual and spiritual awakening. At this time O'Keeffe's landscapes and flower paintings began to reveal a corresponding sense of feminine eroticism.

Working frequently in series, O'Keeffe made two smaller preparatory pastels for *Pool in the Woods, Lake George.*[3] In these works she explores the mysteries of enclosed space, an idea fully developed in *Pool in the Woods, Lake George*, in which she superimposes interior space on exterior space. This work also explores the nature of reflection—a theme that may have evolved from her preoccupation with the analogy between music and visual form. In this pastel the flowing lines shaping the mountain ridge and its reflection seem to conform to inner rhythms just as the dark center acts as a focus from which somber tones can radiate.

A predecessor to her enormously popular flower still lifes, this pastel explores the centrally bisected format containing an ovoid, from which her enlarged flower paintings evolved. In subsequent paintings the ovoid translates into the corolla of a flower as well as a variety of other forms: an open clamshell, or the curl of a leaf on a corn stalk. Other themes explored in O'Keeffe's later work appear in this early pastel. By bringing the distant mountain and rimmed cavity into a single image, she has merged the faraway and nearby. On the reverse of this pastel O'Keeffe has written "pond in center," which supports the notion that the central ovoid found its inspiration in the dark depths of a pond.

Notes

1. Jan Garden Castro, *The Life and Art of Georgia O'Keeffe* (New York: Crown Publishers, 1985), 31.
2. Lewis Mumford, *O'Keeffe and Matisse* (New York Anderson Galleries, 1928; reprinted from *New Republic*, March 2, 1927).
3. *Lake George in the Woods* (c. 1922) is reproduced in *Realism and Abstraction: Counterpoints in American Drawing, 1900–1940* (New York: Hirschl & Adler, 1983), 102, no. 122. *Pond in the Woods, Lake George* (1922, Whitney Museum of American Art, New York).

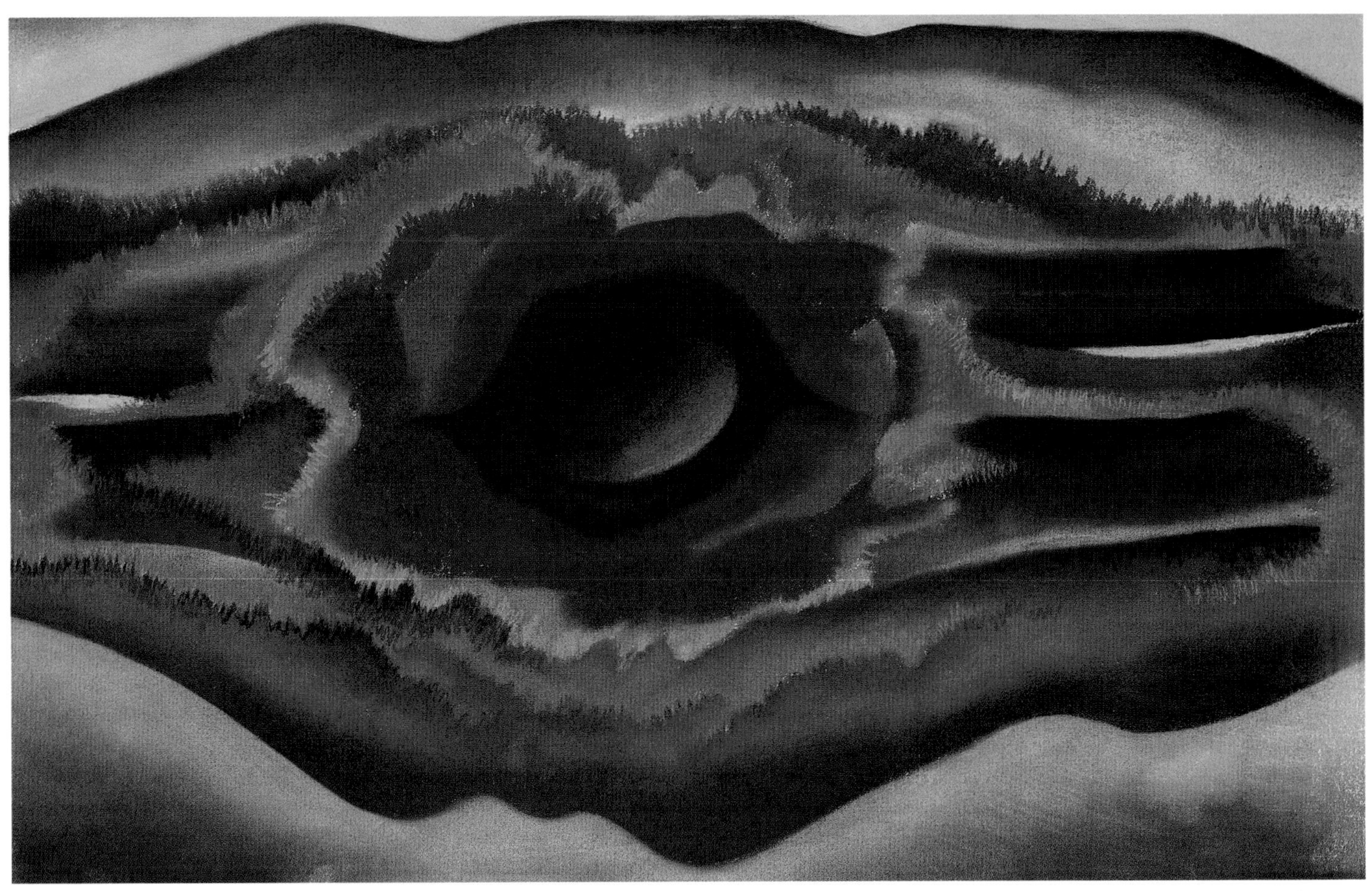

34

Pastel on paper, 17½ x 28 in. (44.5 x 71.1 cm)
Gift of Barbara B. Millhouse in memory of Nancy Reynolds,
Winifred Babcock, and E. Carter

Bootleggers, 1927

Thomas Hart Benton

1889–1975

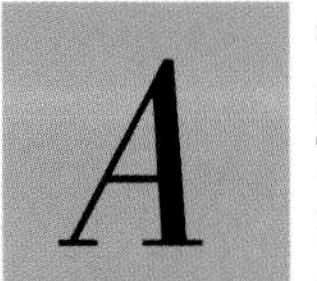

As the son of a Missouri congressman and the grandnephew of the first senator from Missouri, Thomas Hart Benton had been immersed in politics and American history since his childhood. Spending his falls and winters in Washington, D.C., during his father's four terms in the House of Representatives (1897–1905), Benton began his artistic career at the Corcoran Gallery of Art and by age seventeen had landed his first job as a cartoonist for a newspaper in Joplin, Missouri. One year of art studies at the Art Institute of Chicago and four years in Paris (1908–12) introduced him to a variety of avant-garde styles, which he pursued for a number of years. A turning point in his career occurred when he became a naval draftsman during World War I. "The new airplanes, the blimps, the dredges," he wrote, "because they were so interesting in themselves, tore me away from all my grooved habits, from my play with colored cubes and classic attenuations, from my aesthetic drivelings and morbid self-concerns."[1] This was the first contact he had made "as an artist with the actual things of the modern world." Turning away from the prevailing abstract currents of his time, Benton began to develop a dynamic style of realism with which he was to forge a highly visible and productive artistic career.

After his discharge from the Navy, Benton decided to embark upon a monumental series of paintings devoted to the history of the United States. Although he knew that histories were anathema in the New York art world, he nevertheless intended to paint seventy-five large works divided into chapters of five paintings each. The series, the American Historical Epic, was intended to be a people's history; rather than idealizing the American past it was to reflect a radical twentieth-century viewpoint by showing scenes of pioneers and settlers engaged in aggression and exploitation. After completing the first three chapters, Benton became dissatisfied and moved on to a contemporary subject in the hope that his work would gain greater impact. He chose as his subject a nighttime scene of bootlegging. Working for the first time from the real life in the city streets around him, he gained greater authenticity in the figures, and the tension between depth and pattern found resolution. *Bootleggers*, therefore, became a seminal work from which his other mural paintings evolved. Benton identified it as such when he wrote that it is "the predecessor of all later muralistic paintings on American life," and "out of it came the style of the New School for Social Research mural on Contemporary America painted in 1929–30."[2]

Bootleggers is composed of vignettes exposing a chain of events connected with the illegal trafficking of liquor during Prohibition. In the foreground, the bootlegger stands with his back to the viewer next to a case of whiskey.[3] The rippling contours and elongation of his shirt-sleeved arm recall El Greco, a newly discovered Old Master who had considerable influence on the formation of Benton's mature style. On the right a pilot in the cockpit of an airplane resembling *The Spirit of St. Louis*[4] waits for the illegal cargo to be loaded by an anonymous laborer, whose pose resembles Renaissance renditions of Christ carrying his cross to Calvary. Benton's sympathy with the downtrodden is further enforced by the grim reminder of hunger residing in the open can and its spilt contents on the sidewalk.

Benton's attitude toward current events was shaped by the radical politics of the 1920s, especially the progressive liberal views of the well-known historian Charles Beard. By showing the machine as the essential feature controlling modern economic life, Benton demonstrates in images Beard's economic determinist theories.[5] The airplane lifts illegal cargo through the night sky, the express rushes it over the railroad tracks, and the automobile delivers it through the city streets. These new modes of transportation are crammed into the skyways and alleyways, but rather than fulfilling the promise of distributing goods for a better life the new machines are accomplices in crime. Even the telephone lines seem to facilitate the corruption. In this painting Benton, who felt that the underworld played as significant a role in shaping this country as our statesmen, has created a powerful statement about the most explosive issue of the twenties.

After completing this painting Benton abandoned the series, but his reputation had been established as a promising mural painter. His use of deep space and forceful color dissolved walls into dynamic solids and voids to convey powerful statements of modern life. Peopled with laborers, gangsters, politicians, and call girls, his narratives shocked a public accustomed to idealized allegories on the walls of government buildings.

Notes

1. Henry Adams, *Thomas Hart Benton, An American Original* (New York: Alfred A. Knopf, 1989), 87.
2. Letter from Thomas Hart Benton to Barbara B. Millhouse, October 20, 1971.
3. According to Sarah Hunter Kelly and Robert Graham, who remember Prohibition, liquor was not sold in round bottles, but in flasks that were flat and could be hidden. Benton may therefore have included the crate of bottles more as a reference to Cubist still life than an accurate representation.
4. *The Spirit of St. Louis* made its first test flight on April 28, 1927.
5. Emily Braun, *Thomas Hart Benton: "The America Today Murals"* (New York: Equitable Life Assurance Society of the United States, 1985), 24–25.

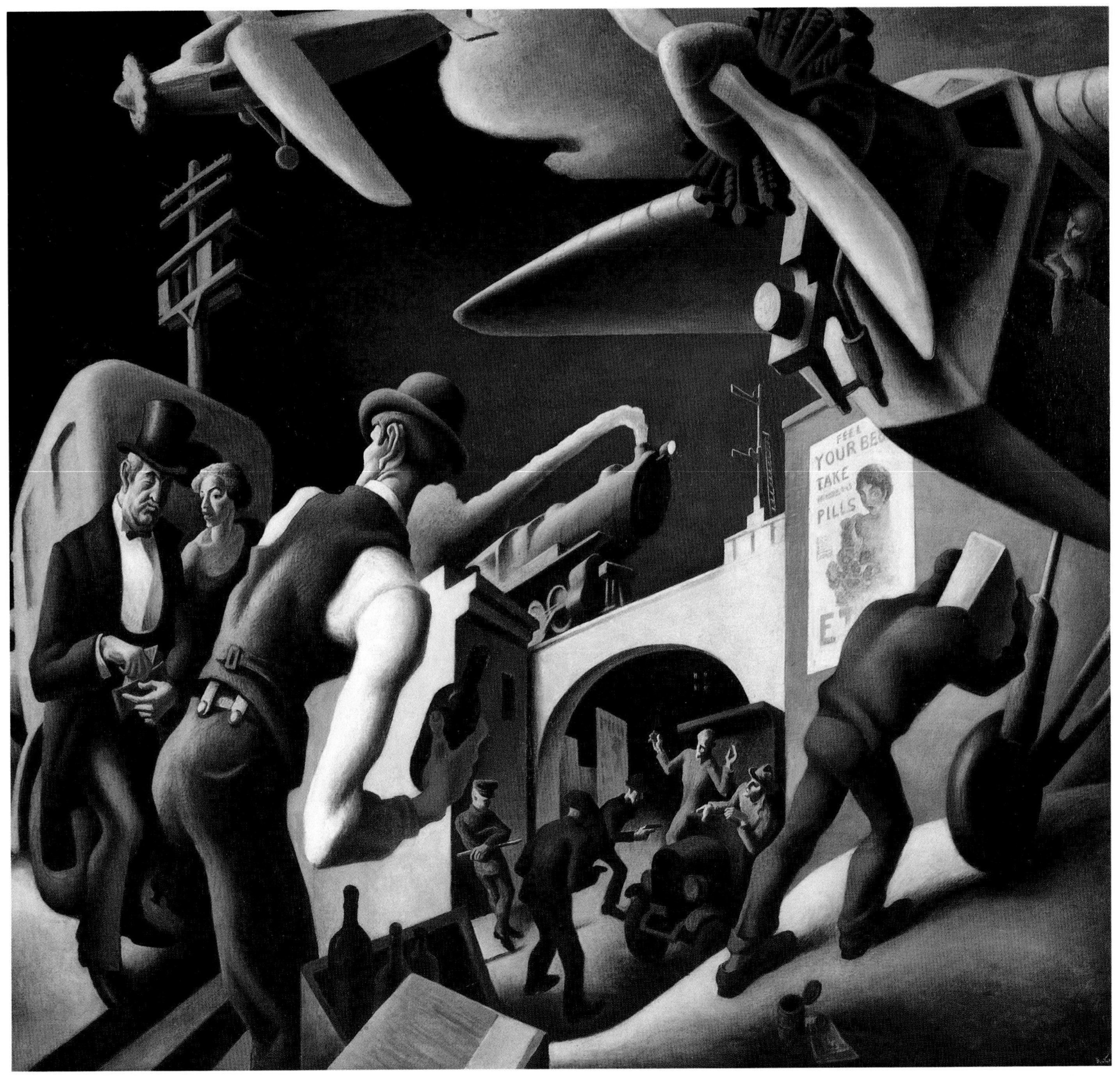

35 Egg tempera and oil on linen mounted on masonite, 65 x 72 in.
(165.1 x 190.5 cm)
Signed at lower right: BENTON
Gift of Barbara B. Millhouse

RAINBOW II, 1928
LYONEL FEININGER
1871–1956

Lyonel Feininger was a master of both music and art. A performing violinist at the age of twelve, Feininger later wrote: "music has always been the first influence of my life, Bach before all others . . . without music I cannot see myself as a painter—although I would never attempt to express the one in the other as many have done."[1] His is an art that may not have been possible had he not first begun his career as a performer and composer of music, and sustained his love for that discipline throughout his life. Feininger's art does not visualize music; it is far more complex. He found in his understanding of musical "law" a structure to assist him in painting—a system whereby he could realize the variety of visual experiences and expressions to which he strove. Inversion, mirror effects, overlapping, interpenetration, and synchronization were all techniques Feininger used to compose fugues. As principles of structure and order, these same techniques have their own form of application in his painting. As is consistent with great music, Feininger's painting has been defined as a process rather than a state of completion. The active participation of the viewer is critical in the unfolding of the overlapping planes, the dynamism of form and color, the reassembling of fractured reality.

Nature is the basis for all of Feininger's art. He reduced his subjects to a minimum few: architecture, an occasional figure, and the sea. Often working in series, Feininger used his painting as a process of clarification and reduction, of continually refining and redefining. His seascapes, of which *Rainbow II* is a notable example, clearly define his working method.

Feininger spent most of his summers on the Baltic sea. Recalling childhood memories of watching the boats on the rivers in New York, he made endless sketches of boats, water, and shore. Boats became critical elements in the construction of space in his paintings. Within the vastness of shore, water, and sky, boats and sails serve as points of reference in the artist's efforts to define nature itself and in his underlying suggestion of man as the definer of that nature.

Rainbow II has its origin in a description written in Feininger's "notes" in the summer of 1924: "I saw, almost frightened, a tremendous double rainbow of incredible sharpness and clarity. . . . Added to this was an intensity of color, the uncanny coppery glow of the sunset hour. The bow stretched across a deep violet sky, and in its midst appeared ghostly cloudheads in stratified rows."[2] From the notes and sketches of this experience, Feininger produced a work entitled *Rainbow*, begun in 1924 and completed the next year. *Rainbow II*, while not a direct recreation of the event, is a synthesized reflection of his memorable encounter with this phenomenon of nature. Included in the Reynolda House painting, however, is a collection of sails that fragment both sea and sky. What begins on the horizon as a scattered world of diffused planes of overlapping and colliding space is unified by the force of the intense arced band of light and color.

NOTES

1. Quoted in Alfred H. Barr, Jr., "Lyonel Feininger—American Artist," in *Lyonel Feininger/Marsden Hartley* (New York: Museum of Modern Art, 1944), 7.
2. Hans Hess, *Lyonel Feininger* (New York: Harry N. Abrams, 1961), 103.

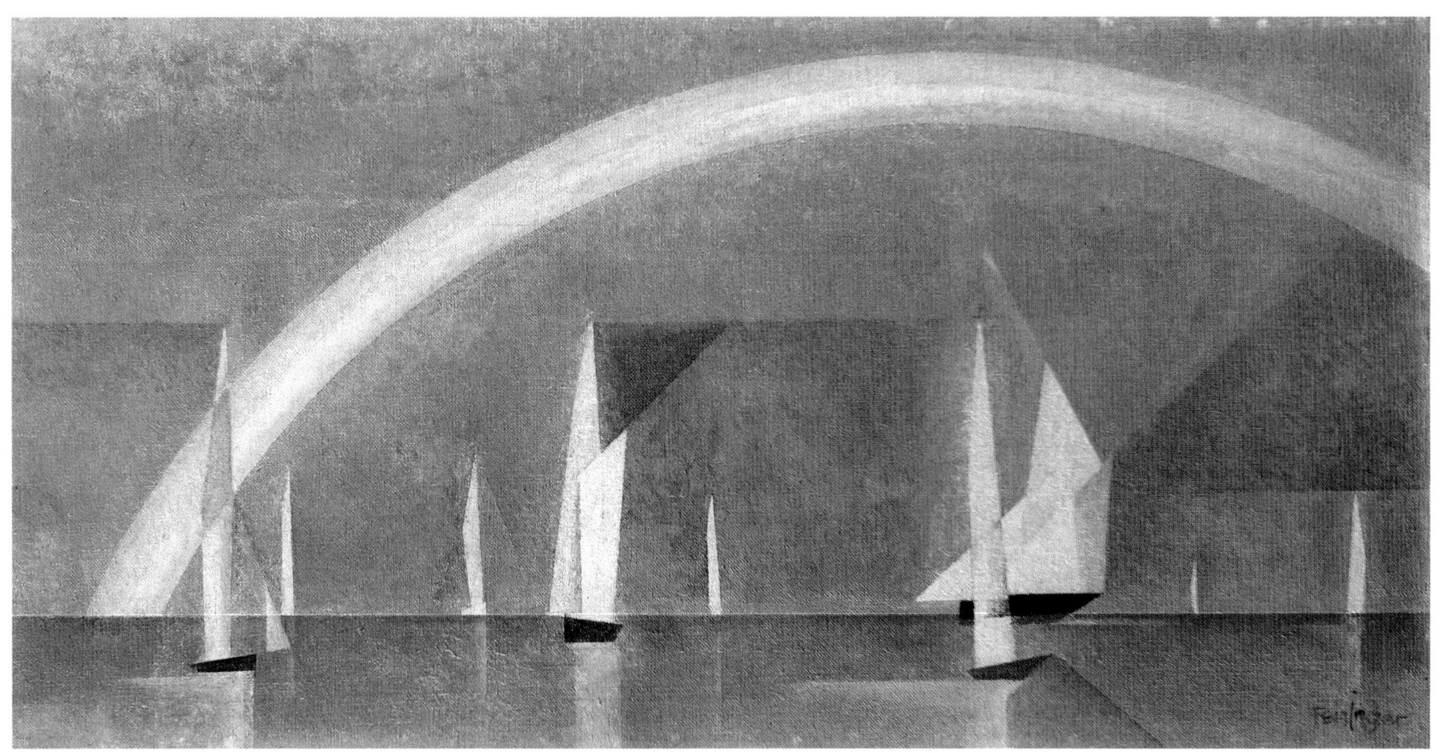

36

Oil on canvas, 11½ x 23 in. (29.2 x 58.4 cm)
Signed at lower right: FEININGER
Written in ink on back of stretcher: LYONEL FEININGER 1928/
REGENBOGEN II
Gift of Charles H. Babcock, Sr.

TREE, CACTUS, MOON, c. 1928

JOSEPH STELLA

1877–1946

After World War I Joseph Stella for the most part abandoned Futurism—for which he had become recognized as this country's leading proponent—in favor of a simplified, restrained style with symbolic and mystical overtones. The evocative power of *Tree, Cactus, Moon,* an example of this late style, seems to surface through its peculiar and subtle fusing of sexual and religious symbolism into simplified natural forms.[1] The long shaftlike shape of the cypress used in conjunction with the concentric circles of the moon contains sexual overtones, and, likewise, the double bloom of the century plant underscores the theme of fecundity. In the 1920s this desert cactus had become the object of considerable attention and its sexual attributes were described by D. H. Lawrence in 1926 in *The Plumed Serpent:* "They cut the great phallic bud and crushed out the sperm-like juice for the pulque."

In this painting, as in most of Stella's other major works, his Italian Catholic heritage is revealed in the shrinelike format common to medieval Last Judgment scenes. He has created a symbolic arrangement on an axis of heavenly and terrestrial domains in which the moon substitutes for the mandorla (the aureole containing the enthroned Christ) and the fiery red ground substitutes for hell, which Stella associated with subway tunnels depicted in several of his celebrated Brooklyn Bridge paintings. He has further defined his religious intentions by drawing into this area the shape of a Gothic arch. In medieval Last Judgment scenes this shape is often found dividing the region of the damned from the heavenly regions. Connecting the infernal to the celestial, the cypress replaces the cross, but it may also point to van Gogh's *Starry Night* (1889), which was widely reproduced at this time.

In this religious context the century plant acquires a role apart from its naturalistic effects or its procreative reading. Its sharp angular leaves recapture the shape of the wings of the archangel Michael, who is often found weighing the souls of the departed at the foot of the cross. Depicted in crude heavy outline, the leaves of the century plant have a transparent quality that suggests at once the transient moment in the plant's life (it dies after it flowers) and the evanescent quality of the angelic apparition for which it serves as a surrogate. The stalks ascend in a serpentlike curve, terminating in clusters colored not their natural white but red—a color generally associated with the sacrificial blood of Christ.[2] Stella has achieved a masterly transposition of a medieval altarpiece into a symbolic landscape.

NOTES

1. Irma B. Jaffe, *Joseph Stella* (Cambridge, Mass.: Harvard University Press, 1970), 104.
2. Ibid., 84. Describing *The Tree of My Life*, Stella writes: ". . . the intense vermillion of the lily, placed as a seal of generative blood at the base of the robust trunk."

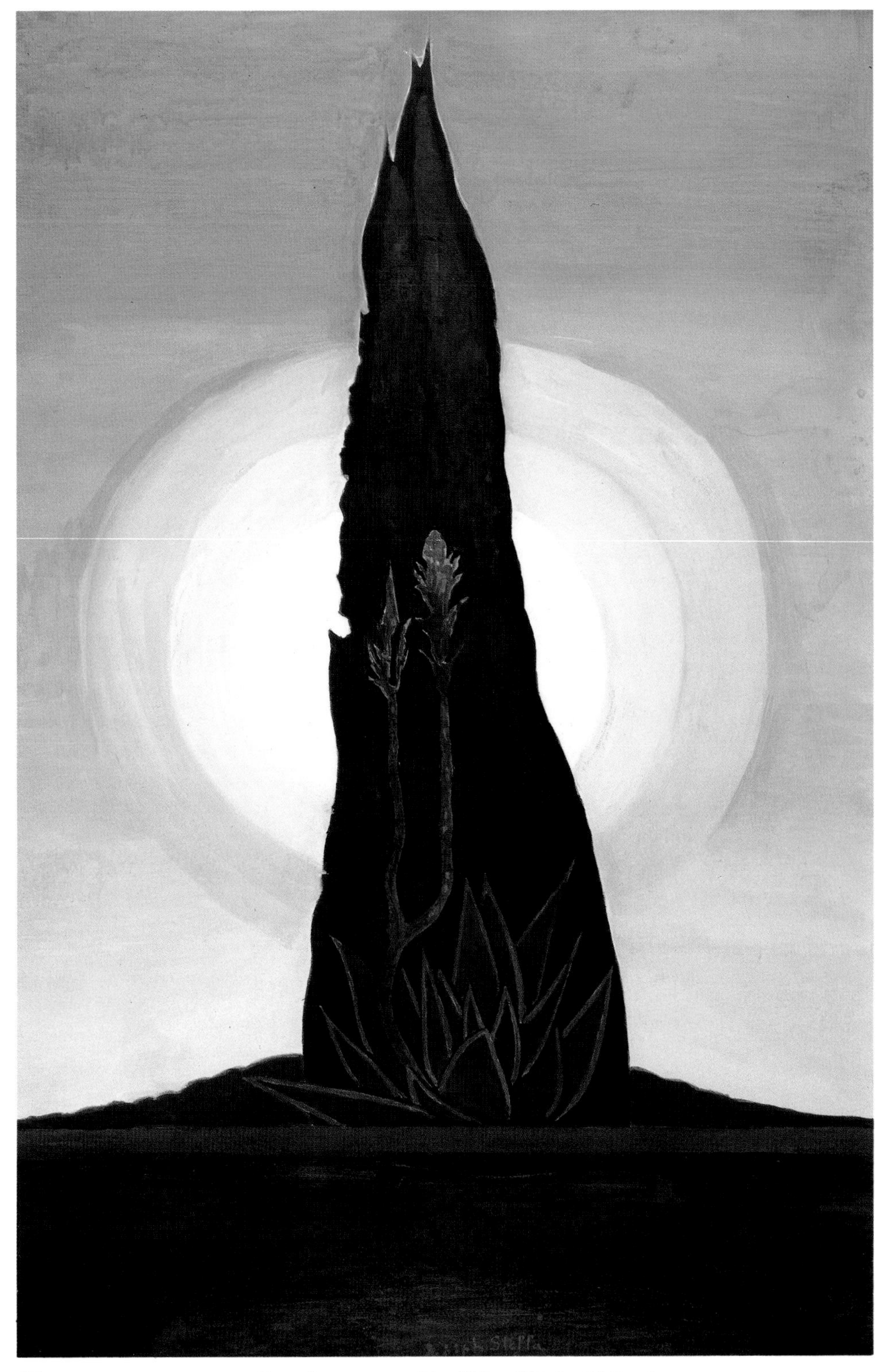

37 Gouache on paper, 41 x 27 in. (104.1 x 68.6 cm)
Signed at lower center and at lower right: JOSEPH STELLA
Gift of Betsy Main Babcock

The Whipping, 1941
Horace Pippin
1888–1946

During his service on the front lines in France in World War I, Horace Pippin began to make drawings of warfare to allay the agony of spending months in the trenches. After his discharge in 1919 images of war continued to haunt him, but he was unable to give them pictorial expression because his right arm was partially paralyzed from a sniper's bullet. In 1925, when he was thirty-seven years old, he discovered an unusual way to make pictures. He braced a hot poker between his disabled arm and his knee, and with his left hand maneuvered a panel against the tip of the iron.[1] In this awkward manner he was able to delineate simple but powerful forms by burning grooves into the wood, which helped contain the paint within the furrows. Eventually his disabled arm began to strengthen, and by 1930 he was able to produce his first oil painting on canvas.

An example of his burnt-wood method, *The Whipping* was inspired by stories of slavery told by his mother. Pippin has depicted a plantation overseer beating a slave whose hands have been tied to a post. Behind him, where paths run between the uncut black grass exposing the packed clay soil, another overseer watches in a commanding pose. In the background a row of log cabins serving as slave quarters are scored to imitate the surface of the rough hewn logs.

After twelve years of working anonymously as an artist, Pippin's work was discovered by the son-in-law of the famous illustrator N.C. Wyeth at the 1937 Art Association Annual Invitational in West Chester County, Pennsylvania, where Pippin spent most of his life. The following year four of Pippin's paintings were selected for the exhibition *Masters of Popular Painting: Modern Primitives of Europe and America* at the Museum of Modern Art in New York. Soon afterward the Philadelphia gallery of Robert Carlen, who had been exhibiting the work of the nineteenth-century folk artist Edward Hicks, began to exhibit Pippin's work, and with this exposure he became widely recognized as a significant black folk artist.

The strength of Pippin's work lies in the directness with which he is able to transpose image into form and color. "The pictures which I have already painted come to me in my mind," Pippin said, "and if to me it is a worth while picture, I paint it. I go over the picture in my mind several times and when I am ready to paint it I have all the details that I need."[2] Although Pippin was entirely self-taught his work shows a remarkable sophistication in conveying its message through formal as well as pictorial means. Background elements seem to take part in the foreground drama. Shaped into an upturned triangle, a cabin roof that appears to be balanced on the overseer's head intensifies the psychological impact of his cruel behavior. The chimney continues the vertical thrust of the brutal overseer's upheld arm and links the foreground to the background, flattening the pictorial space in a modernist manner. Despite Pippin's lack of technical virtuosity, he is able to combine forms into an intense psychological drama, placing him among the best of the twentieth-century American folk artists.

Notes

1. Romare Bearden and Harry Henderson, *Six Black Masters of American Art* (New York: Zenith Books, 1972). Pippin's method is described as follows: "with a poker, he could let the heavy iron support his hand and could manipulate it with the pressure of his arm." Selden Rodman, *Horace Pippin, A Negro Painter in America* (New York: Quadrangle Press, 1947), 11, explains: "Then, one day in 1929 watching the white-hot poker as it lay in the pot-bellied stove, he had a better idea. Holding the handle as firmly as he could in his stiff right hand, and balancing the rod on his knee, he took the extra leaf from the golden oak table, and with his agile left hand maneuvered the panel against the smoking tip of iron. It worked. And this time the design was there to stay, and bitten deeply enough to hold a color."
2. *H. Pippin*, with an essay by Romare Bearden (Washington, D.C.: Phillips Collection, 1976), n.p.

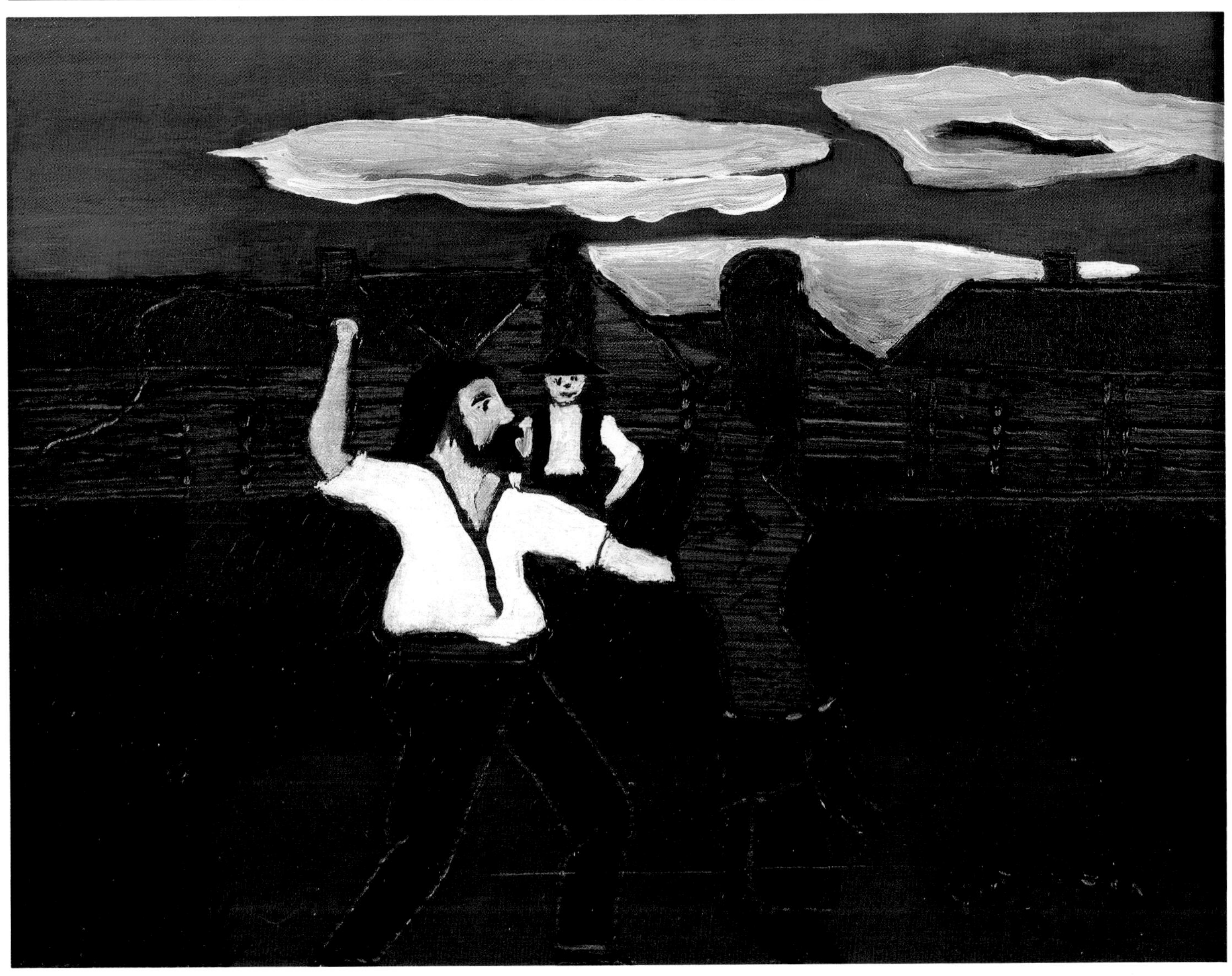

38

Oil on wood, 9 x 11½ in. (22.9 x 29.2 cm)
Signed and dated at lower right: H. PIPPIN 1941
Gift of Lee A. Ault

THE DANCERS, 1948
MAX WEBER
1881–1961

A pioneering American modernist, Max Weber's career spans the first half of this century—a period during which artists in this country began to recognize the dynamics of the European avant-garde. American artists reacted not as a group but as individuals, each creating his own response to challenging innovations in art. When Weber began his struggle for recognition in the New York art world, it was a period of extreme academic control. The progressive concepts of the Fauves led by Matisse and Cubist abstraction as practiced by Picasso and Braque were generally unknown in this country or scornfully criticized and ridiculed by the few dominant voices in art. Weber stands out as an innovative practitioner of modernist ideas in art whose early career is dominated by his aggressive perseverance against his lack of critical acceptance.

Born in Byelostok, in eastern Russia near Poland, Weber immigrated to the United States at the age of ten and was raised in the Jewish community in Brooklyn. Determined to become an artist, Weber entered Pratt Institute, where he studied to be a teacher of drawing and manual training. The highly gifted instructor Arthur Wesley Dow inspired the young Weber with his lectures on the principles of design. Simplicity and harmony within the artist's understanding of mass, line, and form were Dow's guiding principles. After three years Weber left Pratt Institute with a solid training in the rudiments of drawing and mechanical art, as well as more innovative concepts of art and design in general.

As soon as he had saved enough money from his art teaching, Weber left the United States to study in Europe. He settled in Paris and made periodic journeys to Spain, Italy, and Holland. He attended several schools in Paris, including the short-lived academy run by Matisse. Weber visited the exhibition of the Fauves and the Cézanne memorial exhibition of 1907, and exhibited his own work at the Salon des Independants and the Salon d'Automne in 1906 and 1907. He developed friendships with Robert Delauney and the aging Henri Rousseau, and upon his return to America in December 1908 Weber helped spread knowledge of the exciting achievements by artists in Paris during this critical period.

Weber's struggle for artistic recognition in this country is marked by the stylistic variety of his works. His earliest painting introduced Fauve color within reductivist compositions drawn essentially from the figure or landscape. While he relied on nature as a subject, he learned to edit what he saw. The reductivist principles of Dow, synthesized with Weber's knowledge of European modernist ideas, made the artist one of the most radical painters working in New York. As such, he struggled for years before gaining any significant recognition, supporting his wife and two children by teaching and lecturing. At one period between 1912 and 1918, Weber's style of painting derived from his understanding of Cubism, with subject matter often inspired by the thriving urban environment of New York. Yet Weber's abstractions appear gentle and lyrical in comparison to European Cubism. Weber painted in a more personal style, expressing an interest in the character, gesture, stance, and action of the subject. Eventually his work became more representational, dominated by simple and clear forms, and he drew subjects from his own Jewish heritage and his love of the art of the past.

The Dancers is among the late works of the artist, and has thematic parallels to paintings he produced from about 1940 on. *The Dancers* is clearly inspired by Greek vase painting yet it is as personalized a subject as any Weber produced, for while he looked at all other art he rarely quoted it directly. Weber wrote: "The aesthetic grandeur, austerity and certitude in the art of the great ancients of all races and climes are for me a constant source of inspiration and incentive."[1] It is precisely that—the grandeur of the stance of the dancers, the austerity of the surroundings, and the certitude of Weber's use of color, line, and form—that is the essence of this composition. The lyrical beauty of this image, so economically and precisely presented, was Weber's objective in his art; as he wrote: "the basis of any art is simple, natural, spontaneous sensation."[2]

NOTES

1. Joy S. Weber, ed., *Max Weber—Cubist Vision: Early and Late* (New York: Forum Gallery, 1986), 13.
2. Ibid.

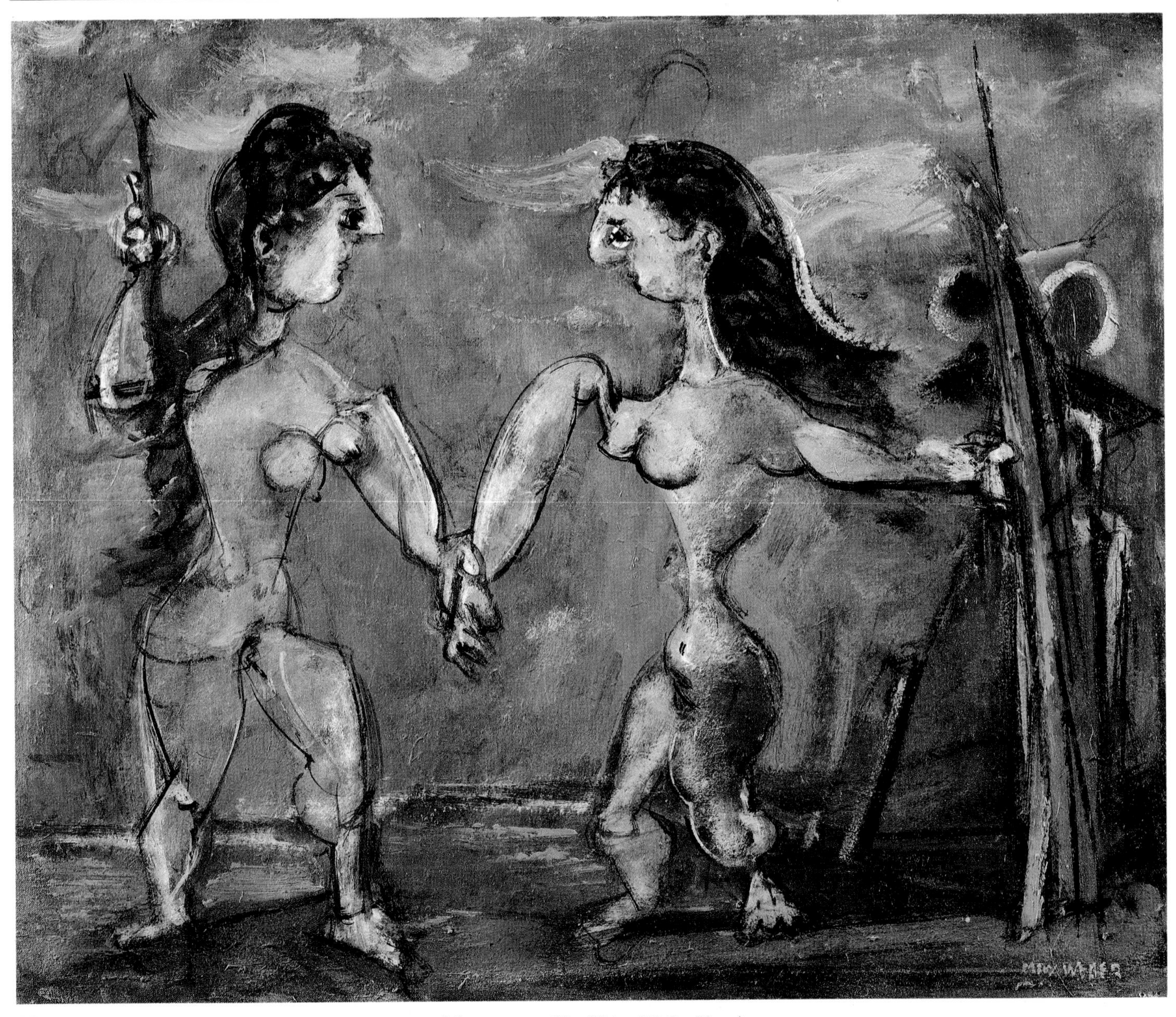

39 Oil on canvas, 20 x 24 in. (50.8 x 61 cm)
Signed at lower right: MAX WEBER
Gift of Mr. and Mrs. Maynard Weber

Conversation Piece, 1952

Charles Sheeler

1883–1965

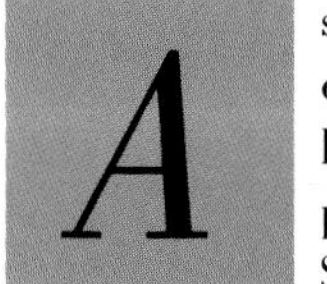

As the influence of the machine aesthetic entered every aspect of life during the 1920s, many artists began to mimic the characteristics of machine production in the process of making their art. Stylistically organized under the heading of Precisionists, these artists eschewed art that relied on spontaneity and elaborate brushwork in favor of planned compositions, smooth surfaces, and clean, precise definition. Charles Sheeler turned from the flamboyant brushwork he learned from William Merritt Chase and worked out a new style appropriate to the depiction of factories, early American interiors, and barn scenes—architectural subjects that displayed the bold proportions of abstract design. Until 1931, when the famous dealer Edith Halpert invited him to join her Downtown Gallery, Sheeler made his living in commercial photography. A retrospective at the Museum of Modern Art in 1939 established him as one of the leading American artists and photographers of the period.

A late work, *Conversation Piece* is nonetheless strongly related in its detached geometry to Sheeler's early Precisionist style. The title of this painting, a term commonly used to refer to eighteenth-century informal group portraiture, reinforces his intention of creating an exchange between a traditional subject and its modernist interpretation. The title may also refer to a dialogue that remained central to Sheeler's artistic vision throughout his career—a dialogue between photography and oil painting. His preoccupation with connections is demonstrated in his frequent use of the prefix *con-*, which is contained in the titles of two other paintings from 1952, *Convergence* (collection of Matthew Wolf) and *Convolutions* (collection of Mr. and Mrs. George Greenspan).

"When we look at any object in Nature," Sheeler wrote, "we inevitably carry over a memory of the object we have just previously seen."[1] In order to capture this perceptual phenomenon, he began in 1946 to use superimposed photographs as the basis of his compositions.[2] An example of this late method, *Conversation Piece* evokes the recollection of barn facades and silos seen over a period of time. A solid white silo, echoed by a less substantial silo, dominates the cluster of transparent, superimposed barn facades. Gleaming white walls show no sign of deterioration. The patch of cloudless blue sky seems airless, almost solid. The densely packed architecture screens out the pastoral setting so effectively that the sole vestige of the natural world is found in the irregular shadow of foliage cast against the barn wall. With the elimination of aging surfaces, enveloping atmosphere, and natural and human presence, Sheeler recollects these barn facades in a cool, detached manner untainted by the nostalgic sentiment associated with the Romantic period.

In the Cubist manner large forms are flattened against the picture plane, with the exception of some tantalizing details that tease the spectator with unexpected penetrations and protrusions. The centrally located roof ventilator, for example, is shaded in three dimension, and the pulley beam above the hayloft breaks into the viewer's space like the illusionistic nail found in several paintings by the French Cubist Georges Braque. The windows, persistent imagery in Sheeler's late work, are arranged to comment upon traditional illusionistic devices. Square frontal windows press against the picture plane, while an oblique window has the ambiguous appearance of puncturing the side wall of the hayloft.

Notes

1. Martin Friedman, Bartlett Hayes, and Charles Millard, *Charles Sheeler* (Washington, D.C.: Smithsonian Institution Press, 1968), 99.
2. The composite photograph and a tempera on artist's board on which *Conversation Piece* is based are in the William H. Lane Collection, Boston.

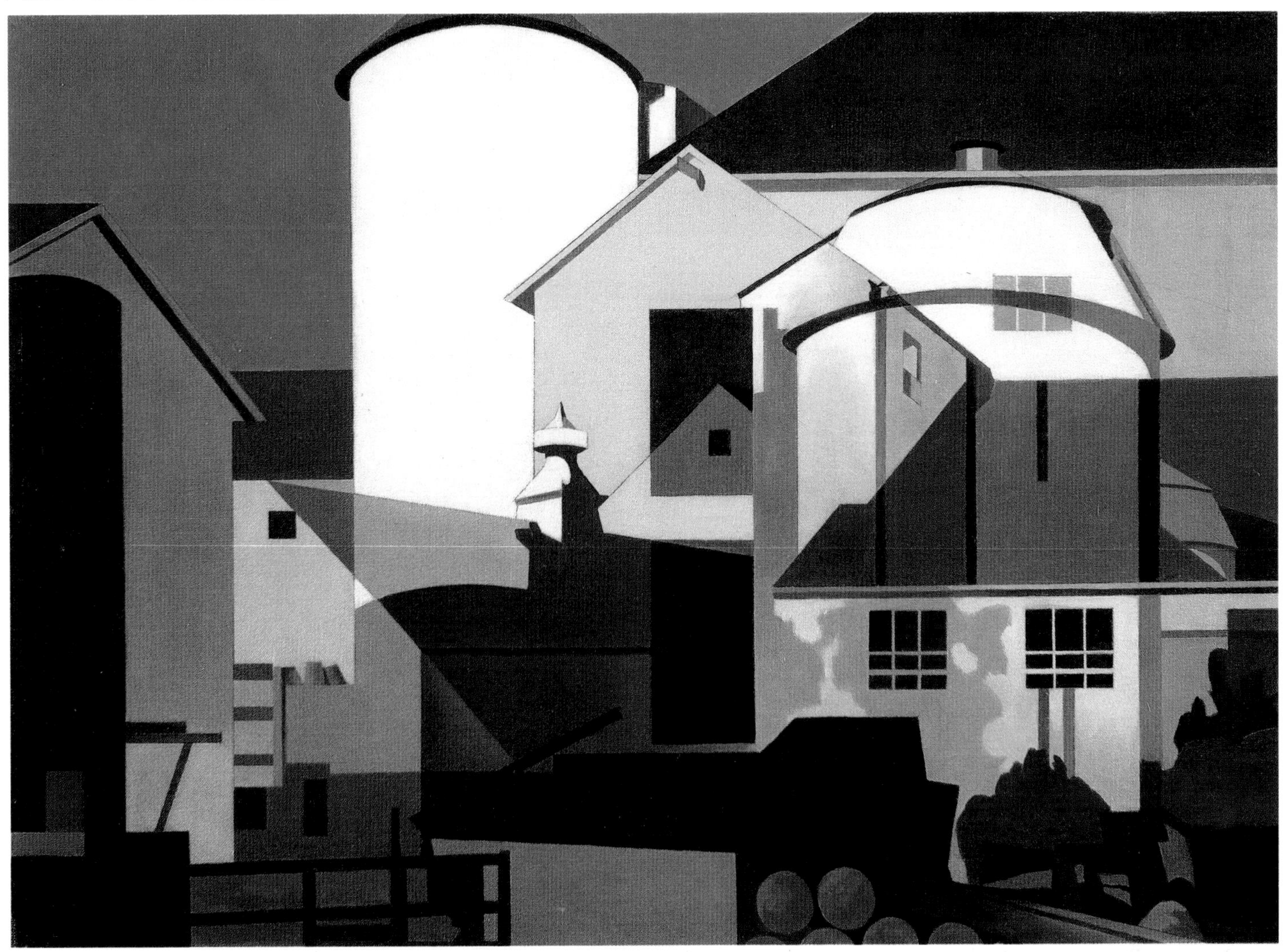

40

Oil on canvas, 18 x 25 in. (45.7 x 63.5 cm)
Signed and dated at lower right: SHEELER/52
Gift of Barbara B. Millhouse

THE WOODPECKER, 1955–63
CHARLES BURCHFIELD
1893–1967

To evoke human emotion through the natural elements of landscape, Charles Burchfield has woven into the rhythmic surface of this painting abstract symbols he invented many years earlier. Reflecting his fascination with the turn-of-the-century fairy-tale illustrations of Arthur Rackham, Burchfield's anthropomorphic response to nature transforms this scene inspired by his backyard in Gardenville, New York, into an enchanted woodland.

Burchfield's style evolved from the Symbolist movement of the 1890s, which used abstract symbols to convey a specific emotion, and the Expressionist movement, which distorted color and form to explore their emotional impact. Both movements were widespread in the first decades of the twentieth century when Burchfield was developing his style. These influences were probably transmitted to him through his teacher at the Cleveland School of Art, Henry Keller, who studied in Germany during the 1890s when the Symbolist movement was at its height.[1] Keller's German ties may also have been influential in shaping Burchfield's affinity with German Expressionism, which was widely accepted by 1916, a crucial year in the formation of Burchfield's style. In his frequent use of cathedrallike groves of trees and mystical undercurrent, Burchfield's art, like that of the German Expressionists, seems to find its roots in a northern Gothic vision.

In his celebrated late work, of which *The Woodpecker* is an example, Burchfield enlarged upon his early style developed in 1916–18 after he graduated from the Cleveland School of Art. He had dropped his interest in fanciful landscape in favor of realistic paintings of factory towns and industrial sites, but in 1943 he reworked some of his early ideas to create the highly individualistic paintings of his late period.

In 1955, when Burchfield completed the main portion of *The Woodpecker*, he recognized that he had made "a bold step in a new direction."[2] John I. H. Baur, the director of the Whitney Museum of American Art, had already chosen the paintings that were to be included in Burchfield's forthcoming retrospective. A correspondence between them ensued over *The Woodpecker*. Baur was delighted with "the imaginative treatment of the woodpecker motif and its brilliant pattern of ascending verticals," but he found "the big hemlock on the right, despite certain conventionalizations, too naturalistic."[3] After this critique Burchfield decided not to send *The Woodpecker* to the Whitney Museum exhibition, but kept it in his studio for eight years during which time he reworked it considerably. A photograph of this painting published in the 1956 winter issue of *Arts* magazine provides evidence that the central woodpecker motif remains close to its original state, but the background has been reworked and the scale increased.

Throughout his career Burchfield used the watercolor medium almost solely, but he frequently had to mount more than one sheet on a board to increase the scale of his works beyond the stock size of the paper. Maintaining the freshness and transparency of watercolor over a large expanse also presented difficulties, but he overcame this by cutting away the areas with which he was dissatisfied and replacing them with new paper. As a result of many revisions *The Woodpecker* is composed of a number of spliced strips of paper mounted on board.

Burchfield wrote in his diaries: "I'm going to give you more sounds and dreams, and—yes, I'm going to make people smell what I want them to, and with visual means."[4] Embodying this concept of synesthesia, *The Woodpecker* reflects Burchfield's belief that art is enhanced when visual forms seem to transpose one sense perception into another. Like the invention of abstract symbols, this concept grew out of the Symbolist movement, and is so powerfully embodied here that the painting seems to evoke a rich, organic odor of decay and decomposition. It also seems to emit the sounds of tapping through the notations that run along the knobby bark of the rotting tree trunks and the vibrating lines that form the shape of the busy woodpecker.

NOTES

1. Charles Burchfield, "Henry G. Keller, an Appraisal by his Best Known Student, Charles Burchfield," *American Magazine of Art* 29 (September 1936): 586.
2. Letter from Burchfield to John I. H. Baur, October 3, 1955 (Archives of American Art, New York, film N648, no.44).
3. Letter from John I. H. Baur to Burchfield, October 11, 1955 (Archives of American Art, New York, film N648, no.41).
4. John I. H. Baur, *Charles Burchfield* (New York: Macmillan & Co., 1956), 63.

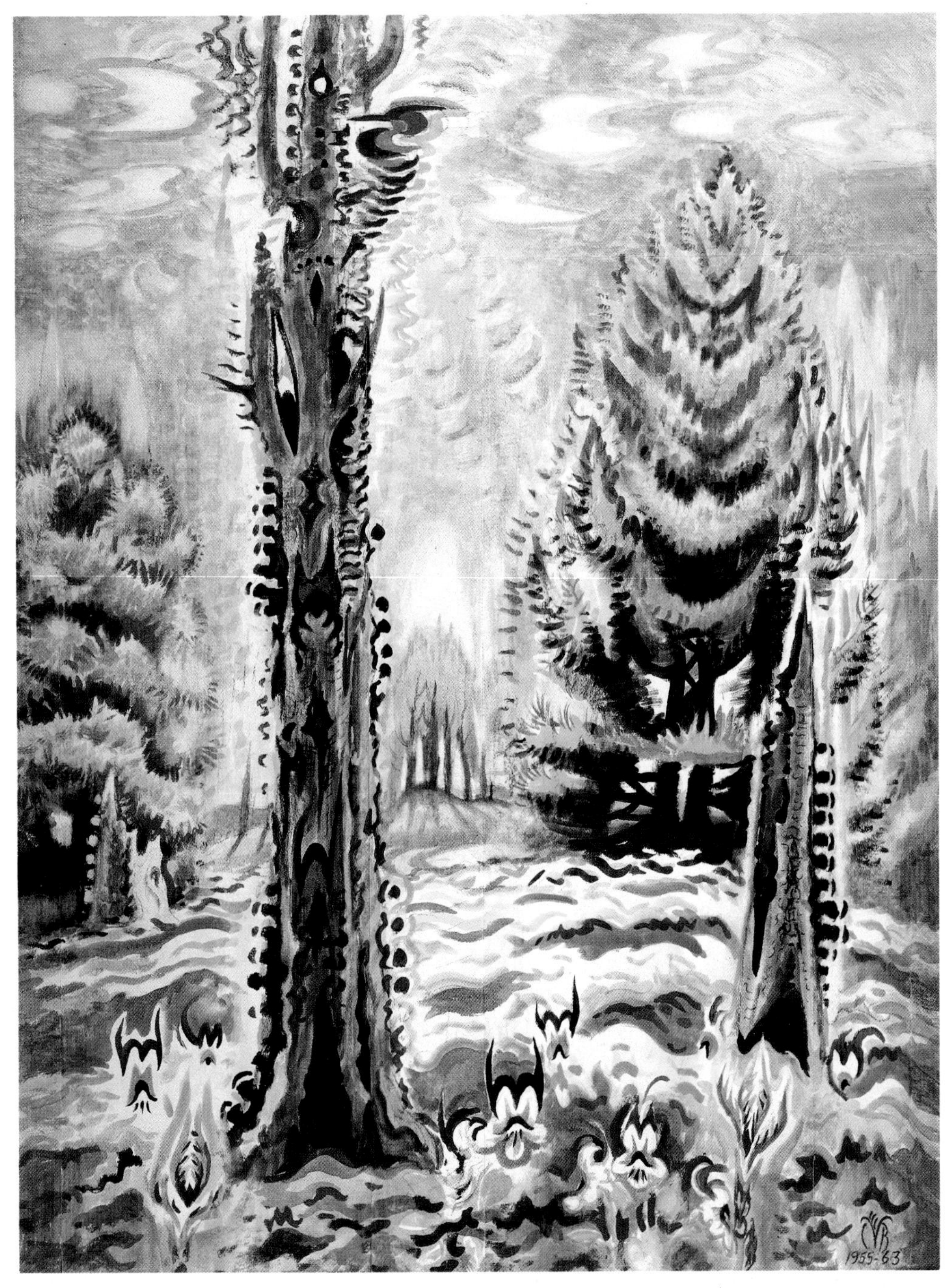

41 Watercolor on pieced paper, 50 x 38 in. (127 x 96.5 cm)
Signed and dated at lower right corner: CEB [monogram]/1955–1963
Gift of Barbara B. Millhouse

Ancient Queen, 1960

Philip Evergood

1901–1973

In *Ancient Queen*, Cleopatra, adorned with the crown of upper Egypt, reclines on a couch with her black slave standing behind her—a scene that recalls Edouard Manet's celebrated *Olympia* of 1863. Leaning on her bony elbows the former temptress and manipulator of Roman emperors, now rejected and frail, is captured at the dramatic moment before her suicide. Between her long, manicured fingers she holds the instrument of her impending demise, a lively green asp. Her ruthless use of sexual allure is suggested by the shrill red of her garment, ironically related in placement and hue to the red stamens of the lilies traditionally found in altarpieces as symbols of purity.

The marital difficulties that plagued Evergood during this period of his life seem to have motivated the choice of this historical enactment. George Rickey, a friend of the artist, wrote in response to a request for an interpretation of this painting: "I would, perhaps, contest that the subject is suicide. I think it is, rather, unrequited love. But it is also glamorous circumstance and legendary grandeur. These topics were always of interest to Phil. The suicide component is an intensifier."[1]

Although Evergood was born in New York City, he grew up in England, where he lived from 1909 to 1923. He graduated from Eton, attended Cambridge for two years, then applied to the Slade School of Art in London. He completed his artistic training at the Académie Julian in Paris and in 1931 he settled permanently in the United States.

Evergood's disregard for pleasing color, flowing line, and polished surface expresses a purposeful revolt against academic realism, which by the twentieth century had become a disparaged and outmoded means of rendering reality. Since the subject of this painting is closely related to the favored harem interiors of the great French academician Jean-Léon Gérôme, the crude, unruly rendering of this scene contains in itself a strong element of satire.

Evergood's content reveals a sophisticated use of references to styles and subjects taken from art history. The muddled vanishing points of the heaving floor, for example, seem to confound the viewer by receding into space on the left and lying flat against the picture plane on the right, but this technique is actually an informed comment on Cubist spatial construction. The manner in which the Queen is posed seems to refer to Matisse's *Blue Nude*, one of the most significant paintings at the Armory Show of 1913. The figure kneeling in the background is possibly a reference to Titian, the Renaissance master of the reclining nude, who included a clothed kneeling figure in the background of his famous *Venus of Urbino*. It might also serve as a wry comment on the obscene background figures of Brueghel, an acknowledged influence on Evergood, or perhaps it is a forthright mockery of the act of worship. Whatever this detail signifies, it is only one of the myriad subtle references that make Evergood's paintings resonate with wit and erudition.

Note

1. Letter from George Rickey to Barbara Millhouse, January 7, 1987.

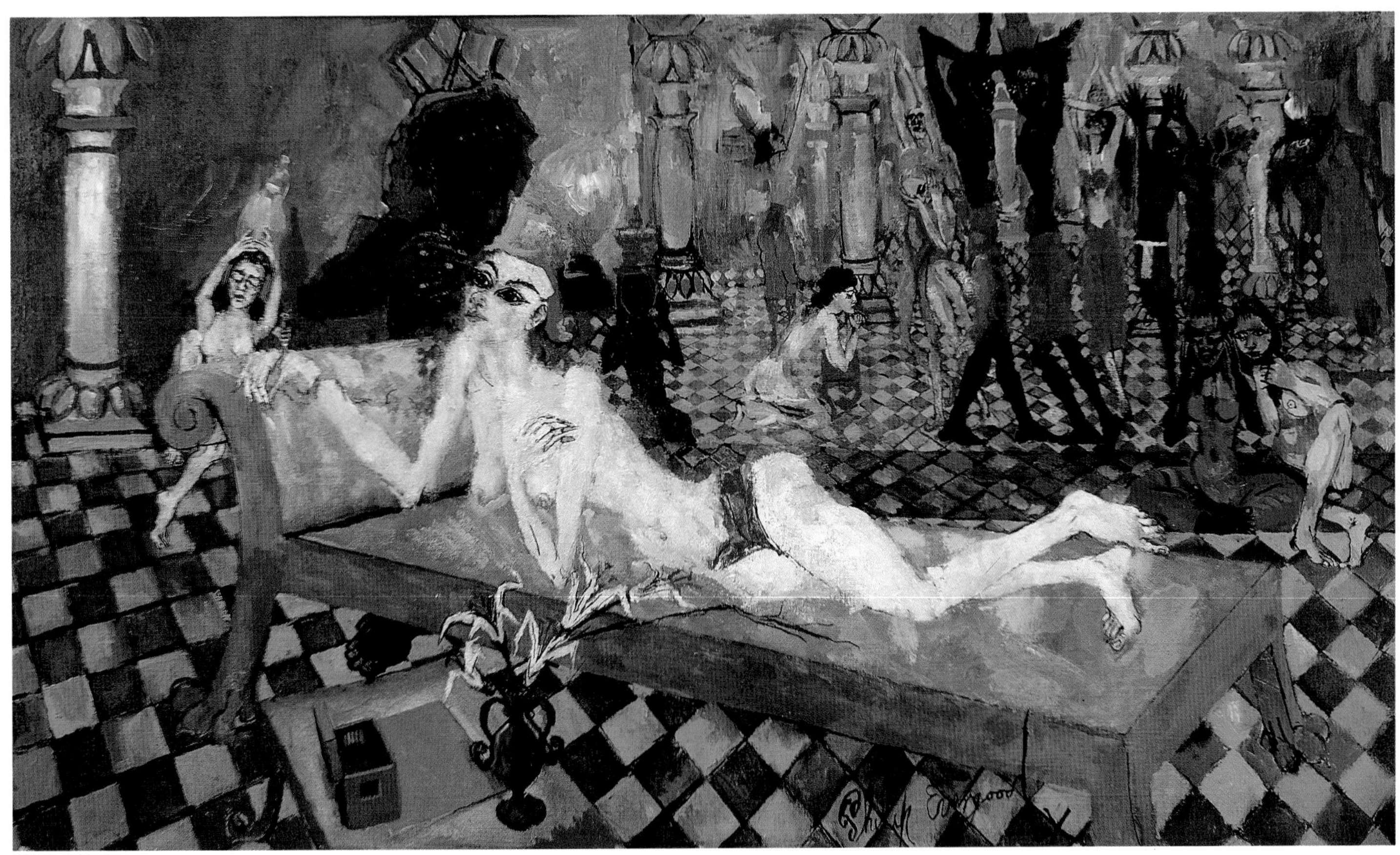

42

Oil on canvas, 28 x 48 in. (71.1 x 121.9 cm)
Signed and dated at lower right: PHILIP EVERGOOD/LX
Gift of Lawrence A. Fleischman

Belle, 1965

Robert Gwathmey

1903–1988

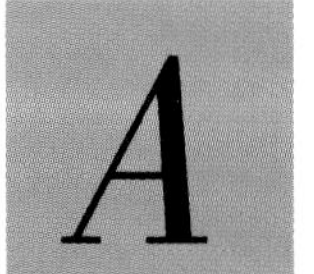

n eighth-generation Virginian, Robert Gwathmey was born and raised in Richmond. As a young man Gwathmey worked at numerous odd jobs to help support his widowed mother and his family. He received art training at the Maryland Institute in Baltimore and the Pennsylvania Academy of the Fine Arts, Philadelphia. After completing his art studies, Gwathmey began a teaching career that included work at Beaver College, the Carnegie Institute, and Cooper Union in New York City. His own working-class upbringing, combined with an awareness of the black man's oppressed position in Southern society, led Gwathmey to develop his art as a statement against the harsh inequalities of his contemporary world.

While little remains of Gwathmey's earliest works, he developed a style of painting consistent with his goal to produce powerful social realist art. Gwathmey uses precise contours that outline graphic shapes in vivid colors, forcing the viewer to read his images much as one would a cartoon or advertisement. While his earlier works generally contain a coherent narrative interweaving a variety of symbols—much like a stage set filled with props and dramatically poised characters—the later works are often a compendium of the symbols themselves. The viewer does not require a translation of Gwathmey's symbols since the artist employs images universally understood (i.e., a burning cross, cotton plant, or hitchhiker), reinforced by the visual tension created by the abstract interplay of shape and color. His attitude toward the South is poignantly stated in *Belle*, which he produced during the height of the civil rights movement.

Belle is a compendium of symbols—some overtly challenging, others requiring the interpretation of their creator. Four southern stereotype characters and a circus performer surround a faded southern belle with her hair in curlers. Gwathmey wrote in a letter to Reynolda House that she "was told that if she read too many books she would limit her chances of marriage. . . . At this late date she still plays the game of he loves me, he loves me not." The preacher holds a Christian cross in front of him and a burning cross behind, as if to say, "Don't let your right hand know what your left hand is doing." The Ku Klux Klansman wears mismatched shoes; one shoe, Gwathmey wrote, "represents the powers that be," while the other "represents the uneducated."

Separated by the trumpet vine, which causes itching when touched, is the half-buried black man with his hands tied behind him so he cannot read the book he holds. The ominous ace of spades and the unlucky number thirteen represent the superstitions of many people. In the center the hungry baby birds, stretching their open mouths toward a mortarboard, symbolize the birdbrained mentality of the characters who will never be able to extricate themselves from their allotted roles. The road signs marked with conflicting arrows mirror the confused life of people going nowhere.

Art critic John Canaday has written: "Robert Gwathmey has been exceptional among the small minority of artists who can be called social commentators. He has managed to capitalize on the sheer pictorial interest of his subject matter without reducing it to picturesqueness; he has recognized the poignancy of the lives he paints without sentimentalizing them, and he has spoken of social injustice without mounting the soapbox."

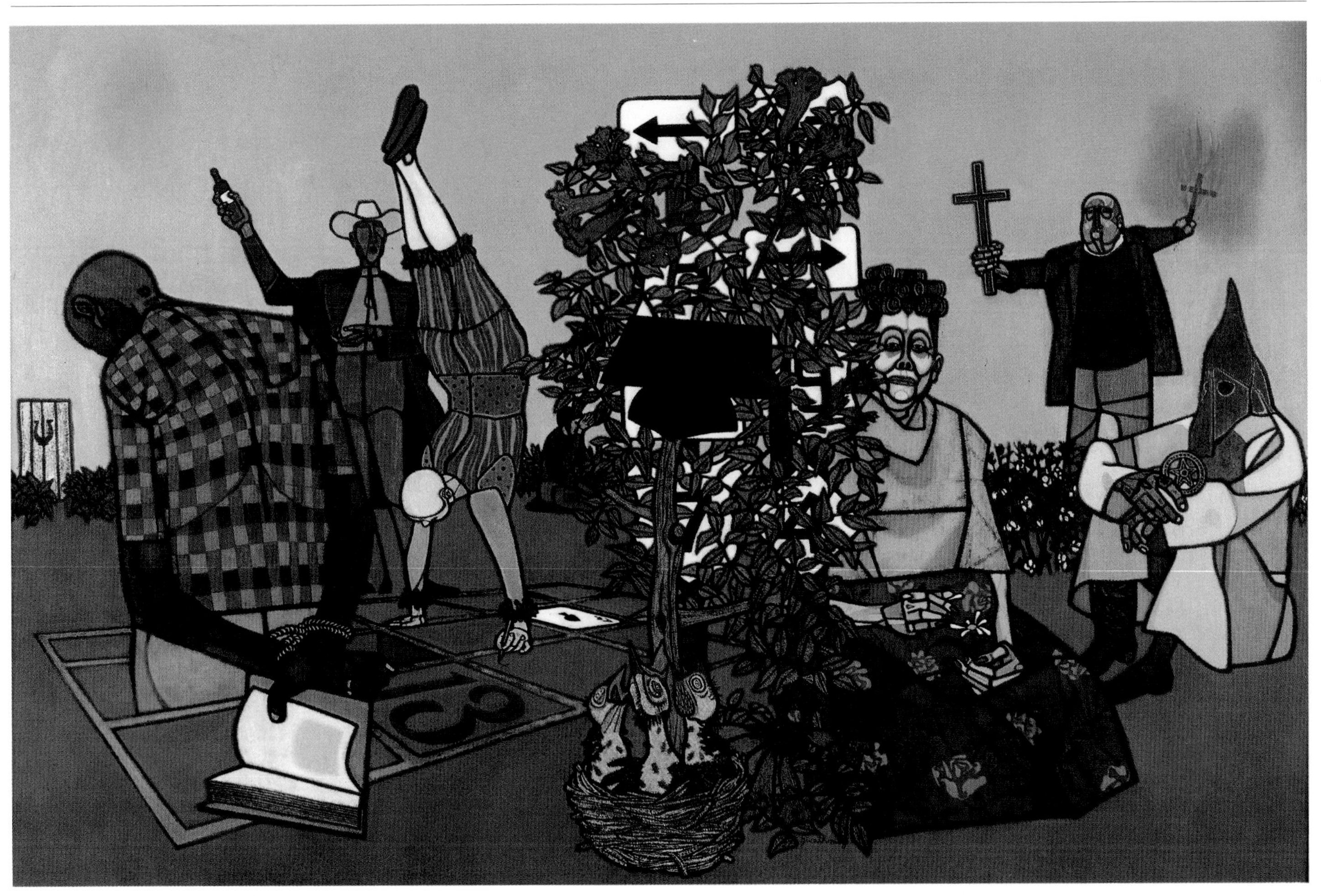

43

Oil on canvas, 40 x 62 in. (101.6 x 157.5 cm)
Signed at lower right center: GWATHMEY
Gift of Barbara B. Millhouse

BUILDERS NO. 2, 1968

JACOB LAWRENCE

b. 1917

In 1968 Jacob Lawrence began a series of paintings based on the theme of builders, recalling his frequent visits to the woodworking shop of the Bates brothers in Harlem, where he had moved with his mother around 1930. The subject continues to occupy him up to the present time and conveys his hope of building a better life for his people by working together in a cooperative effort and can be seen as "the thematic capstone of Lawrence's body of work: visions of people laboring in harmony to fulfill their aspirations."[1]

Although the country was in the midst of the Depression during Lawrence's formative years, the cultural energy of the Harlem Renaissance persisted. Through his studies under the auspices of the WPA at the Harlem Art Workshop, Lawrence came in contact with many dancers, poets, writers, and artists—Charles Mckay, Langston Hughes, Ralph Ellison, Augusta Savage. Although he felt that his greatest influence stemmed from the artists in his own community, he admired the work of German Expressionists Kathe Kollwitz and George Grosz and American modernists Arthur Dove and Charles Sheeler. He made frequent trips to the Metropolitan Museum of Art, where he was especially interested in the early Italian Renaissance paintings by Crivelli and Botticelli. The subject of *Builders No. 2* recalls forcefully the Joseph wing of the fifteenth-century *Merode* triptych (Cloisters, New York), so it seems probable that he knew of this masterpiece as well.

Lawrence's style crystalized in the mid-1930s when he discovered a way of integrating narrative scenes of Harlem life with simplified Cubist spatial constructions. Using water-based paint as his primary medium he created forceful designs composed of clearly defined areas of flat color. In 1941, when the legendary art dealer Edith Halpert invited him to exhibit at her famous Downtown Gallery, Lawrence became the first black artist to be represented by a New York art gallery. *Fortune* magazine reproduced in color twenty-six paintings from this exhibition, and for the next three decades Lawrence was the foremost black artist in the country.

The flat forms and tilted viewpoint are typical of Cubism, a style popular in Harlem in the 1930s because of its widespread influence and African derivations. The Cubist treatment of background and foreground as a single plane enhances the overall design. Precisely delineated areas of warm browns and cool blues are thrust against each other with an impact that parallels in harshness the juxtaposition of diagonals and flat angular planes.

In *Builders No. 2*, the second work of Lawrence's 1968 series, the placement of three carpenters around the worktable, their absorption in their task, and the force of their gestures conjures up images of surgeons performing a critical operation. Lawrence admired hand tools for their beauty and timeless quality, and has placed slide marking gauges protruding from pockets and wood clamps just within a carpenter's reach. The placement of the frenzied hand saws, blades, and wood clamps around the carpenters' heads seem to electrify the workshop with mental exhilaration. Below, a floating hammer, a hand drill, a C-clamp grasping a marker, and a screw embedded in a split block hover in midair as if to signify physical stamina. No element in this painting remains inert; each conveys intense vitality.

NOTE

1. Ellen Harkins Wheat, "Jacob Lawrence and the Legacy of Harlem," *Archives of American Art Journal* 26 (no. 1, 1986).

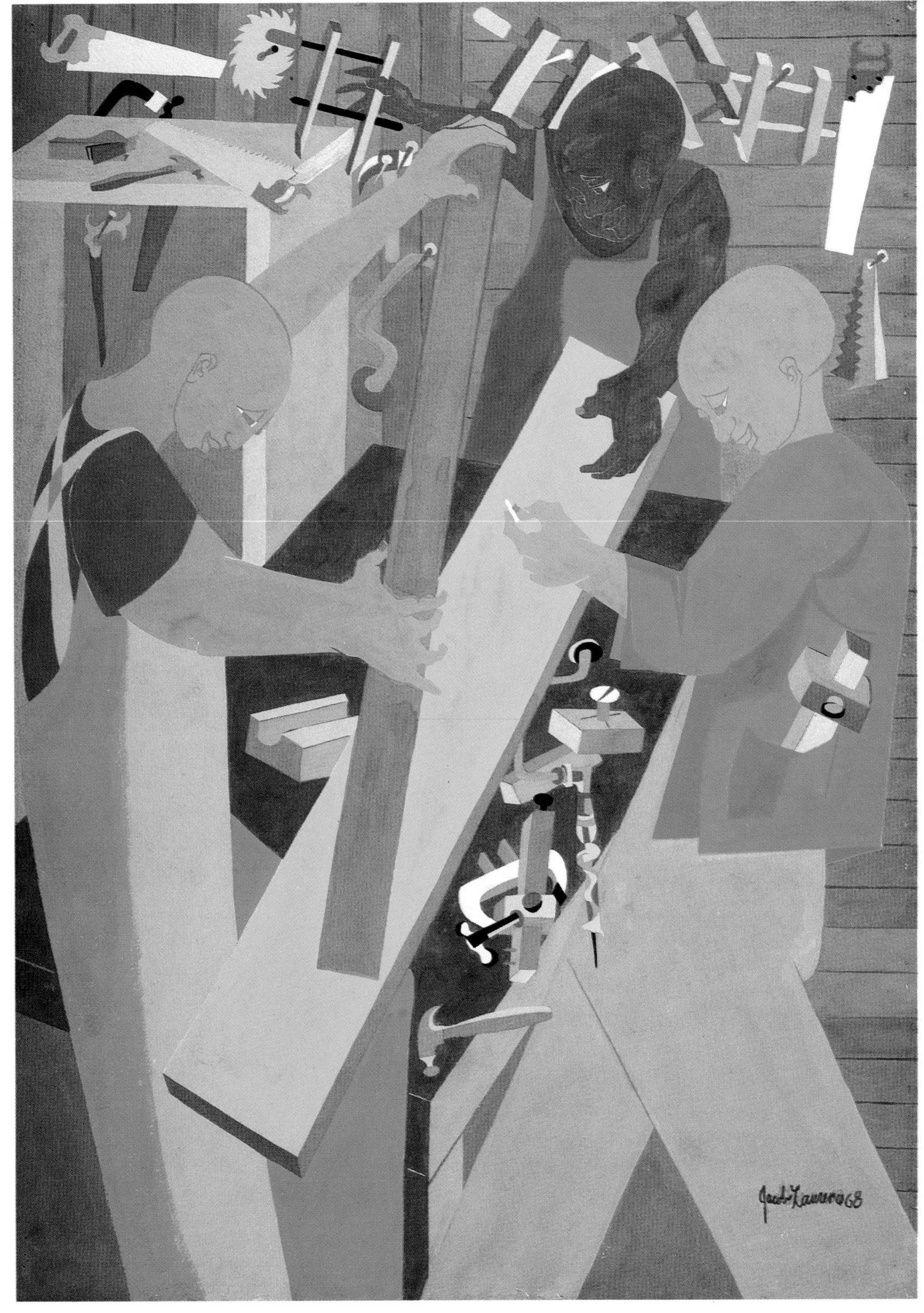

44 Gouache on paper, 30 x 21¼ in. (76.2 x 54 cm)
Signed and dated at lower right: JACOB LAWRENCE 68
Gift of Barbara B. Millhouse

Mr. & Mrs. Jerome Pustilnik
Mr. & Mrs. Walter S. Rosenberry III
Mr. & Mrs. Milton F. Rosenthal
Mr. & Mrs. Richard Rosenthal
Marlene Schiff
Mrs. Marcia Schloss
Mr. & Mrs. Douglas A. Schubot
Mr. & Mrs. Rudolph B. Schulhof
Mr. & Mrs. Joseph Seviroli
Rev. & Mrs. Alfred R. Shands III
Mr. & Mrs. George A. Shutt
Barbara Slifka
Mr. & Mrs. Nathan Smooke
Mr. & Mrs. David M. Solinger
Anne C. Stephens
Mr. & Mrs. James C. Stevens
Mrs. Martha B. Stimpson
Mr. & Mrs. John W. Straus
Mrs. Norman Tishman
Mrs. George W. Ullman
Mr. & Mrs. Michael J. Waldman
Mr. & Mrs. Robert C. Warren
Mrs. Paul L. Wattis
Mrs. Nancy Brown Wellin
Mr. & Mrs. Dave Williams
Enid Silver Winslow
Mr. & Mrs. Bagley Wright
Mr. & Mrs. Howard S. Wright
Mr. & Mrs. C. Angus Wurtele
Mr. & Mrs. T. Evans Wyckoff
One anonymous patron

Staff

Myrna Smoot
Director

Barbara Poska
Assistant to the Director

New York

Exhibition Department

J. David Farmer
Director of Exhibitions

Robert Workman
Administrator for Exhibitions

Marie-Thérèse Brincard
Senior Exhibition Coordinator

P. Andrew Spahr
Senior Exhibition Coordinator

Donna Gustafson
Exhibition Coordinator

Michaelyn Mitchell
Head of Publications

Andrea Farnick
Associate Registrar

Kathleen Flynn
Assistant Registrar

Deborah Notkin
Exhibition Assistant

Film/Video Department

Sam McElfresh
Film/Video Program Director

Tom Smith
Assistant Director Film/Video Program

Thomas Smith
Film/Video Program Assistant

Development, Membership, and Public Information

Susan J. Brady
Director of Development and Public Affairs

Susan Mroczynski
Associate Director, Membership and Special Events

Jillian Slonim
Public Information Director

Jim Gaffey
Grant Writer

Penne Smith
Public Information Assistant

Michelle Graham
Development Coordinator of Annual Giving

Sheila Look
Membership/Director Assistant

Finance and Administration

Mark Gotlob
Director of Finance and Administration

Judith Worman
Controller

Patricia Holquist
Senior Bookkeeper

Yewsheva Wilder
Accounting Clerk

Jane Marvin
Office Manager/Personnel Coordinator

Sabina Moss
Receptionist

Building

Marcos Laspina
Building Superintendent

Alfredo Caliba
Building Custodian

San Francisco

Susan Anthony Loria
Director, Museum Services Division

Nancy Jones
Museum Membership and Marketing Director

Ricki Lederman
Professional Training Director and MMI Administrative Coordinator

Eric Brizee
Museum Service Coordinator/Office Manager

Anna Vandenberg
MMI Research and Membership Assistant

Cassandra Markham
Museum Programs Assistant

Cindy Kiddo
Receptionist

Mary Dalton
Bookkeeper/MMI Assistant

Government Support

National Endowment for the Arts
National Endowment for the Humanities
New York State Council on the Arts
California Arts Council

Corporate and Foundation Patrons

Benefactors

Eastman Kodak Company
Exxon Corporation
The Horace W. Goldsmith Foundation
The Jewish Communal Fund
The Knight Foundation
Metropolitan Life Foundation
Philip Morris Companies, Inc.
The Rockefeller Foundation
Samuel & May Rudin Foundation, Inc.
U.S. West
Lila Wallace-Reader's Digest Fund

Patrons

Drexel, Burnham, Lambert, Inc.
Gorham, Inc.
Samuel H. Kress Foundation
Sacred Circles Foundation
The Andy Warhol Foundation for the Visual Arts, Inc.

Sponsors

Chemical Bank
Cosmair, Inc.
The Cowles Charitable Trust
The Graham Foundation
IBM Corporation
The Interpublic Group of Companies, Inc.
The J.M. Kaplan Fund, Inc.
Lowe Marschalk Inc.
The New York Times Company Foundation, Inc.
McCann-Erickson Worldwide
Paramount Communications
PepsiCo Foundation, Inc.
R.J. Reynolds, Inc.
Sony Corporation
Warner Communications
Wells, Rich, Greene, Inc.

Associates

Arco Foundation
The Laura Bolton Foundation
Chevron Corporation
Donaldson, Lufkin & Jenrette
Fried, Frank & Harris
Generale Bank
Manufacturers Hanover Trust Company

Donors

The Bank of New York
BellSouth Corporation
Champion International Corporation
Compton Foundation, Inc.
Consolidated Edison Company of New York
Estee Lauder, Inc.
Heublein, Inc.
The J.C. Penney Company, Inc.
KMPG Peat Marwick
Kraft Foundation
Lannan Foundation
Mercedes-Benz of North America, Inc.
Mobil Foundation, Inc.
Pfizer, Inc.
Price Waterhouse Company
Reynolds Metal Company Foundation
Rothschild, Inc.
Martin E. Segal Co.
Syntex Corporation
Tandy Corporation
Times Mirror
The Xerox Foundation

Friends

Harry N. Abrams, Inc.
Backer Spielvogel Bates
Ernst & Young
James Felt Realty
General Motors Corporation
Ogilvy Group
Phillips Petroleum Foundation, Inc.

Photography Credits

Photography by Jackson Smith, with the following exceptions: E. Irving Blomstrann, fig. 4; Amon Carter Museum of Western Art, Fort Worth, Texas, fig. 7; The Cleveland Museum of Art, fig. 11; The Corcoran Gallery of Art, Washington, D.C., fig. 9; George C. Cox, figs. 12, 13; The Frick Collection, New York, fig. 8; The Harvard University Portrait Collection, Cambridge, Massachusetts, fig. 5; The Museum of Fine Arts, Boston, fig. 10; Robert E. Nates, Inc., cat. no. 35; National Gallery of Art, Washington, D.C., cat. no. 12; The New-York Historical Society, New York, fig. 6; Dwight Primiano, cat. nos. 3, 6, 10, 15; The Society for the Preservation of New England Antiquities, fig. 3; The Henry Francis du Pont Winterthur Museum, Winterthur, Delaware, fig. 1.

Index

(Page numbers in *italics* refer to illustrations.)